זִכְרוֹן שְׁמוּאֵל

WALKING THE LINE

Hilchot Eruvin from the Sources to the Streets

Rabbi Chaim Jachter

ק
KOL TORAH

Copyright © 2020 by Rabbi Chaim Jachter

First Edition, 2020

All rights reserved. No part of this book may be reproduced in any form on by an electronic or mechanical means, including information storage and retrieval systems, without permission in writing from the author, except by a reviewer who may quote brief passages in a review.

ISBN 979-8-665-01400-5, *softcover*

Kol Torah Publications

Table of Contents

Introduction: Hashkafic Perspectives on *Eruvin* ... iii

The Laws of Creating an *Eruv* 1

Defining the Four Domains 1

A List of Major Cities 10

Highways, Railroads, & Overpasses 22

Constructing the Tzurot Hapetach 30

The Maximum Size of an Eruv 43

Islands and Waterfronts 48

Introduction to Karpeif, Eruv Chatzeirot, & Sechirat Reshut 51

Karpeif and Bodies of Water 66

Eruv Chatzeirot Considerations 72

Demistifying Atu Rabim 78

Eruvin Infrastructure 83

A Lechi on Every Utility Pole? 85

A Tree as a Lechi 95

Lechi Strength 98

Gud Achit Mechitzta and Lavud 104

A Defense of the "Top-side" Wire 110

The Use of Tachuv in Contemporary Community Eruvin 117

Pitcha B'keren Zavit 123

Case Studies 129

Sagging Wire in the Yeshiva University Eruv.............. 131

Mei'achorei Hakotel in Long Island 137

The Boardwalk Railing in Long Branch, New Jersey 141

The Stringency of the Tevu'ot Shor & the Yale New Haven Eruv....146

The 'All-American' Eruv in Champaign-Urbana........... 156

The Lechi Under the Cabin Eaves at Camp Ramah Darom.......... 161

The Delatot of Canarsie, London, Mattersdorf, & Oakland........... 167

Diversity in *Eruvin*............ 181

Sephardic Standards for Defining a Reshut Harabim............183

Eruv Standards According to Sephardic Measurements 188

Chabad and Community Eruvin 196

The Modi'in Eruv & Eruvin Standards in the Jewish State.......... 202

The Machmir & the Meikel Making Allowances for Each Other ... 206

Fighting Price Gouging by Adopting a Lenient Opinion............ 213

Eruv Maintenance............ 217

A Community Model for Eruvin Maintenance in Sharon, MA......219

Managing an Eruv Emergency in Cambridge, MA 223

*The Friday Afternoon the Rabbi Discovered the Eruv Was Broken*227

Eruv Through the Storm 233

The Proper Way to Challenge Authority During Eruv Inspection 239

Eruv Inspections for Yom Tov................. 242

Guidelines for Eruvin Maintenance..246

Standards for Competent Inspection of Community Eruvin..........263

Conclusion: Why Does This Matter to Hashem? ... 271

OU All Daf
Bringing Hilchot Eruvin to Life

We have partnered with the Orthodox Union to produce a video series on *Hilchot Eruvin*. The videos illustrate many of the concepts discussed in *Walking the Line: Hilchot Eruvin from the Sources to the Streets.*

The series may be accessed at
www.alldaf.org/series/bringing-eruvin-to-life/4080

זִכְרוֹן שְׁמוּאֵל
לע"נ הרב שמואל בן הרב הלל

This past year, my beloved father-in-law's *neshamah* returned to the *Olam Ha'emet*. Rav Shmuel Tokayer z"l was born on the Lower East Side of Manhattan to Rav Hillel and Malka Tokayer, z"l. He was the youngest of seven children. Rav Tokayer grew up in the Borough Park section of Brooklyn, New York, and attended Yeshivas Rav Chaim Berlin and Telshe Yeshiva, and received his *semichah* from Chaim Berlin. He and his wife, Chana, started in Queens, NY, as a pulpit Rav in Richmond Hill. They then continued to Wilmington, NC, and finally to Danville, VA, where he served in his last formal pulpit position. Along the way, Rav Tokayer completed a doctorate in School Psychology, and the Tokayer family moved to NJ, where he successfully practiced as a school psychologist for over 30 years and as a clinical psychologist for over 20 years. He was a talented *chazan* from the time he was eighteen years old and practiced *milah* for decades. Rav Tokayer felt a strong sense of responsibility to his community and tried to make an impact wherever he could. He spearheaded the formation of the *chevra kadisha* in his community and ran it tirelessly with warmth and dignity for many years. Rav Tokayer loved learning Torah. He felt deep joy when he attended the Daf Yomi shiurim, completed the Daf Yomi, and participated in the Siyum Hashas. He truly cared about people, and they felt it. He enjoyed life and had a strong faith in Hashem. These were values that he lived by, and that guided his life.

In 1995, I was privileged to become part of the Tokayer family and have Rav Tokayer as my father-in-law. He took great pride in his wife, children, and grandchildren, and was always very supportive of all of my achievements. He was an exceptional role model for me as I watched how committed he was both to his family and his community. I remember individuals would approach him all the time for help and advice, and he would talk to them with warmth, compassion, and insight. It is, therefore, with much gratitude and respect that I dedicate this work to his memory. May his *neshamah* be raised to the highest levels in *Gan Eden*.

Rabbi Chaim Jachter
12 Menachem Av 5780

INTRODUCTION: HASHKAFIC PERSPECTIVES ON ERUVIN

In the pages ahead, we take a deep dive into the intricacies of *Hilchot Eruvin*. Before we embark on our journey, let us explore some of the hashkafic (philosophical) principles that lie behind the details of *Hilchot Eruvin*.

A RELISH FOR AVODAT HASHEM

When taking my older children to visit the celebrated American Revolutionary War site Valley Forge, the guide taught us the secret of the success of the young American army's famous German military adviser Von Steuben. She said that Von Steuben succeeded in instilling a relish for soldiering among the American soldiers. This in great part explains why the outgunned and outmanned fledgling American army was ultimately able to prevail over the mighty British forces during the American Revolution.

The Torah long ago recognized that this indeed is a very potent strategy. One certainly performs far better when one is blessed with a relish for his work. It is for this reason we pray each day to Hashem that He should sweeten the words of Torah in our mouths and in the mouths of our children and future posterity ("*v'ha'arev na et divrei toratecha b'finu...*"). This also explains why we recite Tehillim 100:2, which urges us to serve Hashem with joy, and why Hashem holds us accountable when we fail to do so (Devarim 28:47).

A RELISH FOR ERUVIN

A community *eruv* requires great vigilance, care, and upkeep. The way to ensure the community maintains the *eruv* is to try to instill, as Von Steuben did, a relish for the sacred task. As such, competent *eruv* advisors try to make their interactions with the communities they serve highly interactive, collaborative, and enjoyable. A high compliment is when an *eruv* advisor is told that he makes *eruv* inspection fun and enjoyable.

It is important that those involved in the *eruv* also find it challenging and meaningful – this will maintain their enthusiasm for the holy work. *Eruv* maintenance is inherently challenging. In this introduction, we seek to set forth why it is also deeply meaningful.

HELPING THE JEWISH COMMUNITY

The deep satisfaction one derives from the hard work invested working on an *eruv* begins with the sense of fulfillment one receives when working for the community. Hillel famously remarks (Avot 1:14) that *"keshe'ani l'atzmi mah ani,"* "if I am for myself alone, what am I?" Healthy-minded people instinctively seek to be part of something bigger than themselves. This desire can be channeled into a constructive community project such as devoting time, energy, and talent to the creation and maintenance of an *eruv*.

CONTINUITY

The following story illustrates an even greater level of satisfaction that can be derived from *eruv* work:

When I visited my cousin Yehuda Brandriss for a Shabbat in Modi'in, Israel, he took me to see an ancient *mikveh* (ritual bath) unearthed at the outskirts of modern-day Modi'in, a site he knew I would love. When I looked at the site, shivers ran down my spine. The design of the *mikveh* from two thousand years ago matches exactly the *mikva'ot* we create today. What a stark and stunning example of Jewish continuity!

Although we have not unearthed ancient examples of *eruvin*, the Gemara (Eruvin 11a) describes an *eruv* where an individual planted four poles at the corner of a valley and stretched a vine from one pole to the other until he encompassed the area with *tzurot hapetach* (halachic door frames). The rabbis of the Talmud approved these as valid halachic structures.

When designing a community *eruv*, I sometimes instruct those involved in the project to bear the image of the Talmudic *eruv* in mind when trying to apply the standards set forth by the Gemara to their community. I also take pains to note the grand enterprise in which we are engaged. We are seeking to recreate that which the Gemara describes! To live a life that is deeply and meaningfully connected to the past brings a priceless and profound level of satisfaction. Those who faithfully observe the Halachah experience the exhilaration of being part of a long chain anchored in a rich past, solid present, and an even greater future.

An *eruv* transforms a utility pole into a halachic entity. Talmudic concepts are applied to railroad overhangs, highway embankments, and utility poles. In the process of elevating the ordinary modern day infrastructure into halachic entities, something extraordinary happens. Temporal life is transformed into eternity. For the spiritually astute, this brings an unparalleled sense of intense fulfillment (see Shabbat 33b).

HASHEM'S HELPING HAND

Although it happens at entirely unexpected moments, the sensitive soul can detect the occasional helping hand from Hashem in his *Avodat Hashem*. In the summer of 2019, I believe that I was on the receiving end of such a caress during our yearly walking tour of the Teaneck *eruv*, which I conducted together with my rabbinic colleagues Rav Michael Taubes, Rav Daniel Feldman, and Rav Micha Shotkin. My wife had advised me to buy a pair of sunglasses to use when reviewing *eruvin* on long hot summer days to reduce the stress on my eyes, but my extremely busy schedule did not allow me the luxury of time to make the purchase.

However, five hours into the walking inspection of the Teaneck *eruv*, I noticed a pair of inexpensive sunglasses that were slipped into one of the poles used by the *eruv*. It was apparent that such an item placed in such a public area was deliberately abandoned (*hefker mida'at*) and therefore permissible to take. I seized the opportunity to henceforth use these glasses during my *eruv* reviews, as per my wife's wise advice.

Why did a pair of sunglasses appear ready for the taking on our *eruv* route? I believe it was a caress from Hashem, acknowledging the considerable time and hard work I was doing on behalf of the community.

This is not the only case when I have felt the helping hand of Hashem during my *eruv* work. In the summer of 2018, the grueling but satisfying adventure of walking the greater Teaneck *eruv* took eleven hours. Our eruv walk begins with the most challenging stretch of the day: inspecting the nearly 4-mile-long western border of the *eruv*. This portion of the *eruv* requires intense scrutiny. However, past this point, the *eruv* is able to be easily inspected from within a car. We usually arrange for a friend to drive the rabbis during this portion of the *eruv* to make the inspection more efficient.

In the hurly burly of all the activity, I had forgotten to arrange for a driver. As we approached the area, I became concerned that my oversight would prevent us from completing our task. However, all of a sudden, while passing near a small group of small stores in Northern New Milford we ran into none other than one of my former students with his large van, which easily fit all of the rabbanim (and blessed with potent air conditioning to help us cool down)! He eagerly volunteered to help us and the day was saved!

ESTABLISHING FIRM BOUNDARIES

Someone once called me an hour before Shabbat, noting that he had discovered that the hotel in which he was staying over Shabbat was located a few feet outside the *eruv*. He wondered whether there was some allowance to carry a few feet beyond the *eruv*. After advising him to consult the rabbi for the exact boundaries, I informed him that if the hotel lies beyond the *eruv*, he may not carry beyond the boundary line. *Eruv* boundaries are absolute.

Firm boundaries teach us a lesson of profound importance. A significant part of Torah life is establishing limitations. Boundaries between property, neighbors, males and females, parents and children, are examples of essential hallmarks of proper and appropriate behavior. Tehillim (104:9) states that Hashem establishes boundaries which, if not observed, will destroy the world. Essential to the world's creation is Hashem's setting ironclad boundaries between day and night, land and sea, and even wild animals and humankind (see Rashi to Bereishit 9:2 s.v. *v'chitechem*). We are charged to maintain the boundaries Hashem has set forth for us to follow. Indeed, according to a Gemara cited by Rashi, Balaam's curse was averted due his observation that "the openings of [the Bnei Yisrael's] tents did not face each other so that they should not peer into each other's tents" (Rashi to Bemidbar 24:2).

The establishment of the *eruv* boundary and its weekly inspection, upkeep, and Shabbat observance reminds and reaffirms the notion of an ironclad limit. The *eruv* creates a firm boundary, passed which we may not carry. Before Shabbat, visitors often search for the *eruv* boundaries to see whether they may carry on Shabbat. *Eruvin* are a positive reminder of the essential role healthy boundaries play in our lives.

REACHING BEYOND OUR LIMITATIONS

Every Tefillah is preceded by a citation of Tehillim 51:17 — "*Hashem sefatai tiftach, ufi yagid tehilatecha,*" "Hashem, open my lips, so that my mouth may declare Your praise." Ramban interprets *safah* in this verse to also refer to *sefat hanahar*, the edge of a river. According to Ramban, by reciting this verse, we ask Hashem to free us from our limitations and allow us to accomplish far more than that which our innate abilities allow us to accomplish.

Eruvin express this idea. An *eruv* extends our boundaries beyond their natural limitations. Our homes are our natural boundary, but the *eruv* allows us to carry past them. The redemptive side of the *eruv* lies in its expression of the notion of freeing ourselves from our natural limitations to accomplish far more than that which we deem ourselves capable of. *Eruvin* help us inculcate the value expressed in Sefer Tehillim's dictum (34:15) of avoiding the bad and doing the good — *sur me'ra ve'asei tov*. Respecting boundaries is key to averting the bad, and reaching beyond our limitations allows us to accomplish the good.

ERUVIN AS A WAY OF LIFE

Far from just being an ingenious mechanism that allows us to carry throughout our communities on Shabbat, *eruvin* expresses profound ideas about continuity, community, and commitment. The community *eruv*, therefore, should not merely be viewed as a convenience. It is an institution whose profound ideas are to be contemplated deeply in a manner that elevates and ennobles our lives with rich content and meaning. In *Walking the Line: Hilchot Eruvin from the Sources to the Streets*, we present the technical aspects of *Hilchot Eruvin*, ranging from discussions about the different halachic domains to the best *eruv* inspection practices. In doing so, we hope that the reader will become more aware of *eruvin* in their day-to-day lives, not just in terms of how community *eruvin* are designed and maintained, but also in terms of how *eruvin* have the potential to positively impact the religious climates of the areas they encompass, both on the personal and communal levels. It is our hope that *Walking the Line* will provide an important perspective on *Hilchot Eruvin* in contemporary times.

Section 1

The Laws of Creating an *Eruv*

DEFINING THE FOUR DOMAINS

The construction of *eruvin* has generated much discussion in many Jewish communities. We seek to shed light on the various opinions and practices regarding *eruvin* and thereby encourage mutual respect for the different practices regarding the use of *eruvin* today.

Disagreements about creating an *eruv* center around three primary issues: whether an area is suitable for creating an *eruv*, how to create the *eruv*, and how to rent the enclosed area in a democratic society. We will begin by discussing which areas are appropriate for creating *eruvin*.

THE FOUR DOMAINS

The Gemara (Shabbat 6a) delineates four domains (*reshuyot*) for the laws of Shabbat. A *reshut hayachid* (private domain) is surrounded by walls of a minimum height of 10 *tefachim* (about 40 inches)[1] and has a minimum area of four *tefachim* by four *tefachim*. Common examples of a *reshut hayachid* include buildings and fenced-in yards. One is permitted to carry within a *reshut hayachid* on Shabbat and from one *reshut hayachid* directly into another adjacent one.[2]

A *reshut harabim* (public domain) is an area where carrying on Shabbat is forbidden, such as a city square or a street that passes directly from one end of town to the other. It must

---

[1] A *tefach* is a handbreadth, which is between three and four inches. See *Encyclopedia Talmudit* 20:659.

[2] However, in certain situations, it is necessary to perform *sechirat reshut* and *eruv chatzeirot*, as is explained in the fourth chapter.

be at least 16 *amot* (about 28 feet)[3] wide, unroofed, and with less than three walls (see Shabbat 99a).[4] Rav Hershel Schachter points out that a *reshut harabim* must not be private property (*The Journal of Halacha and Contemporary Society*, 5:12, based on Eruvin 59a; see, however, Rav Dovid Ribiat (*The 39 Melochos* 4:1292) who disagrees). Some opinions maintain that 600,000 people must pass through it daily, and we will discuss this debate later. Additionally, some authorities consider any inter-city highway a *reshut harabim*, even if it does not meet all of the other requirements (Ramban, Eruvin 59a).[5] Carrying four *amot* (about six to seven feet) within a *reshut harabim* on Shabbat is biblically prohibited, as is carrying from a *reshut hayachid* into a *reshut harabim* and vice versa.

A *mekom petur* (literally an "exempt site") is a place within a *reshut harabim* whose area is less than four *tefachim* by four *tefachim* (see *Mishnah Berurah* 345:30). It must also be **either** at least three *tefachim* high **or** enclosed by walls that are three *tefachim* high. One may carry into or out of a *reshut harabim* or a *reshut hayachid* from a *mekom petur*. Common examples include narrow garbage cans and fire hydrants. It is widely accepted that a *mekom petur* exists only in a *reshut harabim*.[6]

---

[3] For summaries of the various opinions regarding the size of an *amah*, see *Encyclopedia Talmudit* (2:28-29).

[4] There is some debate regarding the question of whether such a street also makes all public areas in its town into a *reshut harabim*. This is discussed in the next chapter.

[5] See our separate chapter on *Highways, Railroads, and Ground Levels*.

[6] The Rama (O.C. 345:19) cites two opinions regarding whether or not a *makom petur* can also exist in a *karmelit*. The *Mishnah Berurah* (345:87)

The fourth and final domain is a *karmelit*, where it is rabbinically forbidden to carry. A *karmelit* is essentially any place that does not fit the descriptions of the other domains. This includes the sea and all public places that do not meet the requirements of a *reshut harabim*.[7]

CONVERTING INTO A RESHUT HAYACHID

In order to facilitate carrying in *karmeliyot* and *reshuyot harabim*, these areas must be transformed into private domains. Since the prohibition against carrying in a *karmelit* is only rabbinic in nature, the rabbis made it relatively easy to change a *karmelit* into a *reshut hayachid*. Surrounding it with *tzurot hapetach* (door frames) renders the *karmelit* an enclosed area. A *tzurat hapetach* consists of a horizontal wire (or pole) that passes over the tops of two vertical poles, forming the shape of a doorway. The vertical poles are colloquially referred to as *lechis*

Rav Yehudah Halevi (*Kuzari* 3:51) explains why the rabbis provided a relatively simple way to remove the prohibition of carrying in a *karmelit*, by ruling that *tzurot hapetach* are sufficient to convert a *karmelit* into a *reshut hayachid*. He suggests that they made this enactment to prevent treating rabbinic restrictions with the same severity as the Torah's restrictions and to provide the Jewish people with some freedom of movement on Shabbat.

---

notes that most Acharonim incline to recognize the status of *mekom petur* only in a *reshut harabim*, and the *Aruch Hashulchan* (O.C. 345:45) rules accordingly. Also see *Biur Halachah* s.v. *v'yeish cholekim*.

[7] For a brief summary of the laws concerning these four domains, see Rav Shimon Eider's *Halachos of the Eruv* (pp. 1-4).

The conversion of a *reshut harabim* into a *reshut hayachid* is much more difficult, because the prohibition of carrying in a *reshut harabim* is biblical. A wall or fence must surround the *reshut harabim* in order to change its status.[8] If a *reshut harabim* is enclosed on all sides by doors at night, it ceases to be a *reshut harabim*.[9] The classic example of this phenomenon appears on Eruvin 22a, where the Gemara states that "had Jerusalem's doors not been locked in the evenings, the city would have been considered a *reshut harabim*." In a few locations in the United States, "doors" have been "installed" to encompass an area that might otherwise constitute a *reshut harabim* (this will be discussed at length in a later chapter).[10]

DOES A RESHUT HARABIM REQUIRE 600,000 PEOPLE?

In light of the halachic differences between them, it is quite important to determine if an area is a true *reshut harabim* or merely

---

[8] A fence whose vertical and horizontal links are less than three *tefachim* apart is the halachic equivalent of a solid wall, based on the concept of *lavud*. This principle considers a gap of less than three *tefachim* to be closed off.

[9] While walls undoubtedly turn a *reshut harabim* into a *reshut hayachid*, it is unclear whether doors achieve the same result. The *Avnei Neizer* (O.C. 280) believes they do make the *reshut harabim* into a *reshut hayachid*. On the other hand, the *Chazon Ish* (O.C. 78:1) argues that doors transform a *reshut harabim* into a *karmelit*, but all breaches still require *tzurot hapetach* in order to permit carrying within the enclosed area on Shabbat. We discuss this topic at length in our chapter, *The Delatot of Canarsie, London, Mattersdorf, & Oakland*.

[10] See *Netivot Shabbat* (ch. 23) for a general review of the literature regarding doors that eliminate the status of *reshut harabim*.

a *karmelit*. The precise definitions of these categories have been debated since the time of the earliest Rishonim. The main point of contention is whether an area requires 600,000 people to attain the status of a *reshut harabim*.

RISHONIM

The Rambam (*Hilchot Shabbat* 14:1) does not mention that 600,000 people must be present for an area to be considered a *reshut harabim*. Rashi (Eruvin 6a s.v. *reshut harabim* and Eruvin 59a s.v. *ir*), however, writes that a city that does not regularly have 600,000 people is not a *reshut harabim*, because it is less populated than the Jews' encampment in the desert. The practices and the activities of the Jewish encampment in the desert as recorded in the Torah serve as the paradigm for forbidden activities on Shabbat (see Shabbat 73b-74a). *Tosafot* (Eruvin 6a s.v. *keitzad*) record that the *Behag* agrees with Rashi, whereas *Rabbeinu Tam* finds Rashi's opinion problematic.

A major problem with the opinion requiring 600,000 people for a *reshut harabim* is that the Gemara (Shabbat 6a) describes at length what constitutes a *reshut harabim*, without any explicit mention of requiring 600,000 people. Surely, the Gemara would not omit such a critical part of defining a *reshut harabim*. Rav Aharon Lichtenstein has told me that he believes the opinion of Rashi and the *Behag* is among the most singularly difficult opinions of Rishonim in all of Halachah (though see the Ritva, Shabbat 6b s.v. *kan*, who argues for a basis of this opinion in the Gemara).

THE SHULCHAN ARUCH AND ITS COMMENTARIES

The *Shulchan Aruch* (O.C. 345:7) cites (and presumably accepts) the view that an area is a *reshut harabim* even without 600,000 people. Although Rav Yosef Karo does cite the other view as a secondary opinion,[11] the Rama (O.C. 346:3) indicates that he accepts the requirement of 600,000.[12] Both the *Magen Avraham* (345:7) and the *Taz* (345:6) cite the view of the *Ma'sat Binyamin* (92) and the Maharshal (*Yam Shel Shlomo*, Beitzah 3:8), who rule that the presence of 600,000 people is not required. However, the *Magen Avraham* and *Taz* themselves disagree with these authorities and write that the majority view is that of Rashi, requiring 600,000 people. The *Aruch Hashulchan* (345:17) writes that the *eruvin* in the Jewish towns of Eastern Europe relied on this accepted leniency; otherwise, they could not have used *tzurot hapetach*.

---

[11] The *Shulchan Aruch's* view is somewhat unclear, as he appears to contradict himself in O.C 303:18. There he writes that no places today qualify as *reshuyot harabim*. Presumably, his reason is that he requires 600,000 people for a *reshut harabim*. Regarding the practice of Sephardic Jews today, see our full discussion in our later chapter, *May a Sephardic Jew rely on a Community Eruv*.

[12] This is inferred from the Rama's statement that in our day there are no *reshuyot harabim*. While logic would dictate that the Rama writes this because he believes that only a place with 600,000 people constitutes a *reshut harabim*, this inference presents a certain difficulty. The Shulchan Aruch (O.C. 303:18) also writes that there are no true *reshuyot harabim*, yet he appears to rule that 600,000 people are **not** required for a *reshut harabim* (O.C. 345:7). *Magen Avraham* (345:7) points out this problem.

THE MISHKENOT YAAKOV'S CRITICISM

In the early nineteenth century, the *Mishkenot Yaakov* (O.C. 119-122) strongly criticized the construction of the Eastern European *eruvin*. His criticisms included the fact that their wires sagged[13] and there were no places for hinges on the *tzurot hapetach* (as there are on true doorways).[14] Most of all, *tzurot hapetach* were used to create the *eruvin*, since the towns and villages were seen as *karmeliyot*. He asserted that the opinions of many more Rishonim had been published since the time of the *Shulchan Aruch*.[15] The discovery that many of these Rishonim rejected Rashi's opinion rendered his opinion that requires 600,000 people a **minority** opinion, whereas it had previously been considered the majority view. He argued that even the small towns and villages of Central and Eastern Europe should now be considered *reshuyot harabim*.

---

[13] Sagging wires are problematic, because a *tzurat hapetach* must be constructed in the same manner as people make ordinary door frames (*ked'avdei inshei*; see Eruvin 94b). We address this at great length in our chapter *Sagging Wires in the Yeshiva University Eruv*.

[14] See Eruvin 11b. Our practice is not to require a place for hinges; see *Aruch Hashulchan* 362:31. The *Haghot Oshri* (to the Rosh Eruvin 1:14) already records the widespread practice to not require a place for hinges. He writes that the common practice is based on the *eruv* in the city of Narbonne which did not have a place for hinges.

[15] See Rav Moshe Bleich's article, "The Role of Manuscripts in Halachic Decision Making" (*Tradition* 27:2:22-55), regarding the halachic weight of newly discovered manuscripts of Rishonim.

REACTION TO THE MISHKENOT YAAKOV'S CRITICISM

Halachic authorities expressed mixed reactions to the *Mishkenot Yaakov*'s criticism. The *Beit Efraim* (26) defended the practice to rely on *eruvin* consisting of *tzurot hapetach*, and the *Aruch Hashulchan* (362:18) wrote in the late nineteenth century that it was as if a heavenly voice proclaimed that the opinion requiring 600,000 people for a *reshut harabim* was [still] correct.

The *Mishnah Berurah*[16] strongly urges pious individuals (*ba'alei nefesh*) to be strict and refrain from carrying within an *eruv* that is based on the lenient opinion. However, he writes that one should not rebuke those who do rely on such *eruvin*. For a summary of this issue, see Rav Elimelech Lange's *Hilchot Eruvin* (21-28).

It is interesting to note that even those who are strict and do not rely on an *eruv* might be permitted to ask a Jew who does use the *eruv* to carry for them (see *Teshuvot Igrot Moshe*, O.C. 1:186). Rav Shlomo Zalman Auerbach (*Teshuvot Minchat Shlomo* 1:44) rules that one who embraces the strict opinion in a disputed area of Halachah need not refrain from causing others to follow their practice of relying upon the lenient view. However, he addresses a rabbinic prohibition, and he notes that this matter is subject to debate regarding biblical prohibitions. Regarding *eruvin*, authorities debate whether carrying in a *reshut harabim* enclosed by *tzurot hapetach* is a biblical or rabbinic prohibition; see *Biur Halachah* (364:2 s.v. *vehu* and s.v. *ve'achar*). Elsewhere

---

[16] 345:23 and *Biur Halachah* s.v. *she'ein shishim*. The *Biur Halachah* adds in a parenthetical comment that there is room to be lenient in situations where there is an additional factor to bolster relying on the opinion requiring 600,000 people to create a *reshut harabim*.

(*Minchat Shlomo* 2:35:17), Rav Shlomo Zalman suggests that one who adopts a *chumrah* (stringency beyond the letter of the law) can ask someone who follows the letter of the law to violate this *chumrah*. However, if one is strict because he believes a more lenient view to be mistaken, perhaps he should refrain from asking others to violate what he considers an absolute prohibition. (Even in the latter case, Rav Shlomo Zalman does not issue a definitive ruling.) When Ashkenazic and Sephardic communities follow different opinions, Rav Shlomo Zalman implicitly compares such a situation to a *chumrah*, because the one who causes others to act agrees that Jews from the other community need not be stringent.

A LIST OF MAJOR CITIES

As we explained in the previous chapter, some Rishonim require 600,000 residents for a city to attain the status of a *reshut harabim*. While this position prevents most towns and cities from having to cope with the issues regarding a *reshut harabim*, larger cities might nonetheless face them. In this chapter, we survey the opinions of contemporary authorities regarding certain specific cities.

PARIS: RAV CHAIM OZER GRODZINSKI AND THE CHAZON ISH

In the late 1930s, the rabbis of Paris asked Rav Chaim Ozer Grodzinski (the leading Ashkenazic halachic authority at that time) if they could construct an *eruv* consisting of *tzurot hapetach* around their city. This method would only suffice if Paris were considered a *karmelit*, as opposed to a *reshut harabim*.

Rav Chaim Ozer consulted with the *Chazon Ish* (one of the most respected authorities in the laws of *eruvin*)[17] as well as the rabbis who supervised the Vilna *eruv*. Rav Chaim Ozer (*Teshuvot Achiezer* 4:8) opens his responsum by noting that over 600,000 people reside in Paris, so seemingly all authorities would consider it a *reshut harabim*. Consequently, an *eruv* consisting of *tzurot hapetach* cannot render it a private domain.

However, he notes that walls surround Paris on three sides, rendering it a *reshut hayachid* on a biblical level. There are

---

[17] Rav Hershel Schachter and Rav Chaim Zimbalist have told me that halachic authorities generally treat the *Chazon Ish* more authoritatively than even the *Mishnah Berurah* in the area of *eruvin*.

bridges that pass over the walls, constituting breaches (*pirtzot*) in them.[18] Nevertheless, Rav Chaim Ozer claims that Paris is a *reshut hayachid* on a purely biblical level, since the walls on these three sides cover most of the perimeter (*omeid merubeh al haparutz*). Rav Chaim Ozer argues that while any breach over ten *amot* (roughly fifteen to eighteen feet) invalidates a wall on a rabbinic level, such breaches are insignificant on a biblical level as long as the majority of each of three sides of the perimeter remains enclosed.[19] Since the breaches in Paris's wall are problematic only on a rabbinic level, the erection of *tzurot hapetach* suffices to permit carrying. Rav Chaim Ozer and the *Chazon Ish* thus conclude that *tzurot hapetach* suffice in Paris.[20]

---

[18] See *Noda Beyehudah* (1:42) and *Mishnah Berurah* (*Sha'ar Hatziyun* 363:95).

[19] Rav Moshe Feinstein (*Teshuvot Igrot Moshe*, O.C. 2:90) also rules that a breach of more than ten *amot* constitutes a problem only on a **rabbinical** level. See, however, *Mishkenot Yaakov* (120) and *Mishnat Rabbi Aharon* (1:6:12), who disagree and claim that such breaches invalidate the wall on a **biblical** level.

[20] Also see *Chazon Ish*, O.C. 107:5-7. He addresses a situation where buildings are close enough to one another that they occupy more space than the open gaps between them. After complex calculations, the *Chazon Ish* rules that whenever at least one street ends or curves inside the city, it loses the status of *reshut harabim*. For an explanation of his reasoning, see Rav Hershel Schachter's essay in *The Journal of Halacha and Contemporary Society* (5:15-19) and Rav Yosef Gavriel Bechhofer's *The Contemporary Eruv* (pp. 56-66). See *Beit Yitzchak* 5753, pp. 61-69, for Rav Mordechai Willig's thorough analysis of this issue. Rav Willig notes that the Meiri (Eruvin 20a s.v. *v'yeish*) appears to agree with the *Chazon Ish*. For criticisms of the *Chazon Ish*, see *Mishnat Rabbi Aharon* (1:6:12) and *Teshuvot Igrot Moshe* (O.C. 5:28:1:3). Rav Shlomo Zalman Auerbach (*Minchat Shlomo* 2:35:22) takes the

WARSAW: RAV SHLOMO DAVID KAHANE

Rav Shlomo David Kahane (the Rav of Warsaw during the 1930s) faced an interesting problem with Warsaw's *eruv*. During its construction in the nineteenth century, Warsaw's *eruv* consisted of *tzurot hapetach*. It was effective because fewer than 600,000 people resided within it. However, in the twentieth century, Warsaw's population exceeded 600,000, seemingly invalidating the *eruv*. Rav Kahane (cited by Rav Menachem Kasher in *Noam* 6:44) rules that the *eruv* is nonetheless valid, asserting that the larger a city grows, the less chance there is for any one street to run straight through it, without curving significantly. One requirement for a *reshut harabim* is that a street must go **straight** through the entire city.[21] Accordingly, Warsaw does not meet this requirement and is still not a *reshut harabim*. Rav Moshe Feinstein criticizes this approach (see *Teshuvot Igrot Moshe*, O.C. 1:140), questioning the argument that the street cannot curve. He claims that a street that runs from one end of town to the other turns it into a *reshut harabim*, curves notwithstanding, provided that it meets the other criteria for a *reshut harabim*. Thus, in a place that meets the other requirements for a *reshut harabim*, *tzurot hapetach* do not suffice.

Chazon Ish's view into consideration in case of great need. It is unclear if Rav Chaim Ozer based his ruling in Paris on this opinion of the *Chazon Ish*.

[21] See *Shulchan Aruch* (O.C. 345:7) and Rav Mordechai Willig (*Beit Yitzchak* 25:63-65).

FLATBUSH: RAV YOSEF ELIYAHU HENKIN AND RAV MOSHE FEINSTEIN

During the 1970s, the construction of the *eruv* in Flatbush (a neighborhood of Brooklyn, New York) aroused great controversy. To this day, its permissibility remains disputed. Some rabbis permit carrying inside the Flatbush *eruv*, while many rabbis and *rashei yeshivah* there, such as Torah Vodaath's Rav Yisroel Belsky (personal communication), forbid its use.

Rav Yosef Eliyahu Henkin (*Kitvei Hagaon Rav Y.E. Henkin* 2:25) strongly encourages the construction of *eruvin* in New York's five boroughs, including Brooklyn (whose population easily exceeded 600,000 already in his day). Although Rav Henkin does not explain why these places are not *reshuyot harabim*, a number of arguments have been offered to support his contention that Flatbush is not in this category. First, Rav Shlomo David Kahane's argument regarding the Warsaw *eruv* seemingly applies to Flatbush, too, because no street within the Flatbush *eruv* runs straight from one end of the city to the other.[22]

Second, the ruling of Rav Chaim Ozer Grodzinski and the *Chazon Ish* also seems to apply to Flatbush. The faces of the buildings and the fences along the highways appear to constitute the majority of a wall on three sides.[23] (Ironically, this lenient consideration is most often applicable in densely populated

---

[22] Even Flatbush Avenue and Bedford Avenue bend at various points; Ocean Parkway does not extend from one end of Brooklyn to the other.

[23] The *Chazon Ish* (O.C. 107:5-7) requires that there be at least one street in the town that either bends or ends inside the town. Brooklyn meets this requirement, as we have explained in the previous footnote.

urban areas rather than smaller suburbs, which frequently have much empty space between buildings.)

Third, the *Aruch Hashulchan*'s unique (but highly questionable) approach might be taken into account (O.C. 345:19-24). In his opinion, a street must be the only inter-city thoroughfare or commercial center in that city to be a true *reshut harabim*, with all other streets being minor in comparison. Accordingly, only in the time of the Talmud did true *reshuyot harabim* exist, because it was common for a town to have only one main street.[24] Nowadays, most towns and cities have more than one inter-city thoroughfare and commercial center, so we do not have true *reshuyot harabim*. Brooklyn certainly has multiple commercial centers and inter-city roads, so the *Aruch Hashulchan* would not consider it a *reshut harabim*.

Rav Moshe Feinstein (*Teshuvot Igrot Moshe*, O.C. 4:87) vigorously disputes the *Aruch Hashulchan*'s argument, citing a proof to the contrary from the Gemara (Shabbat 96b).[25] The *Divrei Malkiel* (vol. 3, p. 267) also writes that one may not rely on

---

[24] The *Aruch Hashulchan* refers to the *sratiya* and *platiya* described on Shabbat 6a. It is unclear if the *Aruch Hashulchan* requires that a *reshut harabim* be **both** the only commercial center **and** the only intercity route, or if he suffices with **either** condition. See his comments in O.C. 345:26, where it appears that he suffices with **either** condition.

[25] The Gemara describes how carrying in a **reshut harabim** occurred during construction of the *mishkan*. This work was not done in **the** main thoroughfare of the desert encampment, yet the Gemara states that it was done in a *reshut harabim*. Rav Moshe thus concludes that a city, like the desert encampment, can have multiple public centers and still be a *reshut harabim*, thus disproving the *Aruch Hashulchan*'s opinion.

the *Aruch Hashulchan*'s novel insight, since it does not appear in any earlier source. Rav Aharon Lichtenstein (personal communication) conveyed sentiments similar to those of the *Divrei Malkiel* and Rav Moshe. Moreover, a careful reading of the *Aruch Hashulchan* seems to reveal that he sought to use his novel suggestion only as an adjunct (*senif*) to the view that a true *reshut harabim* requires 600,000 people. He never suggests relying on his idea without other grounds for leniency. Accordingly, the *Aruch Hashulchan*'s view cannot be relied upon as the sole reason for permitting carrying within an area that contains more than 600,000 people.

A fourth defense of the Flatbush *eruv* is the opinion of Rav Efraim Zalman Margoliot (*Beit Efraim*, O.C. 26) that only pedestrians count when determining that 600,000 people travel in a street. He argues that the requirement for 600,000 people is based on a comparison to the encampment in the desert. The comparison can thus be made only to pedestrians, as the 600,000 people who were in the quintessential *reshut harabim* were all pedestrians. The Maharsham (1:162) and Rav Eliezer Waldenberg (cited in *The Contemporary Eruv*, p. 54 note 119) add that trains and cars are private domains unto themselves, so their occupants are not counted among the 600,000 people of a *reshut harabim*. Both Rav Moshe (*Teshuvot Igrot Moshe*, O.C. 1:139:6) and Rav Binyamin Silber (*Teshuvot Az Nidberu* 6:70) reject this argument, pointing out that wagons (*agalot*) were used in the desert encampment's thoroughfares.

Despite all of the arguments in favor of being lenient, Rav Moshe did not endorse the construction of the Flatbush eruv (see *Teshuvot Igrot Moshe*, O.C. 4:87-88). He explicitly rejects all of the arguments presented and rules that the 600,000 people who regularly travel the streets of Brooklyn render it a *reshut harabim*.[26] Interestingly, Rav Ovadia Yosef (*Teshuvot Yabia Omer* 9 O.C. 33) endorsed the creation of an Eruv in Flatbush as acceptable according to baseline Halachah. He accepted the approach of the Beit Ephraim that the occupants of cars do not count towards the count of 600,000 people.

KEW GARDENS HILLS

Although Rav Moshe did not approve of constructing an *eruv* in Flatbush, he did permit the *eruv* in the Kew Gardens Hills section of Queens, New York. Rav Moshe stipulated the following requirements for the *eruv* to be acceptable:

1. All highways (Grand Central Parkway, Long Island Expressway, Van Wyck Expressway) were excluded from the *eruv*, because many authorities maintain that highways always constitute *reshuyot harabim*.[27]

---

[26] Rav Moshe's concern was not for 600,000 **residents** but for 600,000 people **traveling** the streets at any time (drivers and pedestrians) within an area that is twelve *mil* by twelve *mil* (approximately eight miles by eight miles). He thus requires that the population be so great that 600,000 people are regularly found in the streets. Rav Moshe estimates that this requires at least 2.4 million residents. Rav Moshe is the lone authority who requires such a large population, and even he (O.C. 4:87) expresses reservations about his view, noting that no other authorities mention it. Nevertheless, Brooklyn is so populous that even Rav Moshe considers it a *reshut harabim*.

[27] See Ramban to Eruvin 59a (s.v. *verash atzmo*), *Mishnah Berurah* (345:17), and *Teshuvot Bnei Banim* (1:17-20).

2. It was constructed in a manner that greatly reduces the possibility of breakage during Shabbat. A communal *eruv* that uses as many pre-existing components as possible, such as telephone poles and wires, fences, hills,[28] and train overpasses has the greatest chance of remaining intact.[29]

3. An individual was appointed to inspect the *eruv* every Friday; it must be rigorously inspected before every Shabbat (see *Teshuvot Doveiv Meisharim*, 2:28, who addresses of inspecting an *eruv* before Friday).

4. The rabbis of the community were required to approve of the *eruv* and mutually agree that it was built properly, as an *eruv* should promote peace and not be a source of tension within a community (see Gittin 59a).

Regarding the issue of *reshut harabim*, Rav Moshe wrote that "Kew Gardens Hills is small regarding these issues and the reasons I wrote [for not allowing an *eruv* in other parts of New York City] do not apply here." Although the borough of Queens has more than 600,000 inhabitants, Rav Moshe apparently viewed

---

[28] A hill that slopes at a minimum twenty five degree slant qualifies as a *tel hamitlakeit* and constitutes a Halachic wall; however, see *Netivot Shabbat* 15:10 citing the *Chazon Ish* (O.C. 111) notes that great caution must be used in applying this rule, as often what seems at first glance to qualify as a *tel hamitlaket*, under careful scrutiny does not.

[29] See, however, *Teshuvot Igrot Moshe*, O.C. 1:138; though see the *Chazon Ish*, O.C. 79:1, who clearly (see Rav Baruch Simon's *Imrei Baruch, Eruvin UReshuyot* pp. 31-32) does not agree with Rav Moshe's approach to the concept of *pi tikra yoreid v'soteim*.

Kew Gardens Hills as a separate entity. *Tzurot hapetach* thus sufficed, since fewer than 600,000 people resided in it.

Based on this responsum, it seems obvious that it is permitted according to Rav Moshe's standards, to create an Eruv in the Riverdale section of the Bronx. Riverdale is dramatically distinct from the rest of the Bronx, far more than Kew Gardens Hills is distinct from Queens. The same reasoning seems to apply to the Hyde Park neighborhood in the south side of Chicago. However, Rav Moshe in his very brief responsum does not set forth his criteria when he would consider a neighborhood as distinct from the larger city.

TEL AVIV

Not all halachic authorities agree with Rav Moshe's ruling to view certain neighborhoods as distinct entities within a large city. Rav Shaul Yisraeli (*Techumin* 10:140) writes that a city constitutes one halachic entity for purposes of defining a *reshut harabim*. Moreover, the sole halachic criterion defining an area as a city is a contiguity of homes (see *Shulchan Aruch*, O.C. 398), not municipal boundaries. Accordingly, he rules that the entire Tel Aviv metropolitan area (known as Gush Dan which includes Tel Aviv-Yaffo, Ramat Gan, Bnei Brak, Givatayim, Petach Tikva, Bat Yam etc.) should be viewed as one entity regarding the *reshut harabim* issue. Since more than 600,000 people reside in Gush Dan, it constitutes a *reshut harabim*.

The Tel Aviv *eruv* today consists of *tzurot hapetach*, so Rav Yisraeli offers a suggestion for how Gush Dan may yet be a *karmelit*. He explains that the overwhelming majority of the observant community in Tel Aviv relies on the *eruv* because it follows the *Shulchan Aruch*'s presentation (O.C. 345:7) of the view that requires 600,000 people for a *reshut harabim*. He implies that 600,000 people must pass through a **particular street** every day for it to be a public domain. Rav Yisraeli notes that the *Mishnah Berurah* (345:24 and *Sha'ar Hatziyun* 345:25) rules that 600,000 people need not pass through a particular street for the town to be defined as a *reshut harabim*. According to the *Mishnah Berurah*, anywhere with 600,000 residents is a *reshut harabim*.[30]

The residents of Tel Aviv thus rely on an extraordinarily lenient approach. They follow the lenient understanding (*Shulchan Aruch*, to require 600,000 on one street) of the lenient opinion (Rashi, that 600,000 people are required for a *reshut harabim*)! Rav Yisraeli explains that it is possible to be so lenient only because we follow the opinion of those Rishonim (cited in *Biur Halachah*, 364:2 s.v. *ve'achar* and see our chapter on *Demystifying Atu Rabim*) who rule that *tzurot hapetach* suffice on a biblical level for even a *reshut* **harabim**. Because *tzurot hapetach* are only invalid in a *reshut harabim* on a rabbinical level, it is possible to permit lenient practices that would otherwise be unacceptable.

Rav Naaman Wasserzug (*Techumin* 11:163-169) provides a different defense of the Tel Aviv *eruv*. He argues that, on a Torah level, Tel Aviv is a *reshut hayachid*, because it is enclosed by "halachic walls" on three sides.[31] It has the sea on the west, the

---

[30] Rav Moshe Feinstein (*Teshuvot Igrot Moshe*, O.C. 4:88) requires that the 600,000 people be within an area which is twelve *mil* by twelve *mil* (approximately eight miles by eight miles).

[31] This is similar to the ruling of Rav Chaim Ozer Grodzinski and the *Chazon Ish* concerning Paris.

Ayalon Valley on the east, and the Yarkon Valley on the south.[32] According to this approach, the residents of Tel Aviv are not relying on such a radically lenient ruling.

The more straightforward approach to defend the *eruvin* of Gush Dan would be to adopt the approaches we set forth regarding Paris and Warsaw. In addition, Rav Nissim Karelitz is cited (*Ule'areiv Eruvo*, p. 22) defending the *eruv* in Bnei Brak noting that Bnei Brak is a very distinct entity from the rest of Gush Dan. Similarly, the cities comprising Gush Dan are generally perceived as separate entities. For example, the cultural events conducted by each Gush Dan municipality for its residents are not open to residents of other cities of Gush Dan, without paying a higher fee.

Gush Dan differs in this regard from Jerusalem, where the latter is perceived as constituting one municipal entity. Rav Eliashiv is cited (*Ule'areiv Eruvo*, p. 21) as asserting that even Jerusalem's suburb Ramot is considered part of Jerusalem as far as its definition regarding its being a *reshut harabim* since Ramot's residents typically enter Jerusalem even for the most basic purchases (though this is subject to change over time).

CONCLUSION
In addition to the issues discussed in this chapter, my experience indicates that virtually every community *eruv* encounters challenges and difficulties during construction and maintenance. Accordingly, before relying on any community *eruv*, one must consult a halachic authority familiar with both the laws of

---

[32] The Halachah recognizes these places as valid walls; see *Shulchan Aruch* (O.C. 345:2 and 362:3).

eruvin and the details of the *eruv* in question. Our discussion in this chapter only addresses certain issues of interest regarding each *eruv*, but we have not researched the *eruvin* sufficiently to ensure that they are fit for use on Shabbat. Furthermore, due to the difficulties and challenges in maintaining an *eruv*, no one can ensure that *eruvin* that are presently acceptable will remain this way in the future.[33]

---

[33] As discussed at length in our section on *eruvin* maintenance.

HIGHWAYS, RAILROADS, & OVERPASSES

Many community *eruvin* must grapple with the issue of intercity highways. For example, the Jerusalem-Tel Aviv highway is within the Yerushalayim citywide *eruv*, Route 4 runs through Teaneck, New Jersey and the Henry Hudson Parkway enters the *eruv* of the Riverdale section of The Bronx, New York. Different communities grapple with this issue in varying manners and we shall explain the basis for the various practices.

AN INTERCITY ROAD

A most fundamental point is that an *eruv* consisting of *tzurot hapetach* may be constructed only in an area within which it is forbidden to carry only on a rabbinic level. This precludes a *tzurat hapetach* from permitting an individual to carry within a *reshut harabim*. The question, then, is whether an intercity highway is classified as a *reshut harabim*. The Gemara (Shabbat 6a) states that a road that one travels when going from city to city (*seratya*) is categorized as a *reshut harabim*. This passage in the Gemara is codified by the *Magen Avraham* (345:5) and *Mishnah Berurah* (345:17) without dissent. However, there is a question if Rashi's requirement of 600,000 people (see Chapter 1) to designate an area as a *reshut harabim* applies to such a road. If Rashi's qualification of 600,000 people does not apply, then an intercity road could be designated as a *reshut harabim* even if 600,000 people do not travel on it.

Ramban (Eruvin 59a) writes that it is possible that Rashi's leniency does not apply to an intercity road, since such a road is a public domain similar to the *diglei midbar*, the Bnei Yisrael's camp in the desert. This would apply even if 600,000 people do not regularly travel on the intercity road.[34] Rav Hershel Schachter (*Journal of Halacha and Contemporary Society* 5:13 and *Kol Tzvi* 5765, p. 84) explains that this approach views the intercity road as the quintessential *reshut harabim*.[35] Therefore, the intercity road does not have to meet the various conditions that an area usually has to meet to be defined as a *reshut harabim* (such as Rashi's requirement of 600,000 people). An entire city or street that does not run from city to city must have 600,000 people, according to this approach, in order for it to match a highway and constitute a *reshut harabim*.

The *Biur Halachah* (345:7 s.v. *ve'yeish omerim*) cites the suggestion of Ramban, but it is not clear whether he rules in accordance with it. Neither the *Mishnah Berurah* nor *Biur Halachah* clearly write that those who rely on Rashi's lenient approach should refrain from doing so on intercity roads. In fact, the *Mishnah Berurah* (364:8) clearly indicates that the accepted custom runs counter to Ramban's stringency. The *Aruch Hashulchan* (O.C. 345:17) rules that an intercity road requires 600,000 people to be defined as a *reshut harabim*. However, unlike that which is implied by the *Shulchan Aruch*'s presentation, the *Aruch Hashulchan* holds that the 600,000 person threshold does not refer to the number of people who traverse the road each day. Rather, he holds that 600,000 people must pass through the road "in the course of time" in order for it to be defined as a *reshut harabim*.

---

[34] It seems that the *Tosafot Rid* (Pesachim 69a s.v. *matir*) also subscribes to the Ramban's view.

[35] The aforementioned passage in Shabbat 6a seems to support this assertion.

Teshuvot Maharsham (3:188) and Rav Moshe Feinstein (*Teshuvot Igrot Moshe*, O.C. 1:139:5) rule that the 600,000 person requirement applies even to an intercity road. It is clear that Rav Moshe considers the 600,000 person condition to refer to daily passage (*Maharsham* even explicitly writes that the 600,000 person requirement refers only to a city where it is usual to have 600,000 people within it on a daily basis). He does not regard any of the bridges that connect Brooklyn and Manhattan as *reshuyot harabim* since 600,000 people do not travel on them daily, even though 600,000 people definitely pass on these very heavily traveled bridges in the course of time. The *Netivot Shabbat* (3:1 note 9) writes that the *Machatzit Hashekel* (357:11) seems to agree with the *Maharsham* and Rav Moshe.

Rav Mordechai Willig (personal communication) infers that both the *Shulchan Aruch* (O.C. 303:18) and Rama (O.C. 346:3) apply Rashi's leniency of 600,000 people to intercity roads. He deduces this from the fact that both the *Shulchan Aruch* and Rama present Rashi's requirement of 600,000 people by writing that "there is no *reshut harabim* in our times," without stating that intercity roads constitute an exception. Indeed, Rav Willig does not exclude the Henry Hudson Parkway from the Riverdale *eruv* and Rav Eliezer Waldenburg (see Rav Yosef Gavriel Bechoffer's *The Contemporary Eruv*, p. 54 note 119) supports the inclusion of the Jerusalem-Tel Aviv highway within the Yerushalayim citywide *eruv* since 600,000 people do not travel on it daily. Rav Hershel Schachter, on the other hand, rules in accordance with Ramban. His ruling is followed in Teaneck, where the *eruv* excludes Route 4,[36] and Allentown, Pennsylvania, which excludes Route 22 from its *eruv*.[37]

DEFINING AN INTERCITY ROAD

Rav Willig (personal communication) argues further that the Henry Hudson Parkway is not included in Ramban's definition of an intercity road since Riverdale residents commonly use this highway as a convenient and quick manner to travel from one section of Riverdale to another. Indeed, a careful reading of Ramban seems to support this assertion. Ramban speaks of roads that are "outside the city which people use to travel from one city to another and from one country to another until the end of the entire world." The New Jersey Turnpike, which lies (for the most part) outside of city boundaries and is used almost exclusively as an intercity road, serves as a good example.

On the other hand, there are communities in North America that exclude even intercity roads that are fully integrated into the city with traffic lights and side street parking. This approach seems to run entirely counter to the aforementioned words of Ramban.

---

[36] The Teaneck *eruv* does not, however, exclude the exit and entrance ramps of Route 4. This is based on a ruling Rav Schachter (in May 2017) issued to this author that the stringent approach of the Ramban applies only to actual highways but not to the entrance and exit ramps.

[37] The existing infrastructure in Teaneck and Allentown makes this possible. However, in Riverdale and many other communities (such as West Orange, New Jersey and Scarsdale, New York), such an exclusion would be prohibitive in cost and most likely not permitted by the relevant government authorities.

Rav Hershel Schachter adopts a very reasonable approach to this issue. Rav Schachter argues that only a limited access highway is defined as an intercity road for this purpose. Only such a highway can be described as being "outside the city" (even if it runs within municipal boundaries, such as Teaneck's Route 4), since it is set apart from the rest of the city. Thus, Rav Schachter (personal communication in 1990) ruled that Route 34 may be included in the Matawan, New Jersey *eruv* and that Route 46 can be encompassed by the Parsippany, New Jersey *eruv*. There might be an in-between sort of road which is not a limited access highway but is used primarily for an inter-city travel such as New Jersey's 9W (in the portion that runs north of Englewood's East Palisades Avenue) which Rav Schachter might regard as a *reshut harabim*.

RAILROADS

Are railroads considered to be intercity roads for the purposes of *eruvin*? The *Aruch Hashulchan* (ad. loc.) rules that heavily traveled railroads are defined as *reshuyot harabim* and must be excluded from *eruvin*.[38] This ruling is somewhat surprising, as the Gemara (Shabbat 6a) states that a street must be sixteen *amot* wide to qualify as a *reshut harabim* and railroad tracks are not this wide. Indeed, the *Chafetz Chaim* (*Sha'ar Hatziyun* 345:18, following the Rambam in *Hilchot Shabbat* 14:1) rules that even an intercity road must be sixteen *amot* wide to be classified as a *reshut harabim*.

---

[38] Though, the *Aruch Hashulchan* maintains a unique view that a road is defined as a *reshut harabim* only if it is the only major road in the area, see ad. loc. number 20. Rav Moshe Feinstein (*Teshuvot Igrot Moshe*, O.C. 4:87) dismisses this view as entirely unreasonable.

The *Maharsham* (ad. loc.) rules that a railroad does not qualify as a *reshut harabim* since they are not sixteen *amot* wide and do not usually have 600,000 people traveling on it each day. Rav Yeshayahu Bloi (*Netivot Shabbat* 3:1, footnote 3) notes that since railroads are made only for train travel and are not intended for pedestrians, they might not qualify as *reshuyot harabim*. He compares railroad tracks to a sea, which is not defined as a *reshut harabim* (Shabbat 6a) even though many ships may traverse it. The *Shulchan Aruch Harav* (345:19) explains that even though the sea is traveled by many, it is not defined as a *reshut harabim* since it differs so much from the *diglei midbar* where there was ready access to all traffic. We may add that the Rav Bloi's point also applies to a limited access highway where there is no room for pedestrian traffic (and civil laws often prohibit walking along such highways).

I asked Rav Schachter if train tracks that are used only by freight trains (and are not excluded from the Teaneck *eruv*) constitute *reshuyot harabim*. He replied that it might not, since Ramban's intercity road seems to refer to roads where people commonly travel. Indeed, the *Mishnah Berurah* (345:17) writes that an intercity road constitutes a *reshut harabim* since "many people are often there." It is obviously counterintuitive to label a road as a *reshut harabim* if very few people travel on it.

However, Rav Schachter regards commuter train lines to constitute *reshuyot harabim*. He therefore requires that commuter train tracks be excluded from community *eruvin*. By contrast, Rav Moshe Heinemann approved the Sharon, Massachusetts *eruv* despite the fact that heavily traveled commuter railroad trains frequently run through it.[39]

EXCLUDING OVERPASSES

Even those who do not exclude intercity roads from *eruvin* often must address the fact that the highways run above or below the local streets upon which the *eruv* runs. This would be problematic according to the ruling of Rav Yechezkeil Landau (*Teshuvot Noda Beyehudah* 2: O.C. 42), who rules that if a community uses a seawall as a border for its *eruv* and a bridge is constructed above the seawall, then the bridge constitutes a breach (*pirtzah*) in the *eruv* and must therefore be excluded from the *eruv*. He believes than an *eruv* on one ground level is ineffective for a ground level below or above it. According to the *Noda Beyehudah*, if the other ground level is not excluded, the entire *eruv* is disqualified since the area is not completely enclosed and is thus exposed to an area that is not encompassed by the *eruv* (the disqualification of *nifratz le'makom ha'assur lo*).[40] The *Mishnah Berurah* (363:118) and the *Chazon Ish* (O.C. 108:1-2) rule in accordance with the *Noda*

---

[39] Sharon lies in the heart of the Providence-Boston corridor. Significantly, these tracks are not excluded by fences erected for safety purposes. When I showed Rav Zvi Lieberman, the Rav of London's Edgeware neighborhood, some *eruvin* in the United States, he expressed shock that American civil law does not mandate protective fencing to surround railroad lines, as is the law in Great Britain. The safety benefits would provide a halachic benefit as well, as the railroad lines would thereby be excluded from community *eruvin*. See our separate chapter on the Sharon, MA *eruv*.

[40] See our later chapter on *Mei'achorei Hakotel in Long Island* for an example of ground levels.

Beyehudah. The Riverdale *eruv* encounters this problem. Rav Willig created *tzurot hapetach* to ensure that the Henry Hudson Parkway, while not excluded from the Riverdale *eruv*, does not cause a problem of *nifratz le'makom ha'assur lo*. This issue is also successfully addressed in the West Orange and Scarsdale *eruvin*.

CONCLUSION

It is sometimes difficult to fully exclude intercity roads from the *eruv*. Some communities are blessed with the infrastructure to do so. However, for some communities, the cost to exclude intercity highways is exorbitant. (For example, some intercity highways run at ground level and are not separated from local roads with a fence.) Communities which follow a lenient approach in regard to moderately sized intercity roads such as the Henry Hudson Parkway have ample basis for their practice in the rulings of the *Maharsham* and Rav Moshe Feinstein and the practice in Yerushalayim. That being said, it is best (when practical) to exclude such highways from the *eruv*. It is undoubtedly very important to effectively manage any problems posed by highways that run at different ground levels.

CONSTRUCTING THE TZUROT HAPETACH

In this chapter, we will address several issues that arise during the physical construction of an *eruv*. Before beginning to build an *eruv*, it must be determined if the area is a *reshut harabim* or merely a *karmelit*. If the area is a *karmelit*, surrounding it with *tzurot hapetach* suffices, whereas a *reshut harabim* must be enclosed by a wall or, at least, by doors (*Shulchan Aruch*, O.C. 364:2, and *Mishnah Berurah* 364:8).

CONSTRUCTING TZUROT HAPETACH

Constructing a *tzurat hapetach*, literally "the shape of a doorframe," seems to be a simple and straightforward process. The Talmud (Eruvin 11b) states that a *tzurat hapetach* consists of two vertical poles with a horizontal pole directly on top of them (*kaneh mikan vekaneh mikan vekaneh al gabeihen*). However, the laws of *tzurot hapetach* are actually quite complex, particularly when constructing a community *eruv*. Community *eruvin* in North America often use pre-existing structures, which can significantly reduce the costs of building and maintaining an *eruv*. These structures, such as telephone poles, were not built for use in *eruvin* and often introduce halachic complexities.[41]

---

[41] For an explanation of how such structures may be used as *tzurot hapetach* despite the fact that they were not constructed for this purpose, see *Chazon Ish*, O.C. 111:5. See *Mishnah Berurah* (362:64) for more sources on this issue.

MUST THE VERTICAL POLES EXTEND ALL THE WAY TO THE HORIZONTAL ONE?

The Talmud (Eruvin 11b) records a dispute between Rav Nachman and Rav Sheishet about whether the vertical poles of a *tzurat hapetach* must extend all the way to the horizontal pole. The Halachah follows the opinion of Rav Nachman, that if the vertical poles (*lechis*) are ten *tefachim* (approximately forty inches) high and are positioned precisely beneath the horizontal pole, the *tzurat hapetach* is acceptable. The horizontal pole need not touch the vertical poles and may be well above them (*Shulchan Aruch*, O.C. 362:11). The *Mishnah Berurah* (362:62) explains that the basis for this ruling is the principle of *gud asik* (literally, "the wall goes up"), which states that the Halachah views the vertical poles as extending upward to the horizontal pole.

GUD ASIK: EYESIGHT OR PLUMB LINE?

Although vertical poles of a *tzurat hapetach* need not touch the horizontal pole (or wire), they must be positioned directly underneath it. The poles cannot even be off by the slightest amount (see *Mishnah Berurah* 362:63). Halachic authorities debate how to determine the proper positioning.[42] Rav Yosef Dov

---

[42] Measurements for some areas of Halachah are estimated based on what appears correct to people, while other areas require precise measurements. For example, *terumah* (the fiftieth of grain which is given to *kohanim*) must be an estimate and may not be measured to precisely equal one-fiftieth (Terumot 1:7). On the other hand, *techum Shabbat* (the area that one may not leave on Shabbat) must be measured precisely (Eruvin 57b, 58b). In many areas, it is unclear whether an estimate or precise measurement is required. For example, the *Chazon Ish* (*Hil. Tumat Tzara'at* 8:1) writes that measurements for the spreading of a spot of lep-

Soloveitchik (as reported by Rav Yosef Adler) and Rav Moshe Feinstein (reported by Rav Elazar Meyer Teitz, from his uncle, Rav Pesach Rayman) both felt that it is sufficient to estimate the poles' positioning with one's eyes. Rav Zalman Nechemia Goldberg (personal communication) also permits using eyesight, although he requires building very wide vertical beams to allow for a wide margin of error in their positioning.

However, Rav Yitzchak Liebes, Rav J. David Bleich, Rav Hershel Schachter, Rav Feivel Cohen,[43] and Rav Mordechai Wil-

---

rosy are done by estimation. He bases himself on a passage in the Ramban's commentary to the Torah (*Vayikra* 13:5). However, the *Chazon Ish* does not mention that the Rosh (*Tosafot Harosh*, Mo'eid Katan 7a, cited in the *Tur*'s long commentary to *Vayikra* 13:5) requires the use of measuring implements to determine the leprosy spot's growth.

[43] Rav Cohen believes that two sets of vertical poles must be constructed, one set that appears to be under the horizontal pole and one set that has been measured to be precisely under the horizontal pole (if the position determined by sight differs from the position determined by the plumb line). It is not clear, however, that Rav Moshe and Rav Soloveitchik invalidate an *eruv* that was measured by a plumb line. It may be that they also recognize such an *eruv* but add that measuring by eyesight is **also** acceptable. Rav Shlomo Miller (in his letter of approbation for *The Contemporary Eruv*) presents an argument for why constructing an *eruv* with plumb line measurements suffices according to all authorities. See, however, *Teshuvot Avnei Yashfeh* (2; O.C. 43:6) which argues that if a plumb line yields a result that differs from eyesight, than the *tzurat hapetach* is invalid since this is the normal manner in which a door frame is built. The author cites what appears to be Rav Yosef Shalom Eliashiv who endorses this ruling. This approach appears difficult since builders typically use a plumb line when building a door frame. Interestingly, Rav Schachter (personal communication and stated in the 5779 *Hilchot Eruvin* lecture to

lig (all through personal communication) rule that a plumb line (or another device for measuring verticality) is necessary to ensure that everything lines up appropriately. The Gemara (Eruvin 94b) requires constructing "halachic walls" (and presumably *tzurot hapetach* as well) in the same manner that people usually build walls (*kede'avdei inshei*).[44] Builders and carpenters have used plumb lines for thousands of years; they appear in Amos (7:7-8) and the Mishnah (for example, *Kil'ayim* 6:9 and *Keilim* 29:3). Accordingly, a plumb line must be used in constructing a *tzurat hapetach*. Rav Shlomo Zalman Auerbach told me that, while it is best to use a plumb line, one may rely on eyesight alone if it is "impossible" to construct the *eruv* otherwise.[45] When determining whether the *lechi* is positioned directly under the wire, one should be very careful to measure straight up

---

Yeshiva University rabbinical students) believes that while *gud asik* should be measured using a plumb line, there is merit to the view that believes that an eyesight measurement suffices. However, he invalidates an *eruv* where some of the *lechis* are measured by plumbline but other *lechis* are measured by eyesight. Rav Mordechai Willig (personal communication) does not believe that this renders an *eruv* invalid.

[44] The significance of *kede'avdei inshei* is particularly emphasized by Rav Shlomo Kluger (*Teshuvot Ha'elef Lecha Shlomo* 156, 157, 161, 170, 173, 174).

[45] Of course, the definition of "impossible" is debatable. Rav Hershel Schachter (in response to what I quoted from Rav Shlomo Zalman) insisted that it is never impossible to measure precisely, especially with the invention of devices such as laser pointers. Similar to Rav Shlomo Zalman's ruling, the Rama (O.C. 456:3) permits estimating the measurement for separating *challah* when measuring precisely is not feasible (although he addresses a halachic impediment, rather than practical difficulty).

perpendicular to the ground and not in line with the *lechi*. (See the *Chazon Ish* 71:6; this is a common problem.)

Rav David Lifshitz (Rav of Suwalk immediately before World War II) told me that a plumb line was used when constructing *tzurot hapetach* in Suwalk. Rav Ephraim Oshry (Rav of the Kovno Ghetto) told me that in Kovno they relied on eyesight alone. Rav Yosef Singer (Rav of Pilzno prior to World War II) also reported that he believes the rabbis he knew in Europe relied on eyesight alone. Accordingly, this debate has raged for at least 80 years. Rav Meir Goldwicht informed me in 1990 that Israeli communities also have divergent practices regarding this issue. In order to avoid this problem, most North American communities erect vertical poles that reach the horizontal wire or pole. This method avoids the need to estimate from afar if the pole is directly under the wire.

THE TAPERED POLE - THE CHAZON ISH

Telephone and utility poles frequently have wires attached to their sides, rather than on top. It is thus important to determine whether one may use such a wire and pole as a *tzurat hapetach* without affixing additional materials to the telephone pole. One could argue that this would be acceptable, because telephone poles are often thicker on the bottom than they are on top. Therefore, a wire attached to the side of the pole on top passes directly over the extra thickness of the lower part of the pole. Perhaps this thickness constitutes a "vertical pole" of the *tzurat hapetach*. One must check, of course, that the extra thickness at the bottom sticks out under this wire for ten *tefachim* of the pole's height, for every vertical pole in a *tzurat hapetach* must be at least ten *tefachim* high.

Despite the above resolution, the *Chazon Ish* (O.C. 71:12) invalidates a wire on the side of a tapered pole. He adds that if there is an indentation cut in the pole, perhaps this pole and wire may then be used for a *tzurat hapetach*. The indentation must be ten *tefachim* above the ground. The accepted practice is to follow the *Chazon Ish*'s stringency.

PLACING A TZURAT HAPETACH IN A RESHUT HAYACHID

Another important issue in *eruv* construction is whether a component of a *tzurat hapetach* may be located within a *reshut hayachid*. The *Mishnah Berurah* (363:113) cites the *Mekor Chaim*, who invalidates such a *tzurat hapetach*, and the *Mishnah Berurah* accepts his ruling.

The *Mekor Chaim* offers two possible reasons for this strict ruling. One might argue that the *tzurat hapetach* is not noticeable (*nikar*) if it is situated within a *reshut hayachid* (such as a private yard). Alternatively, one might claim that the walls or fences that encompass a *reshut hayachid* are viewed halachically as extending "all the way to the heavens" (see Shabbat 7a), so the airspace above a *reshut hayachid* is halachically impenetrable. For example, a horizontal wire passing through a backyard enclosed by a fence would be invalid according to this opinion, as it is halachically blocked by the "upward extension" of the fence. Rav Hershel Schachter instructs *eruv* planners to be strict on this matter.[46]

---

[46] Rav Schachter discusses this issue in *Be'ikvei Hatzon* (ch. 13).

Other Acharonim disagree with the *Mekor Chaim*'s stringency.[47] The *Chavatzelet Hasharon* (1:20) writes that the custom is to be lenient in this issue. He adds that his father, who was exceedingly strict concerning most halachic matters, ruled leniently concerning this issue. Rav Hershel Schachter (in a lecture given to Yeshiva University rabbinical students in both 5749 and 5779) relates that Rav Mendel Zaks told him that the custom in Europe was indeed to be lenient. However, Rav Schachter strongly urges communities to be strict in this matter. This issue has not yet been resolved, and practices vary from community to community.[48] See our chapter on *The Lechi Under the Cabin Eaves at Camp Ramah Darom* for further discussion of this issue.

FLIMSY AND ZIGZAGGING WIRES

The *Shulchan Aruch* (O.C. 362:11) codifies the Talmud's (Eruvin 11b) requirement that the vertical poles be sufficiently strong that they could theoretically support a door made of straw.[49]

---

[47] The *Aruch Hashulchan* does not mention this stringency. *Teshuvot Chatam Sofer* O.C. 91 and 96 and *Teshuvot Maharsham* 1:207 rule leniently regarding this issue in certain circumstances.

[48] Rav Mordechai Willig once commented to me that, in reality, all communities are lenient on this issue, because cars are considered *reshuyot hayachid*. Virtually every community *eruv* today uses *tzurot hapetach* that pass over cars, and the cars' walls should halachically block them, according to the stringent view. This point is also mentioned in *The Contemporary Eruv* (p. 79).

[49] The thin strips of wire molding used in many *eruvin* today meet this requirement according to most authorities by virtue of the fact that they are attached to the utility pole, which is sufficiently strong (see *Sha'ar*

The *Shulchan Aruch* adds that the horizontal wire connecting the vertical poles does not have to be as strong and can even be made from a very light material, such as reed-grass (*gemi*).

Nonetheless, some suggest that the string may not be so flimsy that it sways in the wind. The *Mishnah Berurah* (362:66) presents two opinions regarding this issue. One focus of the argument is whether the horizontal wire has to be sufficiently sturdy that it can withstand "conventional" winds (*omeid beruach metzuyah*). He quotes the well-known rule that for a halachic wall (*mechitzah*) to be valid, it must be sturdy enough to withstand ordinary winds. This rule undoubtedly applies to the vertical poles of a *tzurat hapetach*, but the *Mishnah Berurah* cites the opinion of the *Machatzit Hashekel* who claims that it does not apply to the horizontal strings (or poles). Another objection to flimsy wires is that normal door frames are not constructed in such a manner (see Eruvin 94b). The *Aruch Hashulchan* (362:37) rules leniently regarding this concern, while the *Chazon Ish* (O.C. 71:10) rules strictly.[50]

In a true doorframe, the horizontal beam goes straight from one vertical beam to the other. When constructing a *tzurat hapetach*, it happens sometimes that the wire will wrap around things, such as trees or poles, which it does not pass over. Con-

---

Hatziyun 363:22). For further discussion of this issue see our later chapter, *Lechi Strength*.

[50] The *Chazon Ish* invalidates the wire as long as the wind can move part of it outside a straight line between the two vertical poles. Rav Nota Greenblatt told me in 1992 that he constructed the Memphis, Tennessee *eruv* with unusually wide vertical poles in order that the wires do not sway beyond the width of the vertical poles.

sequently, the wire, which should parallel the top beam of a doorway, will zigzag between the vertical poles rather than going straight from one of them to the other. One could argue that the status of such a wire depends upon the same dispute as the status of a wire which is blown from side to side in the wind, for both wires move horizontally from being directly between the vertical poles. In defense of the lenient position, Rav Mordechai Willig claims that a minor zigzag is permissible, because the Gemara (Eruvin 11a) describes *eruvin* made of grapevines, which are not completely straight. Nonetheless, a curve of greater than twenty-two degrees would seem to invalidate the *tzurat hapetach*. Rav Yosef Adler reports that Rav Yosef Dov Soloveitchik espouses this position. Rav Meir Arik (*Teshuvot Imrei Yosher* 2:133) claims that the wire is only valid even in case of great need if it does not sway or veer more than three *tefachim* in any direction.[51]

Rav Schachter also does not permit any significant deviation in the wire. Rav Micha Shotkin reports that Rav Shlomo Miller tolerates no deviation in the straightness of the wire. He even uses a plumb line to make sure the line is perfectly straight. Rav Schachter, though, makes no such requirement. We should note, though, that experience teaches that one cannot properly perceive a deviation in the wire at the point of deflection – one needs to take a step back to properly assess the situation.

Rav Moshe Heinemann (as presented in the Star-K's *eruv* webinar) in theory agrees with the view that the wire should be

---

[51] For a criticism of this position, see *The Contemporary Eruv* (pp. 74-75).

straight but in practice he says he views a wire "with an *ayin tov*" (a generous eye) and avoids going out of his way to make sure the wire is absolutely straight. For further discussion of this issue, see Rav Mordechai Willig's discussion in *Beit Yitzchak* (25:99).

SAGGING WIRES

A related issue is whether the horizontal wire may sag. The *Mishkenot Yaakov* (111, cited by *Sha'ar Hatziyun* 362:56) and the *Chazon Ish* (O.C. 71:10) rule that a sagging wire disqualifies a *tzurat hapetach*. If the wire sags, it probably sways in the wind, which is problematic according to some authorities (mentioned above). Furthermore, a *tzurat hapetach* must be constructed in a manner that replicates the way people construct door frames, and people do not manufacture door frames that sag on top. Interestingly, Rav Yosef Dov Soloveitchik (cited in *Nefesh Harav* p. 170) recalled from his childhood that he visited his grandfather, Rav Chaim Soloveitchik, in Brisk and went with Rav Simcha Zelig Riger, the famous *dayan* (rabbinic judge) of Brisk, to check the community *eruv*. During that trip, the *dayan* tightened all the horizontal wires so that they would not sag, apparently following the *Mishkenot Yaakov*'s opinion.

Despite these rulings, Rav Tzvi Pesach Frank (*Teshuvot Har Tzvi* 2:18:8) permits sagging, as long as a significant part of the wire (about ten inches) does not come within ten *tefachim* of the ground. In addition, the *Aruch Hashulchan* does not cite the strict ruling of the *Mishkenot Yaakov*. Rav Hershel Schachter told me that he heard that the practice of most communities in prewar Europe was to follow the lenient opinion and accept sagging wires.

Communal practices today still differ in this area. Some communities follow a compromise approach that the horizontal wire may sag up to three *tefachim* (approximately 9-12 inches),[52] based on the concept of *lavud*, that a gap of less than three *tefachim* is considered closed.[53]

This issue is discussed at further length in our later chapter, *Sagging Wire in the Yeshiva University Eruv*.

SLANTED WIRES

Because a *tzurat hapetach* should be built like a true doorway, a potential problem arises when one pole is taller than the other, putting the horizontal wire on a slant (even though it is taut). One could claim that this should be invalid, as most doorways are built with the horizontal beam perpendicular to the vertical beams. Indeed, Rav Hershel Schachter regards slanted wires as problematic since doorways are not typically constructed in this manner. Moreover, Rav Schachter (in an essay printed in *Sefer Kevod Harav* p. 281) even raises a problem with the floor of a *tzurat hapetach* not being flat since door frames are made only where the floor is flat. However, Rav Schachter acknowledges that many Acharonim (such as *Teshuvot Ha'elef Lecha Shlomo* O.C. 154 and *Teshuvot Melamed Leho'il* O.C 67, based on *Teshuvot Sho'el Umeishiv*) disagree. In practice, this is a very difficult requirement to satisfy.

---

[52] See Rav Shimon Eider's *Halachos of the Eruv* (p. 24).

[53] Another common example of *lavud* is a chain link fence, which serves as a solid wall if the gaps between the links are less than three *tefachim* wide.

Nonetheless, the *Mishnah Berurah* (362:60) rules that even if the horizontal wire is slanted, the *tzurat hapetach* is acceptable. He cites (*Sha'ar Hatziyun* 362:46) the opinion of Rav Akiva Eiger, however, that an exceedingly slanted wire might disqualify the *tzurat hapetach*.

Rav Aharon Kotler (cited in Rav Shimon Eider's *Halachos of the Eruv*, p. 23) rules that a slant of less than forty-five degrees is acceptable even according to Rav Akiva Eiger. Rav Moshe Heinemann (as presented in the Star-K *eruv* webinar) and Rav Mordechai Willig (*Beit Yitzchak* 5753, p. 97) accept Rav Kotler's ruling. In practice, many communities rely on slanted wires in accordance with Rav Kotler's view. In many situations it would be difficult to make the *eruv* without relying on this view (very often tension wires are slanted).

Rav Heinemann similarly cites Rav Aharon Kotler as permitting a *lechi* to slant as long as it is more vertical than horizontal. It is often essential to rely on this view as often the utility wires upon which the *eruv* relies, run a bit off the pole and the *lechi* must be bent in order to reach these wires.

Rav Yosef Shlomo Eliashiv is cited (*The Laws of Eruv*, p. 90) as requiring that the components of a *tzurat hapetach* be straight. Rav Zalman Nechemia Goldberg, though, is cited (ibid.) as disagreeing, noting that for hundreds of years slanted wires and *eruv* poles have been accepted as valid.

One should pay particular attention to not exceed a forty-five degree slant when building a *tzurat hapetach* on a steep hill. The *Netivot Shabbat* (19:27, n. 60) claims that a slant of more than twenty-two degrees is problematic. He also expresses Halachic concerns with building *tzurot hapetach* on a steep hill due to its being a viable Halachic *mechitzah*.

CONCLUSION

We have reviewed some of the major issues concerning how to build a *tzurat hapetach*. While the laws of *eruvin* are complex, it is an area where laymen can make a major contribution. Vigilant laymen who know the locations of their community's *tzurot hapetach* can help ensure its validity by notifying their rabbi whenever they notice downed or sagging wires. Similarly, people can help by noticing when telephone and utility workers make changes in the structure of poles and wires.

THE MAXIMUM SIZE OF AN ERUV

With today's growing Orthodox communities, community *eruvin* are expanding further and further. Is there a point at which an *eruv* is simply too large?

A WORLDWIDE ERUV?
In a fascinating discussion, the Gemara (Eruvin 22b) suggests that the entirety of Eretz Yisrael may be considered a *reshut hayachid* since it is surrounded by natural walls. The Gemara rejects this suggestion, in an equally fascinating manner, for if this were true, then the entire world would be considered a *reshut hayachid* (at least on a Torah level), since it is surrounded by the ocean (i.e. the continental shelf).

TOSAFOT AND RAMBAN
The Gemara summarily dismisses this possibility as untenable since a *reshut hayachid* cannot be so large. *Tosafot* (ad. loc. s.v. *dilma*), however, state that such a limitation applies only to a *reshut hayachid* created by natural boundaries. A *reshut hayachid* created by man-made *mechitzot* is not subject to any size limit.

However, the Ritva (Eruvin 22b s.v. *d'ha makif la perat*) cites Ramban, who asserts that there is a maximum size even to man-made *mechitzot*. Ramban believes that in order for the *mechitzot* to be valid, "one must perceive themselves as inside the *eruv* boundaries."

GENERAL COMMUNITY ERUVIN
Rav Mordechai Willig is of the opinion that the Halachah follows the opinion of *Tosafot* (personal communication). The Ash-

kenazi Chief Rabbi of Israel, Rav David Lau, in a lecture given at Yeshivat Otniel, stated that large Israeli communities, such as Tel Aviv, rely on *Tosafot's* opinion for their citywide *eruvin*.[54] Such an approach seems to be correct by virtue of two points. First of all, the *Shulchan Aruch* does not present a limitation on the size of *eruvin*.[55] Second of all, many *eruvin* today are quite large. The Jerusalem municipal *eruv*, the Los Angeles community *eruv*, and the Baltimore community *eruv* are examples of enormous *eruvin*. These hardly seem to fit the Ramban's requirement that "one must perceive themselves as inside of the *eruv* boundaries."

Alternatively, Rav Moshe Feinstein's explanation of Ramban's opinion is accepted in practice. In his discussion of the Manhattan *eruv* (*Teshuvot Igrot Moshe*, O.C. 1:139:6), he quantifies Ramban's size limitation as an area with a diameter of 32 *mil* (approximately 21 miles).[56]

Rav Moshe bases this on a Mishnah in Bechorot (9:2), which states that in the context of *ma'aser beheimah*, the animals

---

[54] Rav David Lau, *"Eiruvei Arim B'Yisrael Kayom,"* Yeshivat Otniel, www.youtube.com/watch?v=MSFwUOL-s4s. April 2018.

[55] The *Biur Halachah* (346:3 s.v. *karpeif*) does cite the debate between *Tosafot* and Ramban without offering a resolution.

[56] The *Chayei Adam* (*Nishmat Adam*, *Hilchot Shabbat* 49:2) already suggests this measurement. He does not, however, resolve the matter conclusively. In New Jersey's Bergen County, the Englewood, Teaneck, and Paramus *eruvin* are all connected (but they are all independent as well). The distance between Englewood Cliffs (the eastern edge of the Englewood *eruv*) and Paramus is 7.61 miles, according to information accessed at www.distance-cities.com/distance-englewood-cliffs-nj-to-paramus-nj.

are considered to be in one area if they are all located within the area where the shepherd can see them. The Mishnah defines this as sixteen *mil*. Rav Moshe explains that this refers to the radius of the circle. The diameter of the area is therefore 32 *mil*.

Most interestingly, in their famous endorsement of the creation of an *eruv* in Paris, Rav Chaim Ozer Grodzinsky and the *Chazon Ish* agree that Paris satisfies Ramban's criterion since it is an area of which it is "the manner of people to encompass with a wall."

BADATZ OF THE EDAH HACHAREIDIT OF YERUSHALAYIM

It is reported that Rav Yosef Shalom Elyashiv was concerned for Ramban's opinion even regarding an area much smaller than a 32 mil diameter;[57] however, it is not known what he regarded as the maximum size of an *eruv*. The Badatz of the Edah HaChareidit of Yerushalayim divides the Jerusalem neighborhood *eruvin* into many small sectors in order to satisfy this stricter version of Ramban's opinion.

In passing through Ramat Beit Shemesh in January 2019, the great frequency of *eruv* lines struck me as the community's adoption of the stricter version of Ramban's opinion. This appears to be the situation in Lakewood, New Jersey as well.

---

[57] Rav Aharon Lichtenstein, in a personal communication with the author in 1989, disagreed with Rav Moshe's interpretation and felt that Ramban refers to a much smaller area. Rav Lichtenstein's concern for this understanding of the opinion of the Ramban was one of the reasons he offered for why he did not rely upon community *eruvin*. By contrast, Rav Hershel Schachter (in the lecture series on *Hilchot Eruvin* delivered to rabbinical students at Yeshiva University in both 1989 and 2019) presents Rav Moshe's approach as normative Halachah.

Another advantage of a smaller *eruv* is that it is much easier to maintain and ensure that it remains intact throughout Shabbat.

CONCLUSION

Eruvin today worldwide encompass very large areas. Such communities either follow the opinion of *Tosafot* or accept a lenient version of Ramban's view. While there are those communities which make an effort to satisfy the stricter version of Ramban's opinion, community *eruvin* in general adopt a more lenient approach.

POSTSCRIPT – A NEW REASON TO BE LENIENT REGARDING ERUVIN IN ERETZ YISRAEL

While the aforementioned Gemara rejects the idea that natural boundaries free Eretz Yisrael from concern of its status as a *reshut harabim*, the current situation in Israel may actually designate the entire land area as a *reshut hayachid*, as the majority of Israel's borders are surrounded by security fences. The north is surrounded by the fence between Israel and Lebanon, in the northeast there is the security fence separating the Golan Heights and Syria, on the east there is a security fence, and in the south there is a security fence separating Israel and Egypt. Although the fourth side is the sea, on a Torah level, only three walls are necessary to designate an area as a *reshut hayachid*.

Although there are definitely breaches of more than ten *amot* in these fences, according to most *posekim*, on a Torah level, only a majority of wall is required (*omeid merubah al ha'parutz*).[58]

Thus, if Rav Willig and Rav Lau are correct that baseline halachic opinion follows *Tosafot*, then the State of Israel is not a *reshut harabim*. This, in turn, strengthens the basis for relying on community *eruvin* in Israel even in cities such as Jerusalem, whose population now exceeds 600,000 people.

---

[58] See *Teshuvot Achi'ezer* 4:8; the *Chazon Ish*, cited ad loc. and O.C. 107:5-7; and Rav Moshe Feinstein, *Teshuvot Igrot Moshe* O.C. 2:90; this also appears to be the position of the *Bi'ur Halachah* 362:10 s.v. *keshekol haruchot*.

ISLANDS AND WATERFRONTS

Unfortunately, there is no shortage of unfounded rumors about Halachic matters. One of these misplaced rumors is the notion that an island constitutes an automatic *eruv*. While there is a bit of a basis for this idea from the Gemara (Eruvin 22), it is a far cry from constituting normative Halachah. In this chapter, we offer a few reasons why the notion that an island forms an automatic *eruv* is inaccurate.

THE NEED FOR HALACHIC WALLS

Both the *Mishnah Berurah* (363:118) and *Aruch Hashulchan* (O.C. 363:47) rule that the edge of the water constitutes a Halachic wall only if it reaches a minimum depth of ten *tefachim* within an shore distance of four *amot*, which is equivalent to a twenty-five degree decline. This is referred to as a *tel hamitlakeit asara mitoch arba*, which is considered to be a halachic wall. Thus, if an island is surrounded by a beach, then it is not considered to be surrounded by *mechitzot*.

Additionally, when constructing artificial *mechitzot*, the *Mishnah Berurah* even insists that they must be located precisely at the water's edge. If they are not placed at the water's edge, then they do not constitute proper halachic walls. This is true even if a barrier lies within ten *amot* of the water's edge.

Rav Moshe Feinstein (*Teshuvot Igrot Moshe*, O.C. 1:139) adopts this stance as well. However, he is willing to consider the possibility of treating Manhattan Island's edges as viable *mechitzot* only because they are actual sea walls, and not because Manhattan is an island. We should note, though, that ultimately

Rav Moshe does not endorse the idea of an *eruv* in Manhattan due to concern for its being a *reshut harabim* and other issues.

ONE SIDE BOUNDED BY WATER

The *Maharit* (cited by the *Magen Avraham* 363:31) believes that if the fourth side of a *reshut hayachid* is bounded by water, then no *mechitzah* is required for this side. On a Torah level, three *mechitzot* suffice to create a *reshut hayachid*. Chazal require a *mechitzah* on the fourth side due to the concern that one would easily stray outside the enclosed area due to the fourth border not being delineated. The fourth *mechitzah* clarifies the border of the enclosed area. However, there is no need for a *mechitzah* on the fourth side when the fourth side is water, since the water marks the end of the enclosed area. Rav Zvi Pesach Frank (*Teshuvot Har Zvi*, O.C. 2:24) cites the *Me'orot Natan* (number 8), who records that the *Chidushei Harim* relied on the *Maharit* when creating an *eruv* in Warsaw. While he felt that the *Maharit* is highly questionable, he felt that in case of exceptional great need (*bisha'at hadechak gadol*), one may rely on his opinion. Apparently the only way he could make an *eruv* in Warsaw was to rely on the *Maharit*. Rav Hershel Schachter cites from *Chayei Hareiyah* (ch. 13 footnote 123), Rav Moshe Zvi Neriah's biography of the period time of Rav Avraham Yitzchak HaKohein Kook's service as Rav of Yafo, that Rav Kook also relied on the *Maharit's* opinion *bisha'at hadechak gadol*. Rav Kook made two *eruvin* in Yaffo. The larger *eruv* relied on the *Maharit*, while the smaller *eruv* did not. Interestingly, the *Mishnah Berurah* and *Aruch Hashulchan* do not state their opinion, either in a positive or negative direction, regarding the *Maharit's* leniency, despite the fact that the *Magen Avraham* does cite it. Rav Schachter believes (as he stated in his lectures at Yeshiva University in 1989 and 2019), though, that all would agree that it is improper to rely on the *Maharit* if a viable alternative exists.[59]

CONCLUSION

It should be abundantly clear from our discussion that an island itself does not automatically constitute a viable *eruv*. If one visits an island for Shabbat, he should not carry unless he is certain that a competent Rav has certified the existence of a proper *eruv* and is involved in the ongoing upkeep of said *eruv*. Obviously, all other *eruvin* considerations, such as *sechirat reshut*,[60] *eruv chatzeirot*, ground levels,[61] and the size of the island,[62] must be dealt with before finalizing any island *eruv*.

---

[59] For further discussion of this issue, especially the opinion of the *Maharit*, see Rav Baruch Simon's *Imrei Baruch, Eruvin UReshuyot*, pp. 16-18.

[60] The whole island must be rented from the local authorities.

[61] See the earlier chapter on *Highways, Railroads, and Overpasses*. This issue arises with bridges that pass over the island.

[62] As previously discussed, Rav Moshe limits *eruvin* to areas with diameters less than 32 *mil*. Any discussion in regards to the use of islands' natural boundaries as *mechitzot* is limited to islands that do not exceed this maximum diameter. See our discussion in the previous chapter in regard to man-made boundaries.

INTRODUCTION TO KARPEIF, ERUV CHATZEIROT, & SECHIRAT RESHUT

After constructing an *eruv*, three major issues remain: *karpeif*, *eruv chatzeirot*, and *sechirat reshut*.

KARPEIF

A potentially major obstacle in creating a viable community *eruv* is the existence of a *karpeif* within the enclosed area. A *karpeif* is an area at least 100 *amot* (between 150 and 200 feet) by 50 *amot* (between 75 and 100 feet) that is not used for human habitation or other human needs.[63] Accordingly, sports fields, playgrounds, and lakes used for boating do not constitute *karpeifiyot*.[64] *Chazal* forbade carrying within a *karpeif* even if it is located within a *reshut hayachid* created by *mechitzot* or *tzurot hapetach*. This is because the *reshut hayachid* must be encompassed by *mechitzot* or *tzurot hapetach* that were built for the purpose of human habitation (*mukaf ledirah*). A wall or *tzurat hapetach* built to surround an uninhabited forest is not built for the sake of human habitation, so it does not permit people to carry on Shabbat within that forest.

Moreover, the presence of a *karpeif* forbids carrying in the entire enclosed area surrounding it, because an area's walls or *tzurot hapetach* must be erected purely for human habitation.

---

[63] See Eruvin 23a-b and *Shulchan Aruch*, O.C. 358. The Gemara's two primary examples of a *karpeif* are sown fields and water not used for human needs.

[64] See the next chapter for further discussion.

If they also include a *karpeif*, however, they are erected for an area that is not entirely fit for human habitation.[65] My experience indicates that this issue arises much more often in suburban and rural areas than in urban areas, as an urban setting contains fewer undeveloped areas. The *Chazon Ish* (O.C. 88:25) writes that the only way to prevent a *karpeif* from invalidating the rest of the *eruv*'s area is to encompass the *karpeif* with either *mechitzot* or *tzurot hapetach*, thereby excluding it from the *eruv*. The community is then *mukaf ledirah*, while the uninhabited *karpeif* is severed from it.[66]

The lenient positions of some authorities might also solve this problem. The *Biur Halachah* (358:9 s.v. *aval*) cites one such approach from the *Devar Shmuel*. He rules that if a *karpeif* is situated within a city and is only a small part of the city, it does not prohibit carrying within that area.[67] The *Devar Shmuel* rea-

---

[65] For an analysis of the *karpeif*'s impact on the walls, see *Biur Halachah* (358:9 s.v. *hazra'im*).

[66] Also see the *Biur Halachah* (358:9 s.v. *aval*).

[67] Of course, the *Devar Shmuel*'s leniency does not apply to *eruvin* that enclose very large forest areas, since his entire reason is that the *karpeif* is negligible compared to the inhabited area. When I set out to construct an *eruv* in a certain summer community in Connecticut, Rav Hershel Schachter ruled that the *eruv* could not be built, because the *tzurot hapetach* would have had to encompass huge tracts of heavily wooded forest. Rav Schachter also did not permit relying on the extraordinarily lenient views of *Teshuvot Divrei Malkiel* (cited in *Teshuvot Melamed Leho'il* 1:65) and *Teshuvot Even Yekara* (O.C. 16), which would have facilitated constructing the *eruv*, as these views are not accepted by most halachic authorities.

sons that, in such a situation, the *karpeif* is negligible compared to the rest of the city and may be ignored.[68]

Halachic authorities have reacted to the *Devar Shmuel*'s leniency with mixed feelings. On one hand, the *Chazon Ish* (cited earlier) rejects this approach, as he sees no reason for a *karpeif* within a city to differ from one in a more rural area. The *Biur Halachah* expresses serious reservations concerning this leniency, but he seems to accept the conclusion of the *Chacham Tzvi*, that the *Devar Shmuel*'s opinion may be followed where it is impossible to construct an *eruv* otherwise.

This issue remains controversial, as some communities rely on the *Devar Shmuel* while others do not. A number of Israeli rabbis have told me that the practice in Israel is to follow the lenient opinion of the *Devar Shmuel* (except in Bnei Brak, where the *Chazon Ish* resided). This is hardly surprising, since *eruvin* in Israel often encompass entire cities.[69] It is exceedingly difficult to exclude every *karpeif* within Israel's growing cities. Hence, in keeping with the approach of the *Biur Halachah*, they rely on the *Devar Shmuel*'s lenient ruling.[70]

---

[68] Although the *Devar Shmuel* speaks of a city surrounded by walls, his ruling appears to apply equally to a city surrounded by *tzurot hapetach*; see *Teshuvot Melamed Leho'il* (1:65).

[69] For example, according to information received from the Jerusalem Rabbinate in 1991, the circumference of Jerusalem's *eruv* is approximately 110 kilometers. One can only imagine that the size of the general Jerusalem *eruv* has considerably expanded since 1991.

[70] Rav Aharon Gruman of Twin Rivers, New Jersey notes that Rav Moshe Shternbuch permitted a community that otherwise could not reasonably exclude potential *karpefiyot* from its *eruv* to rely on the *Devar Shmuel*. Rav

A number of authorities adopt a compromise approach that distinguishes between different types of *karpeifiyot* (plural of *karpeif*).[71] If a *karpeif* beautifies the city, it does not forbid carrying. If, however, humans in no way benefit from the area, it must be excluded from the *eruv*.

Rav Yechiel Michel Epstein (*Kitvei Ha'aruch Hashulchan* number 64) permits relying on the lenient view regarding *karpeif* in case of pressing need (*sha'at hadechak*). In my experience, adopting a strict view regarding *karpeif* often makes *eruvin* near impossible to maintain. The exclusion of *karpefiyot* from *eruvin* often involves maintaining *tzurot hapetach* in very difficult terrain, which can be extraordinarily difficult, especially during times of inclement weather. When necessary, following the *Aruch Hashulchan's* more flexible approach to *karpeif* often makes the difference as to whether a community is able to maintain its *eruv*.

ERUV CHATZEIROT

Even after a proper community *eruv* has been constructed and the area encompassed is thereby rendered a *reshut hayachid*, one may still not carry within it on Shabbat. Despite the fact that it is biblically permitted to carry from one *reshut hayachid* (one's house) to another (in our case, the outside area enclosed by the *eruv*), the Rabbis prohibited this in many cases. Similarly, this rabbinical prohibition often precludes carrying from one

---

Gruman reports that Rav Shternbuch remarked that many communities rely upon the *Devar Shmuel*.

[71] See *Orchot Chaim* (ch. 358), *Teshuvot Melameid Leho'il* (1:65), and *Teshuvot Har Tzvi* (O.C. vol. 2, Harari Vasadeh p. 249).

household to another even within the same building.[72] For example, this prohibition applies to an apartment building with at

---

[72] If there is only one Jewish resident in the building, this prohibition does not apply (*Shulchan Aruch*, O.C. 382:1). It also does not apply if all of the residents eat together (which applies many times in a hotel setting) or if the landlord stores property in all of the residences (*Shulchan Aruch*, O.C. 370:2,4). Rav Moshe Feinstein (*Teshuvot Igrot Moshe*, O.C. 1:141) rules that a landlord who rents out items (such as stoves or refrigerators) with every apartment is considering to be "storing" his property with the tenants, so no *eruv chatzeirot* is needed. On the other hand, the *Chazon Ish* (O.C. 92) and *Chelkat Yaakov* (1:207) require an *eruv chatzeirot* if the landlord's property in the apartments is rented to the tenants. The *Devar Avraham* (3:30) and Rav Yosef Dov Soloveitchik (cited in *Nefesh Harav*, p. 170) also favor this opinion, although the *Devar Avraham* concludes that he is unsure of the Halachah in such a case. See *The Contemporary Eruv* (p. 110 note 231) for a defense of Rav Moshe's view. Rav Hershel Schachter (in a lecture at Yeshiva University) reported that Rav Moshe encouraged those who do make an *eruv chatzeirot* in such a situation to refrain from reciting a blessing, since he believed that this *eruv* is unnecessary. The *Chelkat Yaakov* also argues that the landlord's ability to unite all of the apartments by storing property in all of them applies only to observant Jewish landlords. Regarding non-observant and non-Jewish landlords, he claims that *sechirat reshut* must be performed even if the landlord stores his personal property in all of the apartments. Other authorities do not appear to accept this qualification. Rav Schachter also quoted Rav Moshe as asserting that his ruling applies even to a co-op, but Rav Schachter noted that this is highly questionable. We should note, though, that Rav Moshe's ruling clearly does not apply to a building where even just a few of the renters purchased and own the appliances that are in their apartments. Thus, one may not necessarily assume that just because it is an apartment building that Rav Moshe's ruling applies.

least two observant[73] families. In such situations, it is required to make an *eruv chatzeirot* (referred to by *Chazal* as an *eruv*) in order to permit carrying.

An *eruv chatzeirot* (literally "mixing the courtyards") consists of every household in the *reshut hayachid* contributing some bread to the collective group of households. The bread is stored in one of the houses within the encompassed area. The Halachah then views the participants as if they all live in that one house, removing the rabbinical prohibition against carrying (see *Shulchan Aruch*, O.C. 366:1).

The Talmud (Shabbat 14b) records that Shlomo Hamelech instituted this requirement, and a heavenly voice acknowledged the profound wisdom in it. The reason for this rule, as explained by the Rambam (*Hilchot Eruvin* 1:4), is that otherwise people would become confused about the laws of carrying. The process of the *eruv chatzeirot* is designed to familiarize the community with the laws of carrying. This goal seems to be a reason for the time-honored practice of storing the *eruv chatzeirot* in the synagogue (see Rama, O.C. 366:3). Rav Elazar

---

We should also note that *Tosafot* (Eruvin 72a s.v. *umodin*) raise the issue that a requirement for an *eruv chatzeirot* is not generated by a guest who may be moved by the owner at will. *Tosafot's* assertion has great ramifications for the discussion of a requirement of an *eruv chatzeirot* in a hotel, Yeshivah or university dormitory, and hospital.

[73] If there are flagrantly non-observant Jews, *sechirat reshut* must be performed. The status of non-observant Jews today is somewhat unclear, as most of them desecrate Shabbat out of ignorance, not out of contemptuousness. See Eruvin 69a and *Chazon Ish* (O.C. 87:14) for a discussion of this phenomenon.

Meyer Teitz told me that his father, Rav Pinchas Teitz (of Elizabeth, New Jersey), prominently displayed the *eruv* in a place within the synagogue where it was easily seen, noting that this was commonly done in Europe. Another advantage of storing the *eruv* in the synagogue is that community members have full access to the *eruv*, which is an important requirement (see Rav Moshe Shternbach's *Teshuvot Vehanhagot* 1:250).

For further debate and discussion of the practice to store the *eruv chatzeirot* in a synagogue, see Rav Baruch Simon's *Imrei Baruch, Eruvin UReshuyot*, pp. 184-188.[74] *Eruv Kehilchato* (Rav Avraham Ades, p. 164) claims that according to Sephardic practice, the *eruv* should be stored in a home.

In practice, we do not require every household in a *reshut hayachid* to give some bread for the purpose of the *eruv*. Instead,

---

[74] All agree that the *eruv* must be stored in a home that it is suitable for dwelling. This entails that the home must be four *amot* by four *amot* in size. Rav Mordechai Willig and Rav Zvi Sobolofsky understand this to mean that even the room in which the *eruv chatzeirot* is stored must be four *amot* by for *amot* in dimension. Therefore, Rav Willig stores the *eruv chatzeirot* for the Riverdale section of the Bronx in his living room and not his kitchen, which is not four *amot* by four *amot* in size. Rav Baruch Simon, though, understands that it is sufficient for the *eruv* to be stored in a home which is four *amot* by four *amot* by size, even though the specific room in which it is stored is less than four *amot* by four *amot*. In helping a community that was changing over its *eruv* from conservative to Orthodox auspices, I was horrified to discover that the Conservative spiritual leader had stored the *eruv chatzeirot* in the Ark along with the Sifrei Torah. It is sad that the Conservative clergyperson was unaware of the lengths at which Chazal went to ensure that food (even holy food such as *terumah*) should not be stored with Sifrei Torah (see Shabbat 14a).

everyone in the community is granted a portion of the *eruv* by the process known as *zachin le'adam shelo befanav*, acquiring something on behalf of another person (see *Shulchan Aruch*, O.C. 366:9-10,15). This is accomplished by one person handing another the *eruv* food[75] and a second person lifting the *eruv* into the air.[76] It is lifted with the intention of acquiring the *eruv* on behalf of all present and future residents of the area encompassed by the *eruv*.

A blessing ("*al mitzvat eruv*") is recited prior to the procedure of acquiring the *eruv* on behalf of the community.[77] Then, the formula of "*behadein eruva*" is recited, explaining the *eruv's* intended purpose (see *Shulchan Aruch*, O.C. 366:15).

Interestingly, the Teaneck, Bergenfield, Englewood, and Tenafly, NJ *eruvin* comprise four distinct *eruvin* that all connect

---

[75] The practice is to use a box or two of kosher-for-*Pesach* matzah; see Rama, O.C. 368:5. Rav Hershel Schachter ("*Eiruvei Chatzeiros*," min. 2-4) on yutorah.org explains that a box of *matzah* is traditionally used for the *eruv chatzeirot* and it works even for Sephardim who would make *mezonot* since it can be *hamotzei* if eaten as a meal.

[76] There is a dispute regarding whether it must be lifted one *tefach* (3-4 inches) or three *tefachim*; see *Shulchan Aruch*, C.M. 198:2 and *Mishnah Berurah* 366:51. In the context of creating an *eruv chatzeirot* lifting one *tefach* suffices.

[77] For an explanation of why a blessing is recited on an *eruv chatzeirot*, see *Teshuvot Chatam Sofer* (O.C. 99). For further discussion as to whether the *berachah* should be recited either before or after the *zikui*, see *Biur Halachah* 366:15 s.v. *b'sha'ah shemezakeh* and *Kitzur Shulchan Aruch* 94:6. Rav Mendel Senderovic told me that the common practice is to recite the *berachah* before the *zikui*, whereas Rav Zvi Sobolofsky believes that the common practice is to recite it after the *zikui*.

to each other. Since they all connect, in order to carry from one community to another, the communities must share an *eruv chatzerot*. On the other hand, since each *eruv* remains distinct, each distinct *eruv* requires its own separate *eruv chatzerot*.

SECHIRAT RESHUT

The procedure of *eruv chatzeirot* is effective solely for Jews who believe in the Oral Law and thus believe in the efficacy of an *eruv*. However, one must rent the apartments, homes, and common areas (such as streets and parks) from every non-Jewish and non-believing Jewish resident of the *reshut hayachid*. This procedure is known as *sechirat reshut*.

Renting every non-Jewish house within the *tzurot hapetach* is a virtually impossible task to accomplish in a community *eruv*. Fortunately, Halachah provides an alternative method of performing the *sechirat reshut* (see *Shulchan Aruch*, O.C. 391:1). The Jewish community may rent the entire enclosed area from the head of the city (*sar ha'ir*) or from one to whom this leader has delegated his authority.[78] The *Shulchan Aruch* rules that the head of the city has the halachic ability to rent out not just the public property within the *tzurot hapetach*, but also the homes of its residents. His ability to rent out private homes stems from his right to quarter soldiers and military equipment in those homes during a time of war without consulting the res-

---

[78] A representative may be used even if this representative knows he is acting against the will of the non-Jewish authority (*Shulchan Aruch*, O.C. 382:11). The *Shulchan Aruch* also discusses who qualifies as a representative.

idents.[79] Democratic countries forbid quartering soldiers under most circumstances. Nonetheless, the *Tikvat Zechariah* (pp. 39-40, cited in *The Contemporary Eruv* pp. 115-117), discussing the possibility of constructing an *eruv* in St. Louis in the 1890s, rules that a city government in America does have the right to lease private homes for *sechirat reshut*. He reasons that local governments may search and inspect private homes, in addition to maintaining the right to expropriate private land for public use (eminent domain).[80]

Others, including Rav Hershel Schachter (in a lecture at Yeshiva University), strongly question this reasoning. They point out that the right of eminent domain is rarely used and is

---

[79] The *Biur Halachah* (391 s.v. *bameh devarim amurim*) adds that the leader must also be capable of deciding when to wage war. Otherwise, his power to quarter troops is irrelevant during times of peace.

[80] Rav Hershel Schachter (in a lecture at Yeshiva University) stated that Rav Moshe Feinstein also permitted performing *sechirat reshut* from a democratically elected mayor based on similar reasoning. See *Chazon Ish* (O.C. 82:9) for an alternative explanation of why *sechirat reshut* may be done from democratic governments. Also see *Teshuvot Minchat Shlomo* (2:35:24), who writes that the *sechirat reshut* performed today "merits investigation" ("*yeish ladun*"). It should be noted that in *Mehudar Eruvin* that are made for some religious neighborhoods in Israel, *sechirat reshut* is conducted with every non-observant Jew and every non-Jew who lives in the area encompassed by the *mehudar eruv*. Very few non-observant or non-Jews typically reside in such neighborhoods and therefore it is feasible to adopt this strict position. It is reported that the *Mehudar Eruvin* are following the instruction of Rav Yosef Shalom Eliashiv who strongly questions the efficacy of a *sechirat reshut* from a government official in a democracy. For further description of *sechirat reshut* conducted in a *Mehudar Eruv*, see *Ul'arev Eruvo*, pp. 127-131.

quite difficult to apply. According to their opinion, it is forbidden to carry on Shabbat (even within an *eruv*) from one's home to the private property of a non-Jew or non-observant Jew.[81] Nonetheless, they acknowledge that the mayor and police do possess the authority to close the public areas of the city. Rav Kenneth Auman of Brooklyn, New York informed me that the Satmar Rebbe was willing to create an *eruv* in the Williamsburg section of Brooklyn for the Shabbat of Sukkot, were it not for the problem of making a community wide *sechirat reshut* in a democracy. Rav Yosef Shalom Elyiashiv is also quoted (*The Laws of an Eruv*, p. 156) as seriously questioning the validity of a community wide *sechirat reshut* in a democracy. Nonetheless, Rav Zvi Pesach Frank (*Teshuvot Har Zvi* O.C. 2:17) indicates that a *sechirat reshut* in a democracy is even more valid than one conducted with a totalitarian regime. A government that is (in the iconic words of Abraham Lincoln in the Gettysburg Address) "of the people, by the people and for the people" is indeed the people's government. Thus, a *sechirat reshut* from a government leader is fundamentally a rental conducted by the official on behalf of the people. It is for this reason, rules Rav Zvi Pesach, that in a democracy the *sechirat reshut* need not be renewed when a new

---

[81] *Netivot Shabbat* (36:27). One could question why according to Rav Schachter the presence of privately owned non-Jewish property inside the *eruv* does not affect the rest of the area. After all, we have already mentioned (regarding a *karpeif*) that a place where carrying is forbidden also prohibits carrying in the rest of the *eruv*, unless special *tzurot hapetach* are erected to separate the forbidden area. While walls enclose the houses themselves, their unenclosed front lawns should invalidate the *eruv*. See *The Contemporary Eruv* (p. 115).

Walking the Line

leader is installed in office. One should consult his rabbi regarding which opinion to follow.

The *Netivot Shabbat* (ch. 37, note 93) notes that all would agree that the mayor and police cannot rent out a foreign embassy located within a city, as international law recognizes it as sovereign territory of the nation it represents.[82] Thus, it would be forbidden to carry into a foreign embassy even in an area encompassed by an *eruv*, such as Jerusalem or Washington D.C., on Shabbat.

In fact, Muammar Gaddaffi's September 2009 visit to New York raised a serious question in regard to the validity of the Englewood, New Jersey *eruv*. The Libyan Ambassador to the United Nations resides in the heart of the Englewood Orthodox Jewish community. During the summer of 2009, in anticipation of Gaddaffi's possible visit to the Libyan property in Englewood in September, extensive work was done on the property. The fences and gates that surrounded the property were temporarily removed. These fences served to exclude the ambassador's residence from the *eruv*, thus ensuring that a *sechirat reshut* would not have to be performed with the Libyan officials. Rav Willig informed us that he had consulted with Professor Louis Henkin, son of the great *posek*, Rav Yosef Eliyahu Henkin, a world renowned expert on international law. Professor Henkin explained that foreign embassies are not technically defined as foreign territory. Under normal circumstances, local authorities grant the embassies a great deal of autonomy as a courtesy.

---

[82] It should be noted that the author of *Netivot Shabbat* resides in Israel, where the laws regarding foreign embassies may differ from those in the United States.

Thus, police would not usually enter a foreign embassy. However, in case of a serious emergency, such as a fire, local officials do enter embassy property even if the foreign representatives protest such entrance. Local authorities would not be able to do so if the embassy area was truly foreign territory.

WITH WHICH GOVERNMENT OFFICIAL SHOULD THE SECHIRAT RESHUT BE PERFORMED?

It is often unclear from which authority the area should be rented from (see *Mishnah Berurah* 391:18). In order to avoid this problem, rabbis often perform *sechirat reshut* from a number of local authorities, such as the mayor and the police chief. A particularly interesting situation occurred when Congregation Kesher Israel of Washington, D.C. established an *eruv* for the community. Due to the ambiguous nature of Washington's municipal authorities, the community performed *sechirat reshut* with United States President George Bush and Washington Mayor Marion Berry, along with the heads of the police and city council.

Rav Mordechai Willig told me that he prefers to perform a *sechirat reshut* with the chief of the fire department, as the fire department enjoys the right to enter a home without warning in case of a fire emergency. Rav Moshe Heinemann mentioned (in a talk delivered to a convention of the National Council of Young Israel rabbis) that when he created the community *eruv* in Baltimore, at the insistence request of a local Rav, he also conducted a *sechirat reshut* with the governor of the State of Maryland.

Rav Zvi Lieberman also told me that when he created the *eruv* for the Edgeware section of London, he conducted the *sechirat reshut* with the representative of the Queen of England for his area, in addition to other government officials. Rav Lieberman reports that the land in England is formally under the control of the queen and thus conducting the *sechirat reshut* with the representative of the queen to Edgware further strengthens the validity of the *eruv*.[83]

EXPIRATION OF A SECHIRAT RESHUT

In addition, a community *sechirat reshut* should not be allowed to expire. Unfortunately, I have encountered more than one community where the local rabbinate unwittingly let the community's *sechirat reshut* expire without renewal. This invalidates the whole *eruv*. When conducting the *sechirat reshut* for the greater Teaneck *eruv*, I rented the area for twenty years (in conformity with Rav Schachter's standards; other *posekim* permit a *sechirat reshut* of a much longer duration). In addition, I stipulated that the *sechirat reshut* would automatically renew in case we forgot to update the *sechirat reshut*. Rav Willig told me that this would be effective as a backup.

Many authorities require the renewal of the *sechirat reshut* when the non-Jewish official with whom it was performed leaves office. The *Netivot Shabbat* (37:28 and notes 96-99) cites these authorities, but he argues that *sechirat reshut* remains effective in democracies even when the government changes.

---

[83] The *sechirat reshut* should be conducted with every municipality that is encompassed by the *eruv*. Rav Elazar Meyer Teitz of Elizabeth, New Jersey reports in a 2007 conversation that he conducted no less than seven *sechirot reshut* since the *eruv* in his community is located in seven different municipalities.

He reasons that a newly elected government is bound by agreements made by its predecessors.

In practice, Jewish communities today usually do not renew the *sechirat reshut* every time the town government changes (also see *Mishnah Berurah* 382:26 and the aforementioned *Teshuvot Har Tzvi*, O.C. 17), although Rav Mordechai Willig informed me that he makes make an effort to renew the *sechirat reshut* for the Riverdale, New York *eruv* when there is a change in the local borough president.

SECHIRAT RESHUT AND ERUV EXPANSION

When expanding a community *eruv*, care must be taken to ensure that the *sechirat reshut* includes the expanded areas. It is for this reason that it is worthwhile to rent the entire area from the government official rather than the area encompassed by the borders of the *eruv*.

Once, when I was inspecting a community *eruv*, I discovered that a tiny portion of the *eruv* juts into the neighboring town from which a *sechirat reshut* was not performed. This disqualified the entire *eruv* since it is *nifratz l'makom ha'asur lo*, exposed to an area in which it is forbidden to carry. It is for this reason that I prefer to conduct a *sechirat reshut* with a county executive. Both Rav Schachter and Rav Willig permit performing a *sechirat reshut* with a county executive. I knows of at least six counties in the United States that were "rented" in such a manner.

KARPEIF AND BODIES OF WATER

An issue that frequently arises when designing an *eruv* is the presence of bodies of water in the area. As previously mentioned, lakes and other bodies of water, depending on circumstance, may be designated as *karpefiyot*, thus mandating their exclusion from the *eruv*. In this chapter, we explore the various opinions in regard to this very important issue.

COMMUNITY USE AND AESTHETIC QUALITIES

As mentioned in our introduction to *karpeif*, in order for an area to be enclosed within the *eruv*, it must be *mukaf ledirah*, fit for human habitation. As such, if a body of water is used for boating or fishing, then it is not a *karpeif*.[84] Additionally, there is a discussion as to whether the aesthetic qualities of a body of water may also remove its *karpeif* designation. For example, a lake that is not used for fishing or boating, yet serves to beautify the scenery of the locale might not be a *karpeif*.

Rav Moshe Heinemann (in a lecture delivered to a conference of Young Israel rabbis) cites Rav Moshe Feinstein as ruling that a body of water's aesthetic qualities does not remove it

---

[84] Regarding watery areas, see *Shulchan Aruch* (O.C. 358:11). Rav Heinemann cites Rav Moshe Feinstein, who rules that in contemporary times, even water that is less than three *tefachim* deep (approximately 9 to 11 inches) should be regarded as a *karpeif*. Although the *Mishnah Berurah* (*Bi'ur Halachah* op. cit. s.v. *vehi*) considers it a problem only if the water is at least three *tefachim* deep, Rav Moshe feels that in contemporary society, unlike in the past (see, for instance, Yoma 77b and Ta'anit 23b), people do not walk through any body of water, even if it is very shallow; thus, no body of water is part of the *dirah*.

from the status of *karpeif*. Rav Moshe's ruling is preceded by similar rulings issued by *Teshuvot Divrei Chayim* (2 O.C. 28) and *Teshuvot Sho'eil Umeishiv* (1:3:131). However, numerous great posekim, such as *Teshuvot Imrei Yosher* (1:170) and the *Nezirut Shimshon* (cited in Rav Bloi's *Netivot Shabbat* 13:13) disagree. In fact, *Teshuvot Chelkat Yaakov* (O.C. 1:181) writes that the consensus of Acharonim adopts the lenient view regarding this matter.

In practice, numerous prominent pre-war communities in Europe adopted the lenient approach to this issue. *Teshuvot Melamed L'ho'il* (O.C. 65) records the adoption of the lenient practice in Cracow (Poland), Lomzha (Lithuania), and Fulda (Germany). *Teshuvot Chelkat Yaakov* (ad. loc.) similarly records that the lenient practice was adopted in Warsaw (Poland), Manheim (Germany), and Antwerp (Belgium). In fact, Rav Yitzchak Isaac Liebes (who served as a leading Rav in pre-war Europe and post-war New York) records (*Teshuvot Beit Avi* 4:68) that almost all pre-war European cities had parks with large flower beds that were not excluded from the community *eruvin*.

It is important to note that the idea that a planted section that serves to beautify the area is considered part of the *dirah* (and hence not a *karpeif*) already appears in the Meiri's commentary on Eruvin 24a. This is quite noteworthy, as the agreement of a Rishon to one side of a disagreement between Acharonim can serve as strong support to that opinion.

However, the Meiri's commentary was most often not available until relatively recently, and thus its Halachic weight is debatable. The *Chazon Ish* famously claims that it does not enjoy much Halachic weight since it was not part of the *mesorah* (tradition) for many centuries. On the other hand, both the *Mishnah Berurah* and Rav Ovadia Yosef frequently quote the Meiri. Thus, the Meiri is an important, though not necessarily decisive, support for the lenient view. [85]

RAV MOSHE FEINSTEIN'S RULING

Although there is ample halachic support for the inclusion of such potential *karpefiyot* in community *eruvin*, the fact that it runs counter to a reported ruling of Rav Moshe Feinstein is no small matter. However, we may take into consideration the fact that (as we mentioned is reported in the aforementioned *Teshuvot Chelkat Yaakov*) the pre-war Warsaw *eruv* relied on the lenient view of the Meiri. Moreover, the *Chelkat Yaakov* notes that the lenient position was endorsed by none other than the *Chidushei Harim*. In general, Rav Moshe considers (as is evident from *Teshuvot Igrot Moshe*, O.C. 5:28:5) Warsaw's *eruv* as setting a significant precedent in the realm of *Hilchot Eruvin*. For example, Rav Moshe's extraordinary ruling (*Teshuvot Igrot Moshe*, O.C. 4:87) that permits the construction of *eruvin* consisting of *tzurot hapetach* in areas with less than 2,400,000 people[86] relies on the precedent of the *eruv* in pre-war Warsaw, where the population was 1.3 million. One might counter that Rav Moshe believed "that accepted leniencies with respect to *eruvin* were needed in

---

[85] See our first chapter for a discussion of the *Devar Shmuel*'s opinion regarding the nullification of a *karpeif* that only constitutes a small part of a city. We also should clarify that the Meiri and the *Devar Shmuel* represent different lines of reasoning. Although some conflate the two, Rav Bloi (*Netivot Shabbat* 13:13 and 15) presents them as distinct ideas.

[86] Rav Moshe argues that 600,000 refers to the amount of people typically in the street during the daytime. In his view, this standard is met in a city with a population of at least 2,4000,000.

prewar Europe, where private homes often lacked basic necessities such as running water making carrying essential. In modern-day cities, an *eruv* is not as crucial and therefore a more stringent approach is warranted" (Rav Francis and Rav Glenner's *The Laws of an Eruv*, p. 151).

One may respond that the aforementioned *Teshuvot Chelkat Yaakov* applies precedents from pre-war communities to post-war Switzerland, an advanced society. Rav Zvi Pesach Frank (*Teshuvot Har Zvi*, O.C. 2:24) and Rav Yosef Eliyahu Henkin (*Kol Kitvei Harav Henkin* 2:32-33) also apply the standards of the Warsaw *eruv* as a precedent to post-war cities in the United States. Similarly, Rav Hershel Schachter (personal communication) holds that one may rely on the pre-war practice to create an *eruv* in a community that has very large flower beds in its parks. Moreover, pre-war Warsaw was a developed city, and, nevertheless, the lenient approach to *karpeif* was relied upon by the community.

Finally, today's reality is that it is crucial for every Jewish community to have an *eruv*, even if it means that the possible *karpefiyot* are not excluded. There are many Jews who find the *melachah* of *hotza'ah* to be especially challenging, and may not necessarily refrain from carrying even in the absence of an *eruv* that encompasses the area. For some, the existence of an *eruv* is a make or break issue as to their decision if they will observe Shabbat altogether. It is quite possible that even Rav Moshe would agree that lenient opinions may be utilized to create an *eruv* in keeping with traditions from Europe in such circumstances. It should be noted that the Israeli rabbinate encompasses all urban Israeli communities with *eruvin* even if all possible *karpefiyot* are not excluded.[87] Likewise, North American communities should be encompassed by *eruvin* even if all possible *karpefiyot* are not excluded.[88]

GOLF COURSES AND CEMETERIES

Rav Moshe Heinemann, in his lecture delivered to the Conference of Young Israel rabbis, felt that sand traps and other hazards on golf courses do not constitute *karpefiyot* despite the fact that they are unused land. He explains that since the hazards are part of the game of golf, it is considered to be a useful portion of the golf course and therefore part of the *dirah*.

There is considerable debate regarding whether a cemetery constitutes a *karpeif*. Rav Eliashiv (*Kovetz Teshuvot* 1:45) rules leniently, as people visit cemeteries, making it part of the *dirah*. Rav Heinemann, though, reports that Rav Moshe Feinstein adopted a strict approach and did not regard a cemetery as part of the *dirah*. The Passaic, New Jersey community excludes cemeteries from its *eruv*. An exception even according to the strict view might be cemeteries of special historic and/or national interest, such as Arlington National Cemetery.

---

[87] *Eruvin mehudarim* (higher standard *eruvin*) in Israel exclude every *karpeif* in accordance with the strict ruling of Rav Yosef Shalom Elyashiv. In January 2019, I saw how a sown field is excluded from the broader Modi'in *eruv*.

[88] We should note that the exclusion of *karpefiyot* is at times exceedingly challenging and sometimes borders on making *eruv* maintenance an unsustainable task for the community.

CONCLUSION

Although it is better to adopt the stricter opinion regarding *karpeif*, in many instances, the stricter view is not a viable and sustainable option. Thus, while those who wish to be strict are encouraged to do so, those who wish to follow the lenient views have ample halachic precedent and rabbinic authority supporting them.

ERUV CHATZEIROT CONSIDERATIONS

A gentleman who is particularly scrupulous regarding Halachah asked if he could carry within White Plains, NY hospital despite the fact that an *eruv chatzeirot* had not been made for this specific location. The White Plains Orthodox community does maintain an *eruv chatzeirot* for its community *eruv*. Even though the hospital is included within the *eruv*, the individual in question wished to heed the *Mishnah Berurah's* call to scrupulous individuals (*ba'alei nefesh*) to avoid the use of community *eruvin*. If he does not rely on the community *eruv*, one could argue that he does not have access to the community *eruv chatzeirot*, and thus he may not rely upon the latter to carry within the hospital. In this chapter, we will explain why it is acceptable even for halachically scrupulous individuals to rely on a surrounding community's *eruv chatzeirot* to carry within areas such as the White Plains hospital despite their reluctance to rely upon community *eruvin*. In the process, we hope to shed more light on the various considerations that should be taken into account when determining whether it is necessary to create an *eruv chatzeirot*.

TEFISAT YAD BA'AL HABAYIT

The first consideration is based on the Halachah that the requirement of an *eruv chatzeirot* does not apply if the landlord stores property in all of the residences (*tefisat yad ba'al habayit*; *Shulchan Aruch*, O.C. 370:2,4). As aforementioned, Rav Moshe Feinstein (*Teshuvot Igrot Moshe*, O.C. 1:141) rules that a landlord who rents out items (such as stoves or refrigerators) with every apartment is considering to be "storing" his property with the tenants, so no *eruv chatzeirot* is required.

This ruling most certainly applies to a hospital, since the hospital stores a lot of equipment in each of the patients' rooms. Although *Teshuvot Devar Avraham* (3:30) and Rav Yosef Dov Soloveitchik (cited in *Nefesh Harav*, p. 170) disagree and rule that the rule of *tefisat yad ba'al habayit* does not apply if the owner places the equipment for the need of the visitor living in that space, we nonetheless may rely on Rav Moshe's ruling as a *senif*, a component of a lenient ruling. This is especially true in the case of great need. Such need is readily apparent in the hospital setting, as observant patients and their families often retrieve Shabbat food and other needs from the hospital kosher room, designed to meet the special needs of Jewish patients.

MATZI L'SALUKINHU

Tosafot (Eruvin 72a s.v. *umodin*) rule that a teacher or scribe that one hosts in his house does not create a need for an *eruv chatzeirot* even if the portion of the house in which he lives has a separate entrance. *Tosafot* present three reasons for this ruling. First, they explain that one does not provide the space with the intent that the guest prohibits him to carry within the home. Second, since the guest relies on the home for his needs such as cooking and baking, he is not considered as a separate entity but rather a member of the household. Finally, the owner is able to remove the guest from his home at will at any time (*matzi l'salukinhu*).
The *Shulchan Aruch* (O.C. 370:3) rules in accordance with *Tosafot*. The *Biur Halachah* (ad. loc. s.v. *einam oserim*) rules that the Halachah applies even if just the last reason of *matzi l'salukinhu* ap-

plies. Accordingly, Rav Moshe Heinemann rules[89] that a hospital does not require an *eruv chatzeirot* since the patients may be moved at the hospital's discretion.

However, the *Chazon Ish* (O.C. 90:32) strongly rejects the *Biur Halachah* and rules that an *eruv chatzeirot* is required unless all three of *Tosafot's* reasons apply. Rav Shlomo Zalman Auerbach (*Teshuvot Minchat Shlomo*, 2:35:24) is concerned for the opinion of the *Chazon Ish*, regarding the specific question of requiring an *eruv chatzeirot* in the hospital.

HOST PROVIDING FOOD
Rav Shlomo Zalman presents another reason to be lenient based on Eruvin 72b-73a and *Shulchan Aruch* O.C. 370:5. The Gemara and *Shulchan Aruch* teach that if the owner provides food for all the residents of the courtyard, an *eruv chatzeirot* is not needed. This reason alone, though, does not suffice to permit carrying without an *eruv chatzeirot* since this Halachah might apply only if the owner lives in the courtyard (see *Bi'ur Halachah* ad. loc. s.v. *v'hani mili*), a condition which does not apply to a hospital.

A RESIDENCE NOT OF ONE'S CHOICE
Rav Zvi Sobolofsky raises another reason to be lenient regarding an *eruv chatzeirot* in a hospital. He cites the Gemara (Yoma 10b) which presents R. Yehudah's opinion that "*dirah ba'al korcha lo shemei dirah,*" if one resides in a place against one's will it is

---

[89] Star K, *The Visitor's Guide to Hospitals*, www.star-k.org/articles/articles/medicine/43/the-visitors-halachic-guide-to-hospitals1.

not considered a residence. Thus, since one could argue that one is hospitalized against his will (as he would much rather not be hospitalized[90]), then his residence does not generate an obligation of an *eruv chatzeirot*. Although this argument is highly debatable (see note 2) one could add it as the long list of *senifim l'hakeil*, components of a lenient ruling.

THE LOCAL COMMUNITY ERUV

Rav Shlomo Zalman Auerbach combines many of the above arguments to not require an *eruv chatzeirot* in a hospital that is encompassed by a community *eruv*. He rules that one may combine the many lenient factors in addition to the fact that a community *eruv* is accepted even by the *Mishnah Berurah* as acceptable as baseline Halachah. Rav Heinemann, though, permits carrying within a hospital without an *eruv chatzeirot* even within a hospital that is not encompassed with a community *eruv*. Rav Natan Gestetner (*Teshuvot L'horot Natan* 5:29:9) rules that one may carry in a hospital without an *eruv chatzeirot* even in a community without an Eruv, especially in case of patient need.

---

[90] This does not, of course, apply to a woman giving birth; however, such a case may allow for its own leniencies. Moreover, it could be argued that those who are hospitalized very much want to be hospitalized since this is the manner which allows them to hopefully save their lives and recover their health. Finally, the fact that the Rabanan reject R. Yehudah and believe that *dirah ba'al korcha shemei dirah*, gives one serious reason to not rely on R. Yehuda's opinion. For further discussion of *dirah ba'al korcha*, see the *Chida's* discussion of the obligation to affix a *mezuzah* to a prison and quarantined area in *Birkei Yosef* Y.D. 286:3).

Based on the five lenient considerations we set forth, I ruled (following Rav Shlomo Zalman's ruling) that one may carry within the White Plains hospital even for those who strictly adhere to higher halachic standards. This is especially so in regard to *eruv chatzeirot* regarding which the Gemara (Eruvin 46a) specifically teaches *"halachah k'divrei hameikel b'eruv,"* the Halacha follows the lenient opinion in regard to disputes in the area of *eruv chatzeirot*.[91]

OTHER AREAS – STUDENTS IN A DORMITORY
If the students all eat together in one cafeteria, an *eruv chatzeirot* is clearly not necessary. However, if they do not, then Rav Schachter believes (as stated in a lecture at Yeshiva University) that nonetheless an *eruv chatzeirot* is not necessary. He combines Rav Moshe's leniency regarding the Yeshiva's property in each dormitory room with the fact that the Yeshiva can change the students' room at will.

However, Rav Schachter quotes Rav Yosef Dov Soloveitchik, who ruled that an *eruv chatzeirot* was necessary in the Yeshiva University dorm. Rav Soloveitchik did not, as noted above, subscribe to Rav Moshe's leniency. Moreover, *Tosafot's* leniency regarding *matzi l'salukinhu* is stated regarding being able to completely remove the resident. However, in the case of the dormitory, while the institution might be able to change the room in which the student is housed, they cannot (under normal circumstances) remove the student entirely from the dor-

---

[91] Though this rule applies only to disputes between the Tana'im according to the Ra'avad cited by the Rashba to Eruvin 47b s.v. *matzati*.

mitory.[92] One could argue, though, that the ability to move the student to a different building is most significant in the context of *eruv chatzeirot*.

If Rav Soloveitchik's view is followed in a secular university campus, a *sechirat reshut* would be required in addition to an *eruv chatzeirot*, unless all of the residents of a particular dormitory are observant and primarily eat from one food source.

HOTELS

If all the hotel guests are observant and primarily eat from one food source, then an *eruv chatzeirot* and *sechirat reshut* are unquestionably unnecessary. If this is not the case, the question depends if one relies on Rav Moshe's furniture ruling. Rav Zvi Sobolofsky adds that one might also consider the fact that the hotel management can (at least in theory) move the guests to another room. In practice, it is best in such cases to make an *eruv chatzeirot* and *sechirat reshut* in such circumstances.

CAMPING GROUNDS

An *eruv chatzeirot* is unnecessary if the observant campers primarily eat together from one food source. If only one observant Jew or family is on the campgrounds, then a *sechirat reshut* is not necessary (as Chazal did not enact the requirement for a *sechirat reshut* in such circumstances; see *Shulchan Aruch*, O.C. 382:1). Otherwise, visitors should conduct a *sechirat reshut* with a park ranger before Shabbat.

---

[92] The *Chida* (*Teshuvot Chaim Sha'al* 2:22) makes such a distinction between the ability to remove a resident as opposed to merely changing their room.

DEMISTIFYING ATU RABIM

The concept of *atu rabim u'mevatlei mechitzta*, "come the many and nullify the Halachic wall," colloquially referred to as *atu rabim*, is a fundamental concept in *Hilchot Eruvin*. However, it is also an elusive concept, both in terms of its meaning and practical ramifications. In this appendix, we will attempt to present a straightforward explanation of this concept and its most important practical ramification.

MISHNAH – CHACHAMIM VS. R. YEHUDAH

The debate surrounding the *atu rabim* has been raging since the time of the Tana'im, and continues to be debated among the later Acharonim. The debate is first recorded in the second chapter of *Masechet Eruvin*.

There, the Mishnah (2:4) discusses a most interesting Halachic concept known as *pasei beira'ot*. This refers to boards that are placed to surround wells to permit drawing water from them on Shabbat to provide for animals to drink. These *pasei beira'ot* require only a limited amount of boards covering a limited amount of space, just four L-shaped corners, considerably less than what is normally needed to permit carrying. This was made as a special concession for those who made *aliyah l'regel* to enable them to provide water for their animals on their way to Jerusalem.

The Mishnah records a debate between the Chachamim and R. Yehudah as to whether *pasei beira'ot* remain effective even if a public thoroughfare passes through them. R. Yehudah rules that they are thereby rendered ineffective, while the Chachamim believe that they remain in full effect.

Tosafot (Eruvin 22a s.v. v'ha) clarify that *tzurot hapetach* are of the same status as *pasei beira'ot* in regard to the question of *atu rabim*. If people nullify *pasei beira'ot*, they nullify *tzurot hapetach* as well.

GEMARA AND RISHONIM

The dispute continues with R. Yochanan and R. Elazar on Eruvin 22a. The fact that the Chachamim disagree with R. Yochanan suggests that the Halachah should follow the majority opinion – the Chachamim. However, the fact that R. Yochanan was R. Elazar's teacher seems to suggest that the Halachah should follow the former.

The Rishonim continue to debate the issue. The Rambam (*Hilchot Shabbat* 17:33) famously rules in accordance with the Chachamim that *"lo atu rabbim u'mevatlei mechitzta."* However, the Rashba (Eruvin 22a s.v. *hacha*) and the Ritva (Eruvin 22a s.v. *Rabi Yehudah*) rule in accordance with R. Yehudah and R. Yochanan.

SHULCHAN ARUCH

The *Biur Halachah* (364:2 *v'hu*) interprets the opinion that requires a *reshut harabim* to have closed *delatot* to transform the area into a *reshut hayachid* as emerging from the opinion of *atu rabbim u'mevatlei mechitzta*. However, the opinion that suffices with doors that merely have the potential to close at night (*delatot re'uyot li'nol*) follows the opinion of *lo atu rabim u'mevatlei mechitzta*.

The *Mishnah Berurah* believes that since the primary opinion in the *Shulchan Aruch* is that doors must be locked each night, the *Shulchan Aruch* must rule in accordance with the opinion that *atu rabim u'mevatlei mechitzta*.

DEFINING THE RABIM

How does one define the *rabim* in this context? The *Biur Halachah* (ibid.) and *Mishnah Berurah* (364:8) rule that the definition of the *rabim* for purposes of designating an area as a *reshut harabim* is also the relevant definition in the context of *atu rabim*.

The *Mishnah Berurah* and *Biur Halachah* further clarify that even if one rules that *lo atu rabim u'mivatlei mechitzta*, the *rabim* still disqualify *tzurot hapetach* on a rabbinic level. Thus, it emerges that the major difference between whether one rules that *atu rabim* or *lo atu rabim* is whether *rabim* disqualify *tzurot hapetach* on a Torah level or a rabbinic level. Almost all community *eruvin* are composed primarily of *tzurot hapetach*.

THE PRACTICAL DIFFERENCE

As we discussed in our first chapter, the definition of a *reshut harabim* is highly debated. One opinion believes that a thoroughfare which is at least sixteen *amot* wide and another opinion argues that it is not a *reshut harabim* unless 600,000 people inhabit the city.

The *Bi'ur Halachah* (345:7, s.v. *v'yeish omerim shekol*) count the Rishonim and concludes that twelve of the Rishonim rule in accordance with the sixteen *amot* view and another twelve Rishonim rule that 600,000 people are required. According to the latter view, if less than 600,000 live in the area, the area is not a *reshut harabim* and all would agree that *atu rabim* is not a concern. The *Bi'ur Halachah* thus concludes that the matter is inconclusive.

The *Mishnah Berurah* (364) and *Bi'ur Halachah* (ibid.) rule that the resolution of the matter depends on whether a *reshut harabim* disqualifies *tzurot hapetach* on a Torah level (*atu rabim*) or only on a rabbinic level (*lo atu rabim*). If one rules that *atu rabim*, then one must be concerned that even just a road that is sixteen *amot* wide disqualifies the *tzurot hapetach*. Since the definition of a *reshut harabim* is the subject of an inconclusive dispute, one should adopt the stricter opinion regarding a Torah level prohibition.

However, if the concern for the validity of the *tzurot hapetach* is only a rabbinic issue, then one may rely on the lenient view since one may adopt the lenient view when there is a doubt about a law on a rabbinic level ("*safek derabanan le'kula*").

THE DISPUTE BETWEEN THE MISHNAH BERURAH AND THE ARUCH HASHULCHAN

The *Mishnah Berurah* acknowledges that the common practice is to follow the more lenient view of the Rambam that *lo atu* and therefore rely on the lenient 600,000 people opinion regarding the definition of a *reshut harabim*. However, since the *Mishnah Berurah* believes that the *Shulchan Aruch* fundamentally adopts the view that *atu rabim*, he urges those who are scrupulous to adopt the stricter view.

The *Aruch HaShulchan* (O.C. 364:1) rules in accordance with the view that *lo atu rabim u'mevatlei mechitzta*. Thus, it is not surprising that the *Aruch HaShulchan* is more supportive of the generally accepted view that a road the width of sixteen *amot* does not nullify the *tzurot hapetach* encompassing the area.

CONCLUSION

As the *kohein gadol* (Yoma, Mishnah 7:1) states in reference to the Torah reading on Yom Kippur, *"yoter mema shekarati lachem katuv kan,"* there is much more written than we have read. We have presented only the surface of the discussion of the rich and longstanding dispute as to whether or not *atu rabim* cancels the efficacy of *mechitzot*. For further discussion, see Rav Baruch Simon's *Imrei Baruch, Eruvin UReshuyot*, pp. 70-81.

Section 2

Eruvin Infrastructure

∝

A LECHI ON EVERY UTILITY POLE?

It might be the most important issue a community must grapple with in constructing its *eruv*. Rav Yosef Gavriel Bechoffer and Rav Moshe Heinemann advise many communities on *eruv* construction and require a *lechi* to be installed on every pole on which a utility wire does not run above the pole. On the other hand, both Rav Hershel Schachter (as heard by myself and Rav Michael Taubes) and Rav Mordechai Willig (personal communication) do not believe that Halachah makes this demand.

This dispute has enormous practical ramifications. Communities that abide by the stricter opinion need to install hundreds of additional *lechis* compared to those communities who do not adopt this practice. At an average cost of fifty to seventy-five dollars per each *lechi* installed by a professional, the adoption of the stricter opinion is extremely costly. Additionally, the associated cost of continual inspection and maintenance of an *eruv* with so many *lechis* is quite steep.

BACKGROUND INFORMATION - TZURAT HAPETACH

We will share perspectives on both opinions, based on thirty years of experience in advising dozens of communities how to construct, expand, and maintain their *eruvin*. We shall focus on the construction of *tzurot hapetach*, which most often constitute the bulk of a community *eruv*. The rationale behind this type of *mechitzah* (Halachic wall) as explained by Rav Hershel Schachter (*Journal of Halacha and Contemporary Society*, vol. 5 p. 9), is as follows:

> Since a house is most certainly a *reshut hayachid* (private domain), even with its door(s) wide open, and even when it has several such

doors, why shouldn't an enclosure surrounded totally by doorways (even when the doors are missing and only the doorframes remain) be considered a *reshut hayachid* as well? All that is needed, for such a door frame *mechitzah* is "a pole on one side, a pole on the other side, and a pole running across the two from above." Strictly speaking, there is no limit to the number of such *tzurot hapetach* which may be employed.

The horizontal wire must run above the *lechis*. If it runs to the side (*tzurat hapetach min hatzad*), it is invalid due to its failure to resemble an actual door frame. Sometimes there will be a series of utility poles over which a wire runs above each and every one of these poles. Such poles are ideal and all agree a separate *lechi* need not be attached to the pole. Often, though, none of the wires run above a series of poles. In such a situation a *lechi* needs to be installed beneath one of the wires that run along the side of the utility pole.

A LECHI ON EVERY UTILITY POLE?

Rav Bechoffer (*The Contemporary Eruv*, 3rd edition pp. 132-133) frames the issue in the following manner:

> There are rabbis involved in the construction and maintenance of metropolitan *eruvin* that are not meticulous in ensuring that every pole in a series have a *lechi* attached to it, so long as the first and last pole in that series have been rectified with *lechayayim*.[1] Their rationale is that the longer *tzuras hapesach* between the first and last pole is sufficient.[2]

Rav Bechoffer's first criticism of this approach is

---

[1] Plural for *lechi*.

[2] This approach argues that *"dal meihacha"* (see Sukkah 2a), that we may ignore the middle poles as halachically insignificant.

its running afoul of the *gezeiras haro'im* (literally, the decree of the onlookers). This principle stated by the *Magen Avraham* (362:20) mandates the maintenance not only of the actual validity of an *eruv*, but also of the appearance of that validity. Accordingly, the *Magen Avraham* mandates the removal[3] of invalid *lechayayim* from the eruv, lest onlookers get a mistaken impression [that a *tzurat hapetach min hatzad* is acceptable].

Rav Bechoffer does not cite any major recent Halachic authority to support his application of the *Magen Avraham* to the contemporary utility pole. It should be noted, though, that two major twentieth century Halachic authorities disagree with Rav Bechoffer. Rav Moshe Feinstein (as cited by Rav Moshe Heinemann and others) did not make such a requirement. Rav Moshe's ruling was applied in practice by Rav Shimon Eider in the 1970s and early 1980s for the *eruvin* he built following Rav Moshe Feinstein's specifications. Rav Moshe is quoted as saying that there is no limit as to the distance between the first and last *lechis* on the series of wires, as long as the wire is relatively straight.

In Israel, the great Rav Zvi Pesach Frank (*Teshuvot Har Zvi*, O.C. 2:18:12), in a brief responsum addressed to rabbis and inspectors of communal *eruvin*, clearly does not subscribe to Rav Bechoffer's application of the *Magen Avraham*. The words of Rav Zvi Pesach are instructive:

> Question: The iron (i.e. utility) [horizontal] wire of the *eruv* runs along a very large area and along its path, the wire meanders and rests on the sides of the poles. However, this happens only on the

---

[3] Of course, Rav Bechoffer does not require the removal of the utility poles, but requires the installation of a *lechi* beneath the wire that runs along the side to eliminate the concern for mistaken impressions.

middle poles. May we rely on the fact that the wires rest on top of the first and last poles in the series?

Response: The *eruv* is valid. See the Rambam (*Hilchot Shabbat* 17:14) who writes "a *tzurat hapetach* that is one hundred *amot* wide is permitted." It is self-evident that the Rambam does not impose a specific maximum of one hundred *amot*. Rather, a *tzurat hapetach* even wider than one hundred *amot* is acceptable.[4] Accordingly, there is no disqualification in the *eruv* due to the middle poles since we view them as if they do not exist. Thus the *tzurat hapetach* created by the *lechis* at the beginning and end of the long stretch of poles is valid and the middle poles do not invalidate the *eruv*.

Note that Rav Zvi Pesach, similar to Rav Moshe, does not advise constructing a *lechi* on the middle poles to satisfy the opinion of the *Magen Avraham*. The question is why these two great authorities did not advise satisfying the *Magen Avraham*, when it is codified by both the *Mishnah Berurah* (362:65) and *Aruch Hashulchan*[5] (O.C. 362:31). One may suggest that Rav Moshe and Rav Zvi Pesach believe that the *Magen Avraham* speaks of a situation where the poles were installed for the purpose of creating a *tzurat hapetach*. In such a situation, the existence of a pole on which the wire rests on its side and remains uncorrected by a Lechi, misleads the observer. However, in contemporary North American urban and suburban *eruvin*, which rely upon modifying pre-existing utility poles to create a suitable *eruv*, the observer is hardly misled. He realizes that the wire

---

[4] The *Shulchan Aruch* (O.C. 362:11), in describing a *tzurat hapetach*, does not mention a maximum distance between *lechis*, which seems to support Rav Frank's approach.

[5] The *Aruch Hashulchan* explicitly states that the *eruv* is not disqualified if the *gezeirat haro'im* is not addressed.

runs on its side not due to Halachic design but owing to the utility company's design. Thus, *eruvin* composed of utility wires need only be valid but need not appear valid.[6]

Indeed, Rav Bloi (*Netivot Shabbat* 19:42, note 95) specifically writes that when constructing an *eruv* using utility poles, a *lechi* is not needed on every pole if the utility wire used as the *eruv* wire runs straight.

RAV BECHOFFER'S SECOND REASON

Rav Bechoffer takes his issue a step further, arguing that failure to install a *lechi* at each pole will likely result in the invalidation of the Eruv. Rav Bechoffer believes that the horizontal *eruv* wire must run in a perfectly straight trajectory in order to be valid. He argues that installing a *lechi* on each pole is the only manner in which to achieve this goal.

As noted, Rav Moshe and Rav Zvi Pesach (as is evident from his aforementioned responsum) do not subscribe to this view. In addition, *Teshuvot Imrei Yosher* (2:133) permits the horizontal wire to deviate up to three *tefachim* (nine to eleven inches). *Teshuvot Sha'arei Tziyon* (number 3) supports the view that the horizontal wire need not be perfectly straight from the fact that the Gemara (Eruvin 11a) describes an *eruv* made of grapevines, which are not completely straight. As previously mentioned in our third chapter, Rav Yosef Adler reports that Rav

---

[6] The fact that the *Magen Avraham* advises removing the pole indicates that he is addressing a situation where we control the installation and removal of the pole.

Yosef Dov Soloveitchik also did not require that the horizontal wire proceed in a perfectly straight trajectory.[7]

Most importantly, wires in a series of poles sometimes do run in a straight line and a *lechi* is not needed on every pole to ensure that the wires of the *tzurot hapetach* are straight. In the Teaneck *eruv*, where Rav Schachter and Rav Willig's approach to this issue is followed, vigilant care is taken to ensure that the wire is straight. This is accomplished even though a *lechi* is not attached to every pole.

A PRACTICAL ADVANTAGE AND DISADVANTAGE TO A LECHI ON EVERY POLE

While Rav Bechoffer makes cogent arguments for the *lechi* on each pole approach, those who disagree make a compelling case as well. Based on my thirty years of experience with *eruv* construction and maintenance, I have concluded that there are practical considerations arguing both for and against the strict approach. The practical advantage to having a *lechi* on every pole is that each *lechi* serves as a pointer so that the inspector can easily recognize which wire the *lechi* is connected to. This helps the *eruv* inspectors properly track the presence of the wire and makes it very apparent if the utility company moved the wire (which they sometimes do).

The practical difficulty with implementing the *lechi* on each pole approach is that it makes *eruv* maintenance very challenging. A typical community *eruv* has a circumference of at least twelve miles. Requiring a *lechi* on each pole often results in

---

[7] *Teshuvot Shaarei Tziyon* notes that the custom in almost all of the *eruvin* in his area (Bilsk, Ukraine) was to be lenient about this matter.

having in the range of five hundred *lechis* to inspect on a weekly basis. Experience teaches that *lechis* must be thoroughly inspected from top to bottom as they are prone to break. It is very challenging for one team of inspectors[8] to thoroughly inspect five hundred *lechis* each week. An average size *eruv* with a *lechi* on each pole needs at least two teams of inspectors on a weekly basis to perform a thorough and proper inspection of the *eruv*. This adds to the cost of *eruv* maintenance. The Gemara's teaching that *"tafasta merubah lo tefasta,"* one who grabs too much will not be successful (Rosh Hashanah 4b), is salient in this context. R. Yochanan ben Zakai teaches the value of *hatzalah purtah*, avoiding overly ambitious goals, which oftentimes do not result in anything.[9]

Cost to the community is an issue as well. It is advisable (and some municipalities require) to hire a professional to in-

---

[8] It is proper for one person to drive the car and another to inspect the *eruv*. One who both drives and inspects the *eruv* does neither task properly. A proper *eruv* inspection includes a full visual inspection of each *lechi*.

[9] Reb Elya Lichter, the great *sofer* who served as the *gittin sofer* for both Rav Moshe Feinstein and Rav Eliyahu Henkin, told me that Rav Moshe would counsel *get* (divorce) administrators to aim to create a *get* that is *kasher b'dieved*, in line with baseline Halachah, as one who seeks to make a *lechatchilah* (ideal) *get* very much risks the halachic validity of the entire enterprise. I have seen this happen with communities who installed a *lechi* on each pole, seeking to make a *"lechatchilah eruv"* and wind up with a disqualified *eruv* since there were too many *lechis* for the inspectors to maintain. An *eruv* with a *lechi* on each pole requires multiple *eruv* inspectors to conduct a proper weekly inspection of the *eruv*. Many communities find it difficult to find even one competent and diligent *eruv* inspector.

stall *lechis* to utility poles. Professionals charge in a range of fifty to seventy-five dollars per each *lechi* installed. Requiring the installation of a *lechi* on each pole dramatically increases the construction and maintenance costs of an *eruv*.

RAV SCHACHTER'S COMPROMISE APPROACH

Rav Hershel Schachter adopts a compromise approach to this issue. He notes that the Gemara[10] (Eruvin 11b) requires that the *tzurat hapetach* must be sufficiently sturdy to support at least a nominal door, namely a door made of straw. Rav Schachter[11] understands this Gemara to mean that the two *lechis* of a *tzurat hapetach* must together be able to at least support a door of marginal weight. Rav Schachter estimates the maximum distance two *lechis* could support a minimal door to be approximately one city block.[12]

---

[10] This Gemara is codified by the *Shulchan Aruch* (O.C. 362:11).

[11] Rav Moshe and Rav Zvi Pesach, who place no maximum on the distance between *lechis*, would explain the Gemara as teaching that each individual *lechi* must be sufficiently sturdy to support a minimal door. Alternatively, as Rav Avi Lebowitz notes, it could refer to supporting a door of a minimal width, ten *amot*. This Gemara teaches that the *lechi* must be made of a substantial material, unlike the horizontal wire which may be made of a most flimsy material (as stated in the *Shulchan Aruch* O.C. 362:11).

[12] Rav Schachter told me this refers to a block such as from 185th street to 186th street in Manhattan (which is approximately 285 feet), making the block to be approximately .05 of a mile. In practical terms this usually means that one may skip a maximum of two poles on which no *lechi* is placed. Rav Schachter told me that in a case of great need, one could tol-

One may support this approach from a comment of Rashi on Eruvin 11a (s.v. *umatach zemorah*), which explains the objective of the *tzurat hapetach*; namely, the emulation of a real doorframe (*me'ein tzurat hapetach*). This understanding fits with the explanation of *tzurot hapetach* we cited earlier from Rav Schachter. One could argue that in a situation where *lechis* are positioned very far away from each other, that what has been created hardly resembles an actual doorframe.

The Teaneck *eruv* follows Rav Schachter's approach to this issue and does not tolerate a distance of more than approximately .05 of a mile between *lechis*. On a practical level, this approach results in the use of a reasonable amount of *lechis*. On the other hand, the relatively frequent *lechis* help inspectors identify the wires that are in use.

CONCLUSION

Although Rav Bechoffer presents a good case for installing a *lechi* on each pole, an equally compelling argument can be made for those who disagree. Those who disagree include Rav Moshe, Rav Frank, Rav Bloi, Rav Schachter, and Rav Willig. Each community must decide what is appropriate based on which approach the Posek for the community finds most persuasive. An assessment also must be kept as to whether adopting the strict

---

erate a distance of up to two blocks (0.1 of a mile or, in most cases, skipping a maximum four utility poles).

approach enhances or detracts from the Halachic integrity and quality of the *eruv*.[13]

POSTSCRIPT

Dr. Bert Miller[14] (*Eruv Manual*, *Eruv* Story No. 30) reports the view of Rav Moshe Heinemann[15] regarding this matter as follows: "The practice of attaching a *lechi* on each pole that runs in a straight line was a stringency." Rav Heinemann believes that the baseline Halachah follows Rav Moshe Feinstein, who believes that a series of utility poles that run in a straight line[16] need only a *lechi* at the beginning and end of the series. Dr. Miller reports that Rav Heinemann was willing to rely on Rav Moshe when building an enclosure to box out a *karpeif* from an *eruv*. However, in the Star K *eruv* webinar, Rav Heinemann was not willing to be lenient about this matter even in case of need.

---

[13] Smaller communities might also have to maintain a more minimal footprint as the local utility may be unwilling to permit the installation of *lechis* on a very large number of poles.

[14] Dr. Miller has worked very closely with Rav Moshe Heinemann for the last forty years to create and maintain the Baltimore *eruv*.

[15] Many *eruvin* in North America, especially those in Chareidi communities, are created and maintained under the supervision of Rav Heinemann.

[16] Rav Yitzchok Frankel told me that Rav Moshe Feinstein did not require the *eruv* line to run in a perfectly straight line. Rav Moshe ruled the line could veer up to three *tefachim* (10 inches according to Rav Moshe's standards) and remain acceptable.

Rabbi Chaim Jachter

A TREE AS A LECHI

It is fairly clear from the Gemara that a tree may be used as a *lechi*. Eruvin 11b records that R. Yochanan ben Nuri stretched a vine from tree to tree and created a *tzurat hapetach* for the purpose of *kilayim* (separating plantings of different species). The Meiri (ad. loc. s.v. *v'achar kach*) clearly indicates that this ruling may be applied to *Hilchot Shabbat* as well.

Thus, we are hardly surprised that Rav Moshe Feinstein (cited in *The Laws of an Eruv*, p. 100) rules that a tree is acceptable as a *lechi*. Rav Hershel Schachter, though, clarifies (personal communication) that we may rely on a tree as a *lechi* only if the wire runs above the central trunk of the tree. Otherwise, the wire is regarded as not being above the "*lechi*" but rather on its side (*min hatzad*).

Rav Mordechai Willig (personal communication) believes that we may rely on a branch off the main trunk if that branch is more vertical than horizontal along its entire length. This follows Rav Aharon Kotler's oft-cited ruling accepting a slanted wire or *lechi* as long as it is longer than it is wide (for a *lechi*) or wider than it is long (for a wire). As long as the branch is longer than it is wide, it is viewed by Rav Kotler as a legitimate extension of the main trunk.

THE PROBLEM WITH THE THEORY
The idea of using a tree as a *lechi* in theory is wonderful. The competent *eruv* planner (especially outside of Israel) attempts to maximize the use of the existing infrastructure. Reducing additional installations reduces costs, makes inspections easier, enhances the *eruv*'s long term sustainability, and reduces the *eruv*'s

footprint (making it more "neighborhood friendly"). This is especially relevant when excluding *karpefiyot*.

The problem with the theory is that trees come down more often than utility poles, especially in settled areas (as opposed to within a forest). In two different communities, I had utilized trees as *lechis*; unfortunately, at a later date, and unbeknownst to the *eruvin* inspectors, the trees were downed. This has brought me to the sad realization that it is best, when possible, to avoid relying on trees as *lechis*.

Other practical considerations include the following realities:

1. Trees grow and may not maintain the same form that allowed for their original use.

2. Trees sway more than utility poles, making the wires attached to them more vulnerable.

3. Smaller trees, which are most often incorporated into *eruvin*, are more prone to break.

4. Trees eventually grow past whatever is placed on them and the *lechi* itself will slowly be swallowed into the tree.

PRACTICAL RECOMMENDATIONS

If the Halachah is carefully followed, there should be no problem with using a properly located tree as a *lechi*. Experience, though, teaches that it is best to avoid relying on a tree for a *lechi* for the long term because *eruv* inspectors are unlikely to notice a missing tree in a settled area. When a community installs a *lechi* on a utility pole, it alerts the inspector of the pole's use in the *eruv*. When a tree unobtrusively serves as a *lechi*, it is easy to forget and overlook its function as a *lechi*.

The use of a tree may be acceptable, though, as a short-term solution to a problem with the *eruv*. Examples of this include the use of the tree in a last minute ad hoc repair before Shabbat or in a situation when construction wreaks havoc on an *eruv*, leaving the community scrambling to find short-term solutions until the construction is completed.

A tree may be used as a *lechi* when it is needed to satisfy what one may regard as a stringency. For example, if the approving Rav of an *eruv* regards Rav Schachter's requirement for there to be a *lechi* every block or block and a half as a stringency (see previous chapter), then a tree may be used as a *lechi* to satisfy this stringency. In such a case, there is less of a concern for the stability of the tree, as even if something would happen to the tree, thereby disqualifying its use as a *lechi*, the *eruv* would still remain kosher according to baseline Halachah.

CONCLUSION

Practical Halachah is not only determined through the examination of the classic sources and consultation with the generation's leading halachic authorities. One must also take into account real-life field considerations in order to implement halachically proper protocols that are sound not only in theory, but also in practice. This once again points to the need for an *eruv* to be reviewed by a Rav with significant field experience in addition to the mastery of *Hilchot Eruvin*.

LECHI STRENGTH

How strong must a *lechi* be? While this might appear to be a simple matter, it is in actuality subject to considerable debate with some very significant implications for best practices regarding community *eruvin*.

GEMARA AND RISHONIM
The Gemara (Eruvin 11b) states that a *lechi* must be sufficiently strong to be able to theoretically support a door (*"beri'ah l'ha'amid delet shel kash"*). The Gemara states that the door to which it refers may even be a minimal one, a door made of straw.

The *Terumat Hadeshen* (74) notes that this Gemara does not seem to fit with his ruling that a thin layer of lime placed on a wall beneath a wire may serve as a *lechi*. How could a thin sheet of lime support even a door of straw? The *Terumat Hadeshen* answers that the lime in combination with the wall on which it is placed is able to support a door of straw. The *Mishnah Berurah* (363:26) and *Sha'ar Hatziyun* (363:22) present this ruling as normative Halachah.

THREE HISTORICAL STAGES OF LECHIS USED IN NORTH AMERICAN ERUVIN
We discern three basic waves of *lechi* construction in North America. In the 1970s and early 1980s, community *eruvin* were designed at the direction of Rav Moshe Feinstein. These *eruvin* utilized forty inch (= 10 *tefachim* by Rav Moshe's standard) 1x2 inch or 2x4 inch pieces of lumber affixed to the pole beneath the wire. Such *lechis* undoubtedly meet the requirement of *"beri'ah*

l'ha'amid delet shel kash." The difficulties with these *lechis*, however, is that they raise questions as to their precise alignment beneath the wire above them. Therefore, the preference in the mid-1980s began to shift towards *lechis* that extend all the way to the wire.

APPLICATION TO HALF INCH GROUND WIRE MOLDING

From the mid-1980s to the mid-2010s, the most common material used for *lechis* the black half-inch grounding wire. The material is fairly flimsy and raises the question as to whether such *lechis* truly are *beri'ah l'ha'amid delet shel kash*. Three approaches have emerged regarding this question:

1. Rav Baruch Simon (*Imrei Baruch, Eruvin Ureshuyot*, p. 142) regards this material as acceptable, as the requirement of *beri'ah l'ha'amid delet shel kash* is met when the strength of the pole to which the *lechi* is affixed is taken into account.

2. Rav Moshe Heinemann (in the *eruv* webinar posted on the Star-K website) argues that the door may even be flimsier than straw. He argues that when Chazal say "straw" they mean to say even the most minimal of materials.[17] Rav Heinemann stated that a *lechi* is acceptable even if it could only support a door made of very thin plastic such as the kind used by dry cleaners to cover cleaned suits.

3. Rav Hershel Schachter (personal communication in 1989), though, is concerned that the half-inch grounding wire is

---

[17] Rav Yaakov Bloi (*Netivot Shabbat* 19:24) also writes that the *delet shel kash* even refers to a *delet kol shehu*, the most minimum of doors.

not *beri'ah l'ha'amid delet shel kash*. He therefore advised that a one-inch by two-inch piece of wood serve as the bottom ten *tefachim* of the *lechi* in order that the *lechi* be capable of supporting a *delet shel kash*.[18]

Rav Schachter argues (personal communication) that the ruling of the *Terumat Hadeshen* cannot be applied to the situation of the half-inch grounding wire since this material does not combine to form one entity as do the lime and the wall to which it is applied. One could respond that indeed the half-inch grounding wire and the pole do combine to form one entity even to the extent that they can combine to create a proper *lechi*.[19] Alternatively, one could argue that although the pole and wire do not combine to form a *lechi*, the pole strengthens

---

[18] Rav Tzvi Fisher, Rosh Kollel of Portland, Oregon, reports that Rav Yaakov Bloi also rules that it suffices for the bottom ten *tefachim* to be capable of supporting a *delet shel kash*. The *Sha'ar Hatziyun* (363:11, at the end) already raises this as a possibility.

[19] Rav Zvi Sobolofsky (personal communication) raises the possibility that the grounding wire and pole do combine to form one halachic entity and can together form a kosher *lechi*. According to this suggestion, if the grounding wire is broken more than three *tefachim* above the ground, the pole to which it is affixed might combine to complete the bottom of the *lechi*. Rav Moshe Heinemann (in the *eruv* webinar posted on the Star-K website) specifically rejects this approach. He understands the *Magen Avraham* (363:28) as teaching that the *lechi* must appear as a side post. Since the pole (or a tree) does not appear to combine with the grounding wire to form a single entity, it does not combine to create an acceptable *lechi*.

the half-inch grounding wire to the extent that it is *beri'ah l'ha'amid delet shel kash*.

TWO PRACTICAL IMPLICATIONS OF THE THREE APPROACHES

Rav Shmuel Khoshermann reports that Rav Heinemann permits the Atlanta *eruv* to rely on an exceedingly thin grounding wire as a *lechi* (see Figure 2). However, in light of Rav Schachter's approach, Rav Michael Taubes and I agree that we would not rely upon this in the Teaneck *eruv*. We feel that while one could argue that the half-inch grounding wire could support a *delet shel kash*, it is quite a big leap to argue that such an exceedingly thin wire meets this requirement.

Rav Avi Lebowitz adds that the *Shiltei Giborim* (*Dafei Harif* 2b) seems to disagree. The *Shiltei Giborim* writes that a *delet shel kash* is very light, and that it is a minimum requirement. Rav Lebowitz also observes that the *Mishnah Berurah* (362:61) notes that the *kana she'al gabeihen* (the horizontal component of the *tzurat hapetach*) does not need to be able to sustain a *delet shel kash*, but cannot be so flimsy that it is "removed by a normal wind." As we are more stringent for the vertical *lechis*, it emerges that the ability to support a *delet shel kash* is a requirement beyond just being sturdy enough to stand up to the wind. Thus, Rav Heinemann's understanding of a *delet shel kash* seems difficult.

In addition, since it appears that Rav Baruch Simon's approach is the most accepted, those responsible for maintaining community *eruvin* should be careful to properly fasten the half-inch grounding wire to the pole, especially in regard to the bottom ten *tefachim* of the wire. The u-bolts that attach the half-inch grounding wire to the utility pole often become detached from the pole. This is a fairly frequent occurrence, and *eruv* inspectors should be alerted to monitor this carefully.

THE NEW APPROACH – HALF-INCH AND ONE-INCH CONDUIT

Since the mid-2010s, it has become common to attach half-inch or one-inch conduit to serve as *lechis* on utility poles (see Figure 3). They have the practical advantage of blending into the poles, as such material is used by linemen on utility poles. In addition, their white color offers a significant advantage in that they are much easier to detect and inspect than the black half-inch grounding wire. Many *eruv* inspectors view this innovation as facilitating a dramatic improvement in both the ease and quality of inspection.

There is also a distinct halachic advantage to using this material, as it is significantly sturdier than the half-inch grounding wire. Therefore it appears to satisfy Rav Schachter's standards for *beri'ah l'ha'amid delet shel kash*. Thus, the members of the Teaneck *Eruv* Rabbinic Board consent to rely on conduit even for the bottom ten *tefachim* of the *lechi*.[20] Nonetheless, it is still worthwhile for *eruv* inspectors to monitor that the *lechi* (especially its bottom ten *tefachim*) remains fastened to the utility pole.

---

[20] Previously in Teaneck, wooden slabs were installed as the bottom ten *tefachim* of each *lechi*, in conformity with Rav Schachter's opinion.

CONCLUSION

Rav Hershel Schachter once told me that there is precious little discussion in the Gemara about *tzurot hapetach*. Most of the issues are left to the Acharonim to address. However, the fact that the Gemara mentions the issue of *beri'ah l'ha'amid delet shel kash* indicates that it is an issue of considerable importance, regarding which it is definitely worthwhile to adopt a stringent approach.

Walking the Line

GUD ACHIT MECHITZTA AND LAVUD

We have previously discussed how the principle of *gud asik mechitzta* allows us to halachically extend a *lechi* upwards so that it is treated as if it is directly in contact with the horizontal component of the *eruv*. However, the question arises if one can likewise halachically extend a *lechi* towards the ground (*gud achit mechitzta*). A *lechi* ideally should extend all the way to the ground. That being said, the ability to halachically extend a *lechi* down to the ground would make *eruv* construction and upkeep much easier; often, the bottom portions of *lechis* are broken by utility workers, snow plows, and weed-wackers. In this chapter, we will address whether *gud achit* can be used in the creation of *tzurot hapetach*.

GUT ACHIT MECHITZTA
The *Chatam Sofer* (*Teshuvot* 34 in the *Likkutim*) permits relying on the principle of *gud achit mechitzta* in *tzurot hapetach*. Faced with the familiar challenge of frequent vandalism to his community *eruv*, he advised his community to rely on a *lechi* that extended down from the wire a minimum of ten *tefachim* from the top and to use the principle of *gud achit* to "extend" the *lechi* down to the ground.

The *Chazon Ish* (O.C. 79:11), however, vociferously objects to the *Chatam Sofer's* ruling. He argues that we may not rely on *gud achit* in the creation of a *tzurat hapetach*. He argues that such construction does not meet the Gemara's requirement that it be made "*k'davdi inshi*," in the manner people normally create items (Eruvin 94b). Since door frames are not created via the principle of *gud achit*, a *tzurat hapetach* may also not be created based on this principle. Common practice follows the ruling of the *Chazon Ish*.

LAVUD IN TZUROT HAPETACH

Even those who reject the use of *gud achit mechitzta* may still allow a three *tefach* or less gap at the bottom of a *lechi* in a *tzurat hapetach*. As we have previously mentioned, the principle of *lavud* allows us to ignore a three *tefach* or less gap in a *mechitzah*. The question emerges if *lavud* may be used in the creation of a *tzurat hapetach*. Twice, the *Aruch Hashulchan* (O.C. 362:36 and 363:46) permits the use of *lavud* to create a *tzurat hapetach*. The *Mishnah Berurah* (363:113) permits this as well. This stands in sharp contrast with Rav Hershel Schachter's view (stated in his lectures to Yeshiva University rabbinical students in both 5749 and 5779) that *lavud* may not be used in such a situation. Although, it should be noted that Rav Schachter told me in 2017 that a very thin break in a *lechi* is acceptable even by his standards.

Although it is usually feasible to satisfy Rav Schachter's stringency in a small *eruv*, it is most often very difficult or even impossible to sustain in a large communal *eruv*. Soil erosion and work on the utility poles often create dozens of situations of *lavud* on the *lechis* that comprise large communal *eruvin*. Such *eruvin* are typically composed of hundreds of *lechis*; experience teaches that it is nearly impossible to ensure that each *lechi* reaches completely to the ground on an ongoing basis.

Interestingly, Rav Bloi permits relying on *lavud* on the bottom three *tefachim* of a *lechi* without citing a dissenting opinion (*Netivot Shabbat* 19:26). Rav Mordechai Willig (personal communication; I saw *lavud* relied upon in the two *eruvin* supervised by Rav Willig, the Riverdale, NY and the Camp Morasha Kollel campus *eruvin*) also rules leniently. Indeed, the Rama (363:7) explicitly permits relying on *lavud* for a *lechi*. Rav Schachter, however, counters that the Rama refers to only a solitary *lechi* that corrects a *mavui* (alleyway that leads from a courtyard to a *reshut harabim*) but not for a *lechi* used to create a full *tzurat hapetach*. However, the *Terumat Hadeshen* (number 74), upon which the Rama is based, explicitly refers to a *lechi* as a component of a *tzurat hapetach*. Moreover, the *Mishnah Berurah* (363:26) also understands the Rama as referring to a *lechi* that is part of a *tzurat hapetach*.

Rav Schachter bases his approach on a very expansive reading of the aforementioned *Chazon Ish* (O.C. 79:11), who writes that "*lavud* cannot create a side-post since such a side post is regarded as *pitchei shimai* (a deformed doorway)." Rav Schachter understands the *Chazon Ish* as completely rejecting the application of *lavud* to create even a small portion of a *lechi*. Rav Schachter explains that just as carpenters do not use *lavud* to create a doorframe, *lavud* cannot be used to create a *tzurat hapetach*. He permits a very thin break since this is commonly tolerated by carpenters when making door frames.

However, Rav Yosef Gavriel Bechhoffer (*The Contemporary Eruv*, pp. 127-131), in discussing the opinion of the *Chazon Ish* in regard to this matter, differs from Rav Schachter's understanding of the *Chazon Ish*. Rav Bechhoffer understands the *Chazon Ish* (based on the *Chazon Ish* O.C. 70:25 and Y.D. 172:1) as disqualifying *lavud* only if *lavud* is used in a continuous manner, where the *lechi* contains many gaps, as in the Gemara's case of "*even nichnas v'even yotzeit*" (Eruvin 11a with Rashi s.v. *shikfi*). Only in such a case is the *lechi* treated as "deformed" since it is not perceived as a doorframe. There is no such issue where the *lechi* is simply missing less than three *tefachim* in one or two places.

Rav Bechhoffer notes that the *Steipler Gaon* (Eruvin 1) permits relying on *lavud* in the creation of a *tzurat hapetach*, without noting any dissenting opinion. It is difficult to assume that the *Steipler Gaon*, the brother-in-law of the *Chazon Ish* (the brothers-in-law both lived in Bnei Brak) was unaware of the *Chazon Ish's* opinion regarding this very common matter.

LAVUD IN THE MIDDLE OF A LECHI

One clarification is needed. The *Aruch Hashulchan* explicitly permits the use of *lavud* for the bottom three *tefachim* of a *lechi* (which is a most common scenario). However, he does not address either explicitly or implicitly the issue of relying on *lavud* in the middle of a *lechi*. The *Mishnah Berurah* (363:113) does explicitly permit relying on *lavud* even in the middle of a *lechi*. Rav Moshe Heinemann (as reported by Rav Micha Shotkin) adopts a compromise approach to this issue. He permits relying on *lavud* for the bottom three *tefachim* but not in the middle of a *lechi*. He regards the use of *lavud* in the middle of a *lechi* as resulting in *pitchei shimai*, a malformed doorway.

POSTSCRIPT - DEFINING THE BOTTOM OF THE POLE

Sometimes, though, it is not easy to define the bottom of the pole. During construction, a small circle of concrete around the utility pole is often removed. Thus, the pole sometimes extends down to three *tefachim* below the ground level. In such a case, must the *lechi* extend all the way to the very bottom of the excavation or just down to the point of the pole where the pole meets the ground?

Rav Mordechai Willig told me that even the *Chazon Ish* would agree that it suffices to extend the *lechi* to the normal ground level. Rav Willig argues that the *lechi* does not have to extend to the bottom of the little hole. He explains that the reason why a *lechi* (or *mechitzah*) that does not extend to the bottom is invalid is due to the fact that the empty space underneath them meets the halachic standard of *gedayaim bokim bo*, a space through which young goats can pass. A barrier with such a breach underneath it does not constitute a valid halachic barrier (Eruvin 16b).

In the case of the small circle of excavated concrete around the utility pole, the cavity is quite small, with insufficient room for a small goat to pass through. In such a case, Rav Willig holds that the *lechi* is not disqualified if it does not extend all the way down to the concrete. Thus, it suffices for the *lechi* to extend only to the normal ground level. In fact, I saw such a *lechi* in use at the *eruv* created for the Kollel at Camp Morasha, located in Lake Como, Pennsylvania.

THE BOTTOM OF A LAMP POST

A similar question arises where a *lechi* must be attached to a lamp post. Must the *lechi* extend to the ground itself or does it suffice for it to reach the top of the rectangular base of the pole? Rav Micha Shotkin reports that Rav Hershel Schachter rules that it suffices to extend the *lechi* to the rectangular base. Rav Schachter views the rectangular base as a legitimate extension of the *lechi* since it is longer than it is wide.

Rav Shotkin reports that Rav Daniel Stein, however, requires that the *lechi* extend all the way to the ground. One could support this view by saying that the rectangular base does not blend in with the *lechi* to constitute a single unit.

A DEFENSE OF THE "TOP-SIDE" WIRE

A very common issue that arises in *eruv* construction in North America is what Rav Gavriel Bechhofer terms the "top-side wire." In this case, as seen in Figure 1, the top wire does not run directly above the utility pole. Instead, it runs atop the insulator which is attached to the top of the pole. In general, a wire must run over the pole and not its side in order for a pole to serve as a proper *lechi*. Rav Bechhofer argues that the "top-side wire" is considered to be on the side of the pole, and, thus, the pole is not considered to be a proper *lechi*. In this chapter, we seek to explain why so many *posekim* regard the top-side wire as, conceptually speaking, running above the pole, thereby treating the latter as a proper *lechi*.

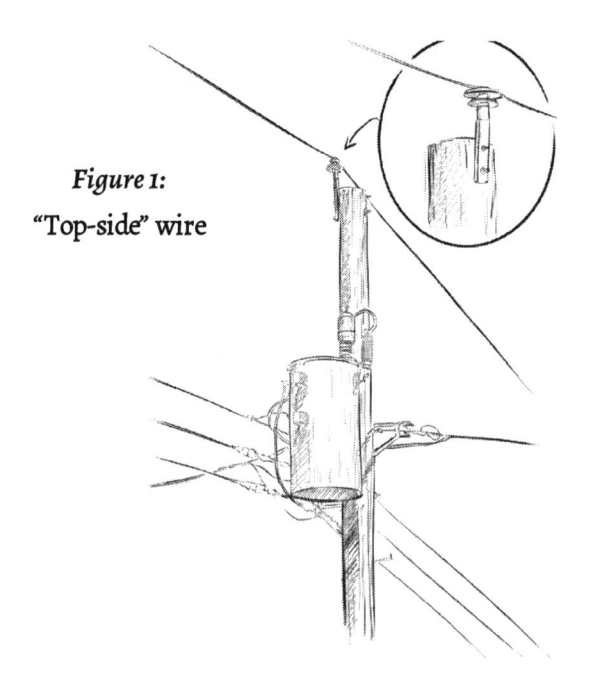

Figure 1: "Top-side" wire

Quite a number of *posekim* from the previous and current generation view the wire in such a setup as running directly on top of the pole. This is significant, as such an approach enables the use of pre-existing unmodified infrastructure for long stretches of the *eruv*, thus saving community funds and making *eruv* inspection easier and more effective. The *posekim* include Rav Aharon Kotler zt"l, Rav Hershel Schachter, Rav Moshe Heinemann, and Rav Mendel Senderovic. The classic *posekim* who permit the use of such *lechis* are the *Teshuvot Machaze Avraham* (2:13) and *Teshuvot Chelkat Yaakov* (O.C. 180).

TESHUVOT MACHAZE AVRAHAM

Rav Bechoffer's primary criticism of the lenient view is that the wire does not run over the utility pole. It should be that the insulator pole itself cannot serve as a *lechi* as it is less than ten *tefachim* long and is more than three *tefachim* above the ground. However, the core of the lenient ruling is that the insulator constitutes a valid extension of the pole. Since it runs over a valid extension of the pole, the wire is considered to be running over the pole itself.

The primary evidence for the lenient view presented by the *Machaze Avraham* is the Gemara (Yoma 44b) and *Tosafot* (ad. loc. s.v. *b'chol yom*) which discuss the special addition made to the *machtah* (firepan) for use in the special *avodah* (service in the *beit hamikdash*) of Yom Kippur. The special addition to the *machtah* is viewed as a valid extension of the latter, as it is nailed onto the original entity.

The *Machaze Avraham* argues that just as the nailed-in and permanently affixed addition to the *machtah* is considered a valid extension of the latter, so too is a pole that is permanently affixed to an original pole. Thus, if the wire runs above the insulator pole (and not the utility pole), it is considered as if the wire runs above the original pole, since the extension of the pole is considered to be part of the pole itself.[21]

CLARIFICATION OF THE TESHUVOT MACHAZE AVRAHAM

It is important to note that just because a pole is permanently affixed to the original pole, it does not necessarily constitute a halachically valid extension of the pole. Both Rav Schachter and Rav Heinemann point out that the added pole must be longer than it is wide (just like the original pole) in order to constitute a valid extension of the original pole.

This caveat generates a tremendous implication. Frequently, the top-side wire runs above the mushroom cap of the insulator, but not above the insulator stick (or utility pole itself). In such a case, the pole does not serve as a kosher *lechi*. This is because the mushroom cap is often wider than it is long and thus does not constitute a valid extension of the utility pole be-

---

[21] Rav Hershel Schachter (personal communication) rules, based on this responsum of the *Machaze Avraham*, that two horizontal wires that touch each other combine to form one wire. This constitutes commonly accepted practice in North American *eruvin*. Rav Moshe Heinemann similarly permits vertical components of a *lechi* to combine into one halachic unit. This also constitutes commonly accepted practice in North American *eruvin*. In regard to horizontal wires, though, it is essential to bear in mind that one must examine the wires very carefully to ensure that they truly touch and thereby form one halachic unit. Experience teaches that at first glance wires appear to touch, but upon close examination it often emerges that they do not.

low it. In order to serve as a kosher *lechi*, the wire must run either above the pole itself or above the stick portion of the insulator. If the wire runs only over the mushroom cap, and does not pass directly above the stick portion of the insulator or the main pole, then the utility pole does not constitute a valid *lechi*.

Rav Willig adds that in order to be designated as a legitimate extension of a pole, the original pole and added pole must be perceived to be one unit (a source for this assertion may be the *Magen Avraham* 363:28, where he disqualifies a wall from serving as a side post of a *tzurat hapetach*; a concern in such a case is that the wall does not give the appearance of a side post). The insulator and utility pole are considered one unit. The insulator thus constitutes a valid extension of the pole. However, Rav Willig rules that a *lechi* and the utility pole itself do not meld into one unit, since they are not perceived as such. Thus, even though two items are permanently attached, the added component does not necessarily constitute a valid extension of the original entity (even if they are both longer than they are wide).

THE VIEW OF RAV MOSHE FEINSTEIN

Rav Shlomo Francis and Rav Yonasan Glenner, in their work *The Laws of an Eruv* (p. 101), cite both Rav Moshe and Rav David Feinstein who are unsure about this issue. However, the authors note that Rav Moshe in this regard follows his opinion that the entire *lechi* must run under the wire in order to be kosher. The authors also note that Rav Aharon Kotler disagrees, ruling that only the top of the *lechi* must run below the wire.

In practice, in North America, the opinion of Rav Kotler is accepted. In fact, many utility poles stand at a considerable slant, making it virtually impossible to create an *eruv* where each *lechi* runs directly under the wire for the entirety of its height. Thus, although Rav Moshe does not endorse the top-side wire, his possible objection is based on an opinion which is not followed in North American *eruvin*.

THE BARRIER CONCERN

Despite his approval of the top-side wire, Rav Heinemann (in the Star-K *eruv* webinar) raises serious concern with the top-side wire if a mushroom cap that is wider than it is long rests (as they often do) above the stick portion of the insulator. Even if the wire runs above the stick and not just the mushroom cap, Rav Heinemann views the mushroom cap as an invalidating barrier (*hefsek*) between the stick and the wire.[22]

Indeed, the *Mishnah Berurah* (363:112) cites the *Taz* (O.C. 363:19) as ruling that a *tzurat hapetach* is invalid if a roof interrupts between one of its vertical poles and the horizontal pole or wire. His reasoning seems to be that *gud asik* (the theoretical "stretching" of the vertical pole to reach the horizontal one) applies only when there is no obstruction between the poles.

---

[22] Rav Heinemann is quite strict in regard to barriers between the *lechi* and the top wire. As reported by Rav Micha Shotkin, Rav Heinemann does not permit another utility wire to intervene between the *lechi* and the utility wire that is used in the *eruv*. In such a case, one could argue (as does Rav Mordechai Willig in a personal communication) that the other utility wires are part of one unit and do not constitute a *hefksek*. Moreover, Rav Heinemann (as he states in the Star-K *eruv* webinar) regards even tree leaves and branches as a *hefsek* between the *lechi* and wire. By contrast, *Netivot Shabbat* (19:27 note 62) rules that non-permanent "obstructions" (such as tree branches) should not be regarded as a *hefsek*.

However, the *Chazon Ish* (O.C. 104:6) rules that an obstruction narrower than three *tefachim* (approximately nine to twelve inches) and perhaps even less than four *tefachim* does not constitute a *hefsek* between the *lechi* and wire. A mushroom cap is certainly less than nine inches wide.

Moreover, both the *Tosefet Shabbat* (O.C. 363:64; cited by the *Pri Megadim* 363: *Mishbetzot Zahav* 19) and the *Shulchan Aruch Harav* (O.C. 363:32) reject the *Taz*. They note that the Gemara (Eruvin 11b) approves the use of an archway as a valid *tzurat hapetach* as long as a minimum of the first ten *tefachim* of the archways walls are straight. These authorities note that the rounded portions of the archway create a barrier between the straight portion of the wall and the archway's lintel. This seems to indicate that there is no concern for a barrier between the *lechi* and wire above it. The *Aruch Hashulchan* (O.C. 363:46) rules in accordance with this rejection of the *Taz*.

Thus, the mushroom caps do not create a problem both according to the *Chazon Ish* and the *Aruch HaShulchan*. Moreover, the mushroom caps should not create a problem even according to the *Taz* and *Mishnah Berurah*. This is because the defense of the *Taz* from the Gemara's case of the archway is that the straight portion of the arch and rounded portions of the archway constitute one unit and thus the rounded portion does not create a *hefsek*.

Similarly, one may argue that the mushroom cap and the insulator constitute one unit and that the mushroom cap does not create a *hefsek* between the insulator stick and the wire that runs above it. Indeed, Rav Schachter accepts the use of a top-side wire even if the mushroom cap that is wider than long runs above the insulator stick, as long as the wire runs directly above the insulator stick. This would present a problem according to Rav Heinemann even if the wire runs directly over the pole. Common practice in many North American *eruvin* is to accept such poles as valid *lechis*.

TOP-SIDE WIRE BY CURVED ROADS

In a case where the wire runs only above the mushroom cap, but neither above the pole or the insulator stick, Rav Schachter agrees that it is not a valid *lechi*. This frequently occurs with utility poles installed along areas where the adjacent road curves. In such a case, the wire does not run along the center rung of the mushroom cap, but rather is typically installed on the side of the rung.

CONCLUSION

The arguments that support the use of the top-side wire are quite compelling. Moreover, there is more than ample room to argue against Rav Heinemann's barrier concern. It is no wonder why so many North American community *eruvin* rely on the top-side wire, even when the mushroom cap that runs over the insulator stick is wider than it is long.

POSTSCRIPT

A similar issue arises in regard to street signs attached to a post where the *eruv* wire runs above the street sign but not the post. If the sign is longer than it is wide, Rav Heinemann regards the sign as a valid extension of the post. Thus, the sign could serve as a valid *lechi* if the *eruv* wire runs directly above the street sign, even it does not run above the post.

THE USE OF TACHUV IN CONTEMPORARY COMMUNITY ERUVIN

The Gemara relates that in a valid *tzurat hapetach*, the horizontal pole is placed atop the vertical poles. Furthermore, if the vertical poles are not under the horizontal one, but to its side (*tzurat hapetach min hatzad*), the *tzurat hapetach* is unacceptable (Eruvin 11b). A major area of debate in regard to *tzurot hapetach* is the status of *tachuv*, where the horizontal pole (or wire) does not rest atop the vertical poles, but is attached to a bolt which is drilled through them instead (see Figure 2), a situation not directly addressed by the Gemara. Cases of *tachuv* frequently arise today, as many wires on utility poles, especially those used for cable television, are attached to bolts that pass into holes in the poles. The issue of *tachuv* arises dozens of times in a typical North American community *eruv*. In this chapter, we will present a survey of the various positions regarding the use of *tachuv* in community *eruvin*.

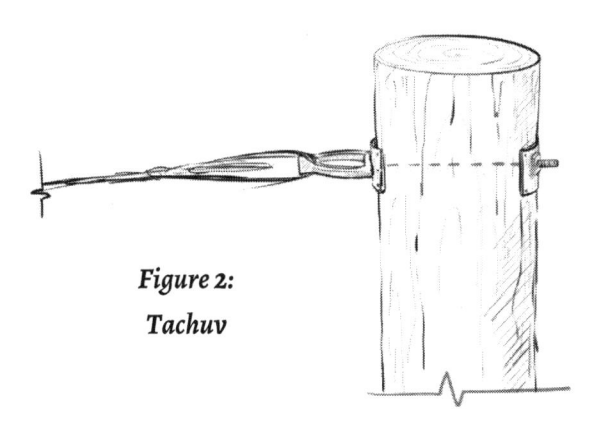

Figure 2: Tachuv

THE BASIC DEBATE

The *Acharonim* debate the acceptability of such a *tzurat hapetach*. The *Mishnah Berurah* (362:64) notes that the *Pri Megadim* was uncertain regarding this issue and therefore was inclined to rule strictly. On the other hand, Rav Shlomo Kluger (*Ha'elef Lecha Shlomo*, O.C. 164), the *Aruch Hashulchan* (O.C. 362:32), the *Chazon Ish* (O.C. 71:9), and Rav Tzvi Pesach Frank (*Teshuvot Har Tzvi*, O.C. 2:18:3) rule that such *tzurot hapetach* may be used. They argue that as long as the horizontal pole passes through the vertical poles at a point higher than ten *tefachim* off the ground, the portion of the vertical pole that is above the horizontal pole is ignored.[23] The *Chazon Ish* notes that if a horizontal pole was placed on top of a vertical pole and then another vertical pole was placed on top of the first one, the original *tzurat hapetach* remains acceptable. Similarly, a horizontal wire that passes through a hole in a vertical pole should be acceptable.

This issue has not been resolved; some rabbis who advise communities regarding *eruv* construction rely on the lenient opinion, while others follow the strict one. Rav Dovid Feinstein told me that although baseline Halachah accepts *tachuv*, this leniency should not be employed in community *eruvin*. Rav Yitzchok Frankel told me that this was also the approach adopted by Rav Moshe Feinstein. Rav Shlomo Zalman Auerbach (*Teshuvot Minchat Shlomo* 2:35:25), though, writes that *tachuv* is undoubtedly acceptable. Rav Yehuda Amital told me in 1990 that the practice in Israel is to be lenient on this issue (Rav Eliyahu Haddad, though, in 2020 reports that *tachuv* is far less common-

---

[23] The principle of ignoring what is unnecessary is known as *dal meihacha*. See, for example, Sukkah 2a.

ly used *eruvin* even for standard citywide *eruvin*; in the army, though, it remains more commonly used). Rav Hershel Schachter (in his 5779 *Hilchot Eruvin* lectures to Yeshiva University rabbinical students) cites Rav Yosef Shalom Eliashiv who believes that one should follow the stricter view regarding *tachuv*.

SURVEY OF POSEKIM WHO PERMIT TACHUV

How unfortunate it is for *The Laws of an Eruv* (p. 201) to state that *tachuv* is "not used in normative *eruv* construction." This statement is shocking, considering that the following *posekim* permit reliance on *tachuv*: *Aruch Hashulchan* (O.C. 362:32), Rav Shlomo Kluger (*Ha'elef Lecha Shlomo*, O.C. 164), *Teshuvot Maharsham* (1:162 and 2:149), the *Chazon Ish* (O.C. 71:9), *Teshuvot Divrei Malkiel* (3:16, who is inclined to permit), *Nefesh Chaya* (number 34), Rav Tzvi Pesach Frank (*Teshuvot Har Tzvi*, O.C. 2:18:3), *Teshuvot Chessed L'Avraham* (number 21), *Teshuvot Zekan Aharon* (1:19), *Teshuvot Chelkat Yaakov* (O.C. 1:180), and Rav Shlomo Zalman Auerbach (*Teshuvot Minchat Shlomo* 2:35:25). In fact, Rav Yaakov Bloi in his *Netivot Shabbat* (19:31) essentially rules in accordance with the lenient view; though, he notes that there are those who are strict about this matter. Rav Hershel Schachter, Rav Mordechai Willig, and Rav Zecharia Ben-Shlomo ((*Orot Hahalachah*, p. 616) all permit relying on *tachuv* in a community *eruv*. Rav Naphtali Burnstein informs me that Rav Shlomo Miller permits the Buffalo, New York community to rely upon *tachuv* in its community *eruv*. How spot on is Rav Baruch Simon's remark (*Imrei Baruch, Eruvin UReshuyot*, p. 114) that "it emerges that many Acharonim rule leniently in regard to *tachuv*." Considering the strong basis and considerable support of *posekim* current and past, it is my fervent hope that future editions of *The Laws of an Eruv* retract this most unfortunate statement.

THE MAHARSHAM'S ARGUMENT IN FAVOR OF TACHUV

Moreover, Rav Simon (op. cit. pp. 112-113) presents the *Maharsham's* compelling argument in favor of the acceptability of *tachuv*. The *Pri Megadim* is inclined to be strict regarding *tachuv* due to his understanding of the *Haghot Oshri* (Eruvin 1:14), who quotes the *Or Zaru'ah* as saying that "the *eruv* wire should not be *tachuv* (embedded) between the poles in their middle." The *Pri Megadim* infers from this statement that the *eruv* wire must rest above the pole and not be embedded in the pole. However, the *Aruch Hashulchan* (op. cit.) understands the *Haghot Oshri* as referring to a situation where the wire runs to the side of the pole, not through the pole. The *Maharsham* supports the *Aruch Hashulchan's* understanding of the *Haghot Oshri* by referring to the actual language of the *Or Zaru'ah*. The *Or Zaru'ah* does not use the word *tachuv*; rather, he describes the disqualification as a case where "he placed the wire between two poles in the middle but not on their tops." The *Maharsham* argues that it is clear that the *Or Zaru'ah* and the *Haghot Oshri* both speak of a situation where the wire rests on the side of the *lechi* and not where the wire runs through the pole.[24]

---

[24] In terms of the use of *eruvin* that employ *tachuv* by Sephardic Jews, it should be noted that although the *Kaf Hachaim* (362:106) adopts the position of the *Pri Megadim* (Mishbetzot Zahav 363:19), the fact that the *Yalkut Yosef* accepts (as baseline Halachah) a typical community *eruv* indicates that he regards these *eruvin* as acceptable for Sepharadim, despite their use of *tachuv*. Indeed, Rav Zecharia Ben-Shlomo (*Orot Hahalachah*, p. 616)

SURVEY OF POSEKIM WHO FORBID TACHUV

On the other hand, the *posekim* who rule strictly in addition to the *Mishnah Berurah* (364:64) are *Teshuvot Beit Shlomo* (2:167), *Zechor L'avraham* (O.C. 70), and *Teshuvot Minchat Yehudah* (number 25). In addition, Rav Moshe Feinstein (as I heard from Rav David Feinstein in 1989) did not want community *eruvin* to rely on *tachuv*, even though he believes that *tachuv* is acceptable according to baseline Halachah. Rav Yosef Shalom Eliashiv (as reported by Rav Hershel Schachter in his 5779 lecture delivered to Yeshiva University rabbinical students) also rules strictly regarding *tachuv*. Thus, if some of a community's Rabbanim prefer not to rely on *tachuv*, that opinion should also be respected.

LIMITATIONS OF TACHUV

One must bear in mind a few points regarding *tachuv*. Rav Hershel Schachter will accept *tachuv* only if the bolt enters and leaves the pole in the same straight line as the wire leading into it (as seen in Figure 1). Rav Mordechai Willig, though, believes that *tachuv* is acceptable even if the bolt does not run in a straight line along with the wire. The *Mishnah Berurah*'s (362:64) citation of the *Tiferet Yisrael* as the authoritative opinion seems to support Rav Willig's view.

One must also be careful to avoid what we may call "false *tachuv*." This refers to a situation where the bolt does not run through the utility pole but rather is attached to a brace that envelopes the pole. A cursory glance leads one to think these wires

---

permits all Jewish communities to rely on *tachuv*. It is also noteworthy that all the standards Rav Ben-Shlomo presents for *eruv* construction are identical for all groups of Jews.

lead into a bolt through wire and are legitimate *tachuv*. Hence, one must look carefully at the wires and its connecting bolts before concluding that a wire qualifies as proper *tachuv*.

Metal poles pose a special challenge in this regard. The wire may appear to be bolted-in continuously, but on closer inspection it is often not. One must exercise extra caution in regard to metal poles before deciding that it is actually genuine *tachuv*.

CONCLUSION

Making use of *tachuv* eliminates the need to install dozens of *lechis* in a typical community *eruv*. Not only does this save the community money, but it also makes *eruv* inspection significantly more efficient and reduces the *eruv's* footprint. Many communities in North America rely upon *tachuv*, and there is ample support and basis among classic and contemporary sources for this practice.

PITCHA B'KEREN ZAVIT

Halachah tolerates breaches up to ten *amot* (approximately fifteen to twenty feet) wide in a halachic *mechitzah* (Mishnah Eruvin 1:8). However, the Gemara (Eruvin 6a and 94b) presents a significant exception. If the breach is in a corner (*pitcha b'keren zavit*), then the wall cannot be used as a part of the *eruv*. This is because people do not normally make openings in corners, *pitcha b'keren zavit lo avdi inshi*.

There are considerable debates about the parameters and scope of this Halachah, from which emerge many practical considerations in the construction of community *eruvin*. We will set forth six major debates that concern this interesting and practical issue.

TORAH OR RABBINIC LAW

It would seem that a *pitcha b'keren zavit* should pose a problem only on a rabbinic level. After all, most Acharonim (such as the *Chazon Ish*, O.C. 107:8 and Rav Moshe Feinstein, *Teshuvot Igrot Moshe*, O.C. 2:89) rule that an opening even greater than ten *amot* wide constitutes a breach only on a rabbinic level[25] if the majority of that side of the *eruv* is enclosed with a valid *mechitzah* (*omed merubeh min ha'parutz*). Thus, it would seem that a less than ten *amot* wide opening at a corner should pose a problem only on a rabbinic level. Indeed, Dayan Weisz (*Teshuvot Minchat Yitzchak* 8:32:3) rules that a *pitcha b'keren zavit* is a prohibition on the rabbinic level.

---

[25] In accordance with the view of *Teshuvot Beit Ephraim* (O.C. number 27), unlike *Teshuvot Mishkenot Yaakov* (O.C. 121).

However, the *Chazon Ish* (O.C. 72:1) regards a *pitcha b'keren zavit* as a problem on the Torah level. This is quite a surprising ruling in light of what we noted above. Nonetheless, the *Chazon Ish* believes that the side terminates at the end of the wall and thus, the gap in the corner is not part of the side which has a majority of wall. Therefore, the *Chazon Ish* concludes that a *pitcha b'keren zavit* constitutes a Torah level concern.

MISSING PART OF ONE SIDE OR TWO SIDES
Rashi (Eruvin 94b s.v. *kegohn*) believes that an opening constitutes a *pitcha b'keren zavit* only when parts of both of the walls that constitute the corner are missing (Figure 3). Rambam (*Hilchot Shabbat* 16:20), though, rules it applies at any corner even if only one side is missing (Figure 4). The *Mishnah Berurah* (361:8) rules in accordance with Rashi. Rav Bloi (*Netivot Shabbat* 14:4, footnote 8) writes that "the *posekim*" write that the Halachah is in accordance with the *Mishnah Berurah*.

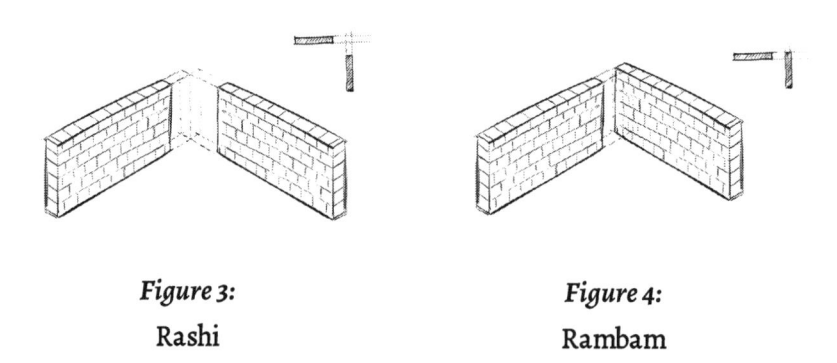

Figure 3:
Rashi

Figure 4:
Rambam

MISSING TWO SIDES IN THE MIDDLE OF A SIDE
There is another debate regarding a situation where two sides are missing in the middle of a *ru'ach* (side). Rav Hershel Schachter (personal conversation) and Rav Mordechai Willig (personal conversation) both permit such an opening. The *Mishnah Berurah* (ibid) supports this view, as he rules that the Halachah of *pitcha b'keren zavit* applies only at the edges where the two sides would otherwise converge. The *Mishnah Berurah* is supported by the *Taz* (O.C. 373:3) and *Eliyahu Rabbah* (373:4).

Nonetheless, *The Laws of an Eruv* (p. 134) cites Rav Moshe Feinstein who rules that although there is room to be lenient regarding this matter, he believes that the custom is to correct such a breach with a *tzurat hapetach*. Significantly, though, the *Taz, Eliyahu Rabbah,* and *Mishnah Berurah* do not mention such a custom. In fact, *Teshuvot Avnei Yashfeh* (2, O.C. 43:1) cites who appears to be Rav Yosef Shalom Eliashiv, who rules that this configuration does not constitute a *pitcha b'keren zavit*.

HOW MANY CORNERS CAN THERE BE IN AN ERUV?
I was privileged in November 2018 to witness Rav Schachter and Rav Willig debate how to understand the *Mishnah Berurah's* ruling limiting a *pitcha b'keren zavit* to the corners of the *eruv*. What if an *eruv* has many corners? As most *eruvin* are not perfect squares or rectangles, it is common for *eruvin* to contain many corners.

Rav Schachter believes that in such a case, a *pitcha b'keren zavit* can exist in any corner within the *eruv*. Rav Willig, on the other hand, believes that an *eruv* should be viewed as having only four corners even if it is not a perfect rectangle or square. In such a case, Rav Willig rules that one should look at the big picture and determine the four fundamental corners of the *eruv*. The problem of *pitcha b'keren zavit* has the potential to arise only in these four basic corners. Rav Willig's position drastically limits the issue of *pitcha b'keren zavit* in community *eruvin*.

The debate between Rav Schachter and Rav Willig has another important ramification. Recall that an opening of up to ten *amot* is acceptable only if the majority of the side in question is physically enclosed with a proper *mechitzah* (*parutz merubeh min ha'amud*). The question is how to determine a side. Once again, Rav Willig argues that we should look at the big picture and the *eruv* should be viewed as having only four sides. In contrast, Rav Schachter believes that an *eruv* can have more than four sides. Therefore, according to Rav Schachter, one must determine if the standard of *parutz merubeh min ha'amud* is met for each and every one of these sides. Thus, as long as the standard of *parutz merubeh min ha'amud* is met from a "big picture perspective," Rav Willig will tolerate a breach up to ten *amot* wide along any of the four sides of the *eruv*. For Rav Schachter, each of the potentially many sides of a community *eruv* must be treated as distinct, and a ten *amot* or less break in any given side will not be acceptable unless the majority of that side is physically enclosed with a proper *mechitzah*.

THE SIZE OF A PITCHA B'KEREN ZAVIT

The *Mishnah Berurah* presents two opinions as to the minimum size of a *pitcha b'keren zavit*. He first cites the *Pri Megadim*, who rules that a break up to one *amah* or less is acceptable even at a corner. However, he then notes that the Rashba disagrees.

However, the *Mishnah Berurah* also notes that the Rashba rules that if the break is less than three *tefachim* wide, it is viewed as a solid wall through the principle of *lavud*. A three to four *tefach* wide break at a corner can be corrected with two *lechis*, while a break wider than four *tefachim* at a corner can only be corrected with a *tzurat hapetach*.

The fact that the *Mishnah Berurah* cites the Rashba after he cites the *Pri Megadim*, and the fact that the Rashba is a prominent Rishon and the *Pri Megadim* a much later authority, both indicate that the Rashba's stricter opinion is accepted in practice.

A POLE AT THE CORNER TO CORRECT A PITCHA B'KEREN ZAVIT

The *Chazon Ish* (O.C. 72:2) rules that the problem of *pitcha b'keren zavit* can be corrected through the placement of a single pole at the convergence of what could have been the end of the two perpendicular walls (see Figure 5). One could have potentially rejected this view by applying the principle of *"ati avira d'hai gisa v'hai u'mevateil leih l'mechitzta,"* which nullifies a *mechitzah* that is surrounded by openings wider than it on both sides.

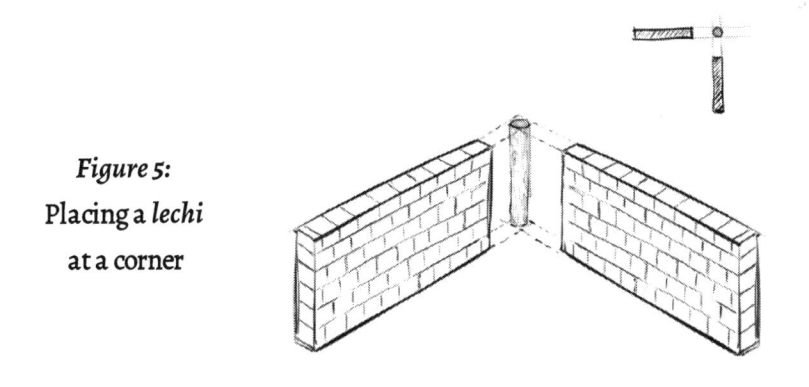

Figure 5:
Placing a *lechi*
at a corner

However, the *Chazon Ish* argues that the placement of a pole at the point of convergence does not run afoul of *ati avira*. The pole in the corner does not constitute a wall; it merely serves to formally demarcate the edge of the side of the *eruv*. Once the dge of the *eruv* is demarcated, the missing pieces of the walls do not give rise to the problem of *pitcha b'keren zavit*, as the ends of both walls are followed by breaches that are less than ten *amot* wide. In addition, there is no *avir* (empty space) on the other side of the pole since it is considered to be the end of a side of the *eruv*. Rav Bloi (ad. loc.) rules in accordance with the *Chazon Ish* regarding this issue.

CONCLUSION

A *pitcha b'keren zavit* can potentially create considerable challenges when designing a community *eruv*. However, the extent of the challenges will depend on how the above issues are resolved. The extent to which one will be strict regarding these issues depends in part on whether one follows the *Chazon Ish* or the *Minchat Yitzchak* as to whether a *pitcha b'keren zavit* creates a problem on a Torah or rabbinic level.

Section 3

Case Studies

∝

Rabbi Chaim Jachter

SAGGING WIRE IN THE YESHIVA UNIVERSITY ERUV

A few years ago, while I was passing through the Washington Heights section of Manhattan, I noticed a significant peculiarity in the Yeshiva University *eruv*. Someone had tied a shoe to an *eruv* string, causing the string to sag severely, all the while remaining more than ten *tefachim* above the ground. I immediately called Rav Mordechai Willig, who told me that while this should be upgraded, the severe sag did not disqualify the *eruv*. On the other hand, Rav Moshe Heinemann (Star-K webinar) permits only a moderate sag in the *eruv*. Moreover, when touring the Modi'in *eruv*, its administrator, Rav Eli Haddad, took great pride in the fact that the *eruv* wires in the Modi'in *eruv* are quite taut and do not sag at all. What is the basis for the variety of opinions?

TESHUVOT MISHKENOT YAAKOV

As we mentioned in an earlier chapter, the *Teshuvot Mishkenot Yaakov* (O.C. 123) adamantly opposes *eruvin* whose wires sag. He notes three issues with such wires. First, the Gemara (Eruvin 11a) defines a *tzurat hapetach* as two side posts with a pole above the side posts. The *Mishkenot Yaakov* argues that a sagging wire does not run above the side posts. Accordingly, the *Mishkenot Yaakov* does not even accept a situation where the wire sags less than three *tefachim*.

One could argue, though, that it suffices for the lintel (*mashkof*) to run above each pole, even though the wire sags in between the poles. The Gemara's requirement for the lintel to run above the two side posts might refer only to the points where the lintel connects to the vertical poles, and not to the entirety of the lintel.

Second, the *Mishkenot Yaakov* argues that if the wire sags, it will sway in the wind. A *tzurat hapetach* that sways even in a normal wind is not an acceptable *tzurat hapetach*, as noted by the *Magen Avraham* (363:4).

A problem with this approach is the fact that the Yerushalmi, cited by the *Mordechai* (first chapter of Eruvin) and codified by the *Shulchan Aruch* (O.C. 362:11) accepts a lintel even if it is a made of a very flimsy material. The *Aruch Hashulchan* (O.C. 362:37) observes that such materials will inevitably sway in the wind. Moreover, the Mordechai writes that the *eruv* wire must not be removed by the wind. The *Aruch Hashulchan* observes that the Mordechai never said that the wire cannot sway in the wind.

Moreover, the *Mishnah Berurah* (362:11) cites as the primary opinion the *Machatzit HaShekel*, who argues that the *eruv* wire is secondary in importance to the side posts. The side posts, he believes, constitute the essence of the *tzurat hapetach*, and only the side posts must be sufficiently sturdy so as not to sway in the wind. However, it is acceptable for the *eruv* wire to be moved by even a common wind.

A third issue is that the *Mishkenot Yaakov* believes that the top post must run straight and not in an arc (either upwards or downwards) in order to constitute a valid *mashkof*. However, the *Shulchan Aruch* (O.C. 362:12) seems to run counter to this ruling, as he validates an arch as a valid *tzurat hapetach*.

Rabbi Chaim Jachter

IS THE MISHKENOT YAAKOV'S OPINION NORMATIVE?

The question becomes whether the *Mishkenot Yaakov's* opinion is accepted in practice. We have already noted that the *Mishnah Berurah* presents the *Mishkenot Yaakov* as the secondary opinion. The *Aruch Hashulchan* (ad. loc.) rules in accordance with the lenient opinion; he does not even cite the stringent view of the *Mishkenot Yaakov*. The *Chazon Ish* (O.C. 71:1 and 77:6), however, rules in accordance with the *Mishkenot Yaakov*.

In Eretz Yisrael, where communities create their own *tzurot hapetach*, every effort is made to satisfy the *Mishkenot Yaakov*. They have even developed clever devices to ensure that *eruv* wires remain taut and free of droops. However, North American communities, following in the footsteps of Rav Moshe Feinstein, rely on the existing utility wires to create community *eruvin*, adopt the lenient opinion.[1]

The question is what was the custom in the learned and devout Jewish communities of pre-war Europe? As mentioned in an earlier chapter, Rav Simcha Zelig Riger, the famous *dayan* (rabbinic judge) of Brisk, followed the opinion of the *Mishkenot Yaakov*. However, this seems to be the exception to the rule. Rav Ben Zion Shternfeld, the Rav of turn of the century Bilsk (locat-

---

[1] I was most impressed in June 2011 to see how Rav Zvi Lieberman of London's Edgeware neighborhood designed his community's *eruv* to satisfy the view of the *Mishkenot Yaakov*. Edgeware's *eruv* does not rely on utility wires; instead, the community installed thirty nine perfectly made *tzurot hapetach*. However, this required a massive effort to obtain permission to make such installations. In fact, it took the Edgeware Jewish community no less than fifteen years to obtain such permission! For a description of how this *eruv* was constructed, visit www.tinyurl.com/eruv-edgeware.

ed in the Ukraine), in *Teshuvot Sha'arei Tziyon* (number three) records that the common practice in almost all of the *eruvin* in his region was to permit *eruvin* that sag. The early twentieth century *posek*, Rav Meir Arik (*Teshuvot Imrei Yosher* 2:133; Rav Arik served as a Rav in Galicia), similarly notes the commonly accepted custom to be lenient.

The *Sha'arei Tzion* presents evidence to his opinion from the paradigmatic *tzurat hapetach* recorded in Eruvin 11a. The Gemara describes four poles placed in four corners of the area, with vines running from the tops of each pole to another. The *Sha'arei Tziyon* notes that vines hardly run in a straight line. They typically sag and veer slightly off course, and, nonetheless, the Gemara declares them acceptable for use in a *tzurat hapetach*. This seems to be a compelling disproof of the *Mishkenot Yaakov*. Rav Ovadia Yosef (*Teshuvot Yechave Da'at* 7:72) rules in accordance with the *Teshuvot Sha'arei Tziyon*, against the *Mishkenot Yaakov*, in regard to the *eruv* in Netivot. He even adds that he believes the custom in Jerusalem[2] is to follow this lenient opinion.

However, Ashkenazic Chief Rabbi Rav David Lau, in his lecture delivered on the topic of communal Eruvin in Israel at Yeshivat Otniel, reported that he made every effort to keep the *eruv* wires in Modiin from sagging in order to conform with the strict view of the *Mishkenot Yaakov*. He noted that those who are lenient have ample halachic basis upon which to rely.

---

[2] Rav Yosef composed this responsum in 1976.

HOW MUCH OF A SAG MAY BE TOLERATED?

Even according to the lenient view, how much of a sag may be tolerated? Rav Shimon Eider (*Halachos of the Eruv*, p. 24) presents the opinion of Rav Moshe Feinstein that the horizontal wire may sag up to three *tefachim* (approximately 9-12 inches, as an application of the concept of *lavud*. *Teshuvot Imrei Yosher* also adopts this standard.

Rav Heinemann was willing to tolerate a sag of even more than three *tefachim*, as long as the wire does not sag beyond "normal." This seems to mean a reasonable droop in the wire which is the normal "give" that a wire has so it will not snap under pressure.[3] The *Aruch Hashulchan* also seems to adopt this position.

Rav Zvi Pesach Frank (*Teshuvot Har Zvi* 2:18:8) adopts the most lenient view regarding this matter. He permits a *lechi* to sag as long as the wire does not droop below ten *tefachim*. This seems to be the most compelling view, since once a wire sags, it should not make a difference if it sags in a moderate or dramatic fashion, as long as the wire does not dip below ten *tefachim*.

Rav Heinemann would say that a severe droop, such as the one I noticed at Yeshiva University, constitutes a *pitchei shimai*, a malformed doorway (see Eruvin 11a with Rashi). However, the fact that common practice in North America is to not be concerned for the *Mishkenot Yaakov* indicates that we are not concerned at all for *pitchei shimai* in the context of *tzurot*

---

[3] Rav Micha Shotkin told me that the lineman's (the professionals who install utility wires) guide book mentions that the wires are supposed to sag and there is a proper degree the wires should sag.

hapetach. The *Netivot* (in his outline of *Hilchot Eruvin*) indeed rules this way. The *Shulchan Aruch*, *Mishnah Berurah*, and *Aruch Hashulchan* all do not raise concern for *pitchei shimai* in the context of *Hilchot Eruvin*, seeming to agree with the approach of the *Netivot*. Indeed, it is the *Mishkenot Yaakov* who emphasizes concern for the issue of *pitchei shimai* in the context of *tzurot hapetach*.

In defense of Rav Heinemann, he could argue that if the *eruv* sags drastically, it no longer qualifies as a *tzurat hapetach*.[4] In other words, although the concern for *pitchei shimai* may not apply to *tzurot hapetach*, the latter must still reasonably resemble a door frame in order to be regarded as a legitimate *tzurat hapetach*.

Shockingly, Rav Frank even permits an *eruv* wire to sag below ten *tefachim* provided that the area below the sagging wire is less than three *tefachim* wide.

CONCLUSION

By design, utility wires have some give and are not completely taut. Thus, communities that rely upon utility wires to create their *eruv* perforce must rely on the lenient opinions of those who do not accept the stringent stance of the *Mishkenot Yaakov*. While it is preferable to permit only a moderate slant, in case of need we may rely on the opinion of Rav Zvi Pesach Frank, as was followed by the Yeshiva University *eruv* for many months until the aforementioned issue was addressed.

---

[4] A similar approach in a similar context is presented in the name of Rav Moshe Feinstein in *The Laws of an Eruv* (p. 92).

Rabbi Chaim Jachter

MEI'ACHOREI HAKOTEL IN LONG ISLAND

When designing a Long Island community *eruv*, we had to take into consideration a railroad that runs straight through the town. As discussed in an earlier chapter, there is room to be lenient in regard to designating a railroad as a *reshut harabim*, as railroad tracks are less than sixteen *amot* wide. However, in this case, the railroad raised a variety of issues that had to be dealt with. In this chapter, we will delve into these issues, namely, the concepts of ground levels and *mei'achorei hakotel*.

GROUND LEVELS

The railroad runs aboves the *mechitzot* of the *eruv*. As previously discussed, the *Noda Beyehudah*, *Mishnah Berurah*, and *Chazon Ish* all invalidate such *eruvin*.[5] Since the railroad tracks run above the *mechitzot* of the *eruv*, the *mechitzot* are ineffective as far as the railroad tracks are concerned. Thus, the railroad tracks must be excluded from the *eruv* to ensure that the *eruv* is not exposed to an area that is not enclosed within it, *nifratz lemakom ha'assur lo*.

Fortunately, a fence runs along both sides of the tracks, thereby almost completely excluding the tracks from the *eruv*. However, in the area of the train stop there is a break in the fences to allow passengers access to the trains. We erected *tzurot hapetach* across these fences (with the wire sufficiently high that it not cause a safety hazard); however, the railroad company would not permit us to install the *lechis* within the fences, but only on the outside side of the fences, which raises the issue of *me'achorei hakotel*.

---

[5] See our earlier chapter on *Highways, Railroads, and Overpasses*.

THE ISSUE OF MEI'ACHOREI HAKOTEL

Mei'achorei hakotel refers to the placement of *lechis* behind a wall or walls. Rav Yaakov Bloi writes (*Netivot Shabbat* 19:46) that "there are those who disqualify such an arrangement." He does not cite opinions that permit it. The *Chazon Ish* (70:21) is cited as the primary authority who forbids such an arrangement.

In our case in Long Island, *mei'achorei hakotel* is the only manner in which we could install a *tzurat hapetach* to exclude the railroad. As per *Netivot Shabbat*, it seems that such a *tzurat hapetach* is not acceptable. Is there a substantial basis upon which to rely in a case of great need, such as ours?

RABBEINU YEHONATAN

The *Steipler Gaon* (*Kehillot Yaakov, Eruvin* number 4) notes that the *Chazon Ish* was strict about this matter. He cites Rabbeinu Yehonatan (Eruvin 2b in the pages of the Rif s.v. *va'afilu*), who explicitly writes that the side posts of a *tzurat haptach* must at least slightly reduce the size of the area it seeks to enclose. Thus, the *lechis* must be placed on the inside of the fence. The reasoning for this strict approach is that in a normal doorway, the side posts reduce the width of the opening. In our case, the area that we sought to enclose was bounded by the fences lining the railroad. As such, the placement of the *lechis* outside of the fences expanded and did not minimize the gap between the fences.

However, the *Bach* (O.C. 363) cites Rabbeinu Yehonatan and observes that "we do not know from where Rabbeinu Yehonatan derived this rule. Perhaps it is because this is the manner in which a door frame is typically made, but this does not at all constitute baseline Halachah."

Rav Baruch Simon (*Imrei Baruch, Eruvin UReshuyot*, p. 137) explains that the *Bach* subscribes to the view articulated in *Teshuvot Chatam Sofer* (O.C. 87) who permits a *tzurat hapetach* that passes over water, despite the fact that people do not typically construct a *tzurat hapetach* in such areas. The *Chatam Sofer* explains that the disqualification of an *eruv* due to its dissimilarity to the manner in which door frames are normally constructed is limited to the cases specifically set forth in the Gemara.[6]

THE MISHNAH BERURAH'S OPINION

Interestingly, *The Laws of an Eruv* (p. 110, footnote 27) cites the Israeli *eruv* expert Rav Moshe Berlin as permitting in a case of great need a *tzurat hapetach* whose *lechis* are *mei'achorei hakotel*. Rav Berlin's ruling seems to be supported by the fact that the *Mishnah Berurah* (363:52 with *Sha'ar Hatziyun* number 37) clearly permits *lechis* that are located *mei'achorei hakotel*.

CONCLUSION – A S'NIF L'HAKEIL

Although it is proper to adopt the strict view whenever possible, in case of great need, one may rely on the lenient view regard-

---

[6] For a discussion of the *Chatam Sofer*'s view of the issue of *mei'achorei hakotel*, see chapter 12 of Rav Hershel Schachter's *B'ikvei Hatzon*. Rav Simon adds that a *tzurat hapetach* that does not reduce the gap between the walls would be acceptable according to the *Netivot* (as set forth in his *Tikkun Eruvin*), who believes that the disqualification of *pitchei shimai* applies only to mezuzot and not to *tzurot hapetach*.

ing *mei'achorei hakotel*, especially since it is supported by the *Mishnah Berurah*.

This is especially so in our case in Long Island, since the *Chatam Sofer* (O.C. number 89) disagrees with the aforementioned *Noda Beyehudah* and rules that *eruvin* are also effective for elevated ground levels that are higher than the *mechitzot* of the *eruv*. Thus, according to the *Chatam Sofer*, the railroad tracks in the Long Island *eruv* need not be excluded from the *eruv*. Although this view is normally not followed, in case of great need we may rely upon it as a *s'nif l'hakeil*, an adjunct to a lenient ruling. This is especially true as Rav Shmuel Wosner (*Teshuvot Sheivet Halevi* 8:97) notes that many Acharonim defend this ruling of the *Chatam Sofer*.

THE BOARDWALK RAILING IN LONG BRANCH, NEW JERSEY

In the extension of the Long Branch, New Jersey *eruv*, we rely on the railing of the local boardwalk as the *eruv's* eastern boundary. In this chapter, we seek to demonstrate how the railing can act as a halachically legitimate *tzurat hapetach*.

RELYING ON TACHUV

As seen in Figure 1, although the top pole does not run above the pole, it does run through the pole at a height higher than ten *tefachim*. As we discussed in an earlier chapter, this is known as *tachuv*. As previously noted, the *Aruch Hashulchan* and the *Chazon Ish*, along with many other *posekim*, permit the use of *tachuv* in *tzurot hapetach*. Rav Hershel Schachter and Rav Mordechai Willig also support the use of *tachuv* in community *eruvin*.

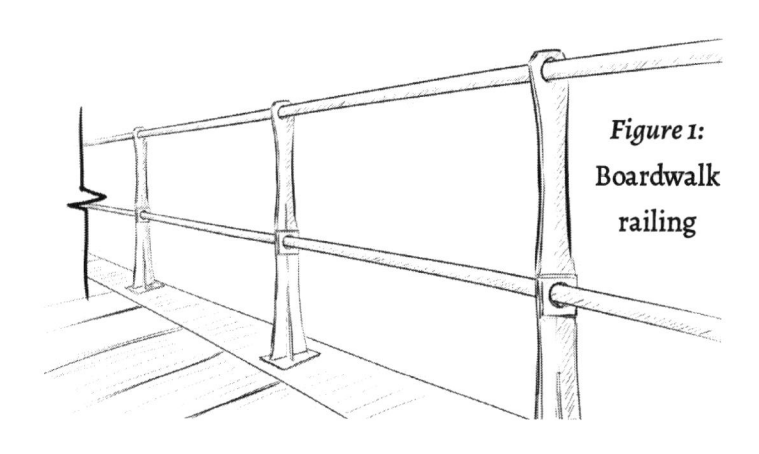

Figure 1: Boardwalk railing

BLOCKAGE WITHIN THE TZURAT HAPETACH

One Rav who lives in a nearby community challenged the use of this railing as a *tzurat hapetach*, noting the many Acharonim who believe that the *tzurat hapetach* should not be obstructed. In the case of the boardwalk railing, the middle horizontal bar obstructs the *tzurat hapetach*. Indeed, there is considerable discussion and debate concerning this matter.

Some argue that a *tzurat hapetach* must create a *petach* (opening), and just as a *petach* is not obstructed, so too a *tzurat hapetach* must not be obstructed. Others, though, argue that since a *tzurat hapetach* is designed to enclose an area, a *tzurat hapetach* is more effective if more of the area within it is filled in. Moreover, one may argue that the goal of an *eruv* is not to create a *petach* but rather to eliminate *pirtzot* (breaches).

The Acharonim debate this matter vigorously. *Teshuvot Teshurat Chai* (1:327) leads the list of those who rule strictly, and *Teshuvot Avnei Neizer* (O.C. 295) is among those who adopt the lenient approach. It should be noted that the lenient view enjoys strong support since the *Maharil* (*Likkutim* number 15), a Rishon, supports this view.

POSEKIM WHO FUNDAMENTALLY ACCEPT THE LENIENT OPINION

Rav Moshe Heinemann stated (Star-K webinar) that he follows the Tchebiner Rav (*Teshuvot Doveiv Meisharim* 1:3), who adopts the stricter approach in practice but fundamentally (*me'ikar hadin*) rules in accordance with the lenient approach in regard to an obstruction in the *tzurat hapetach*. Indeed, the Tchebiner Rav writes that "those who follow the lenient approach certainly have a legitimate view upon which to rely."

Rav Hershel Schachter (personal communication in 1989) agrees with the lenient opinion since we are interested in creating a *tzurat hapetach* and what transpires in the area below it is irrelevant. Rav Zvi Pesach Frank (*Teshuvot Har Zvi*, O.C. 2:18:4) also rules in accordance with the lenient view. Rav Yaakov Bloi (*Netivot Shabbat* 19:9) presents this issue by stating that "there are those who permit" without noting those who rule strictly in the body of the text, indicating that he fundamentally rules in accordance with the lenient view.

EVEN THOSE WHO RULE STRICTLY MIGHT AGREE

Rav Heinemann (Star-K webinar) notes that even according to the strict view, the *tzurat hapetach* may have some obstructions. He rules that as long as there is some place within the *tzurat hapetach* where one can pass, it constitutes a proper *tzurat hapetach*. This argument is supported by the Satmar Rebbe (*Teshuvot Divrei Yoel*, O.C. 21:13).

I showed Rav Mordechai Willig and Rav Baruch Simom a picture of the Long Branch boardwalk railing in 2000. Both Rav Willig and Rav Simon ruled that this is a proper *tzurat hapetach* since there is enough room for one to climb through the railing to the other side. I tried in practice and indeed was able to climb through the railings.

One cannot argue that the stricter opinion requires that one walk upright through the *tzurat hapetach*. The minimum height of a *tzurat hapetach* is ten *tefachim*, which, according to the maximalist conversion, is not taller than forty inches. Almost all adults would have to bend to be able to pass through such an opening, and it is nonetheless undoubtedly defined as a *petach*.

A SIMILAR SITUATION IN THE PRINCETON UNIVERSITY ERUV

Based on the ruling of Rav Willig and Rav Simon, the same approach was followed in the *eruv* created in Princeton, New Jersey. In the planning for this *eruv*, a few gaps wider than ten *amot* were discovered. Since Princeton University is quite particular in maintaining the high aesthetic quality of their campus, simply constructing a *tzurat hapetach* would simply not fit into the landscape. Instead, split rail fences, like those shown in Figure 2 above, were added in two locations to close the gaps. The possible objection in this case is that the top horizontal pole only partially runs through the vertical pole. However, both Rav Shlomo Zalman Auerbach (*Teshuvot Minchat Shlomo* 2:35:25) and Rav Mordechai Willig (personal communication) rule that even a partial *tachuv* is acceptable, as we may ignore the rest of the vertical poles' width through the use of Talmudic principle of *dal mehacha*.

Figure 2: Princeton fence

CONCLUSION

The extension of the Long Branch *eruv* to cover the areas where all of the Orthodox Jews reside required the use of the boardwalk railing. As mentioned previously, it is imperative for each community to have an *eruv* even if it cannot satisfy all opinions. In the case of the Long Branch *eruv*, there is abundant basis to rely on the boardwalk railings (and the Princeton community relying on split rail fences) as *tzurot hapetach*, especially as it seems that the stringent opinion is satisfied in this situation as well.

Walking the Line

THE STRINGENCY OF THE TEVU'OT SHOR & THE YALE NEW HAVEN ERUV

While reviewing the Yale New Haven *eruv* in the summer of 2019, I was quite concerned with how the *eruv* was set up near the Yale New Haven hospital. There was only a narrow corridor within the *eruv* through which one could enter the hospital. It was very easy for a well-meaning individual to mistakenly stray outside the *eruv*, since there was little margin of error. I urged the two local rabbis, Rav Alex Ozar and Rav Schneur Roth to find an alternative arrangement to allow for easier and much broader access to the hospital on Shabbat.

After a few weeks, Rav Ozar and Rav Roth developed an alternative route. The problem, though, is that their approach relies on a less than 10 *amot* gap (the gap is approximately 12 feet wide) between a *tzurat hapetach* and a wall of a building. In this case, attaching a *lechi* to the wall in question would have been cost prohibitive. Additionally, it would be highly unlikely that the relevant authorities would have granted them permission to attach the pole and wire to the wall.[7] In this chapter, we will discuss the extensive and rich debate surrounding the stringency of the *Tevu'ot Shor* in regard to this situation.[8]

---

[7] Rav Heinemann (in the Star-K *eruv* webinar) states that building an *eruv* without permission violates Halachah and creates a terrible *chillul Hashem*. I heard (in 1985) Rav Yosef Dov Soloveitchik similarly instruct community Rabbanim to refrain from building an *eruv* without permission.

[8] Rav Baurch Simon, in his *Imrei Baruch, Eruvin UReshuyot* (pp. 128-131), presents a magnificent summary of this captivating debate.

THE STRINGENCY OF THE TEVU'OT SHOR

As we have previously discussed, the Mishnah (Eruvin 1:8) does not treat a ten *amot* or less gap (15-18 feet) in the *eruv* as a breach, provided that the majority of the side of the *eruv* that contains the gap consists of valid *mechitzah* (or the area covered by *mechitzot* is at least equivalent to the open spaces). The *Tevu'ot Shor* (to Eruvin 11b, cited by the *Sha'arei Teshuvah* O.C. 363:26) argues that this leniency does not apply to a gap between two *tzurot hapetach* and a gap between a *tzurat hapetach* and a wall.

The *Shulchan Aruch* and its most authoritative commentaries, the *Magen Avraham*, *Taz*, and *Vilna Gaon*, do not mention this stringency. Indeed, there has been vigorous debate as to whether the Halachah accepts the stringency of the *Tevu'ot Shor* altogether.

THREE REASONS FOR THE TEVU'OT SHOR'S STRINGENCY

The *Tevu'ot Shor* believes that just as a single lone *lechi* may not be positioned more than three *tefachim* from a wall (Eruvin 14b), so too, a vertical pole of a *tzurat hapetach* may not be positioned more than three *tefachim* from a wall.[9] The *Tevu'ot Shor* tries to demonstrate that *Tosafot* (Eruvin 11a s.v. *ipcha*) support his opinion,[10] and the *Netziv* (*Meromei Sadeh*, Eruvin 2a s.v. *tzurat*

---

[9] A single *lechi* placed more than three *tefachim* away from a wall in a *mavui* does not serve as a proper *hekeir* (signifier) to notify people that they are about to enter a *reshut harabim*.

[10] However, Rav Chaim Shaul Greinemann, in his *Chidushim U'biurim* to the Mishnah Eruvin 2:10, disputes this inference.

hapetach) argues that one may infer this position from Rashi (ad loc. s.v. *tzurat hapetach*) as well.

Teshuvot Avnei Neizer (O.C. 287) offers a second explanation for the *Tevu'ot Shor's* stringency: While a *tzurat hapetach* does enclose an area, it does not factor into the assessment of whether the side of the *eruv* is *omeid merubah al haparutz*. For all intents and purposes, the *Avnei Neizer* does not treat *tzurot hapetach* as *mechitzot*.

Finally, the *Chazon Ish* (O.C. 6:14) supports the *Tevu'ot Shor*, arguing that a *tzurat hapetach* should be made in the manner in which a normal door frame is constructed. Thus, since when making a doorway one does not distance its frame from the door, so, too, one should not place a *tzurat hapetach* at a significant distance from the wall.[11]

Thus, according to the *Tevu'ot Shor*, the new proposed route to the hospital would be invalid due to the space between the *tzurat hapetach* and the wall.

FIRST ARGUMENT IN SUPPORT OF THE NEW YALE ERUV ROUTE

Despite the considerable support enjoyed by the *Tevu'ot Shor*, nonetheless, there is considerable reason to permit the new Yale *eruv* configuration. The first argument is based on the *Netivot*

---

[11] However, one may counter that even a regular door frame is positioned three *tefachim* or less (*lavud*) away from the opening, and yet all agree that the *tzurat hapetach* may be positioned within three or less *tefachim* from a wall. One could argue that just as the principle of *lavud* is employed in regard to the positioning of a *tzurat hapetach*, so, too, a gap of ten *amot* or less may be relied upon when positioning the *tzurat hapetach*.

(*Tikkun Eruvin*), who follows the *Tevu'ot Shor* only if both ends of the *tzurat hapetach* are located ten *amot* or less from the wall. Many Acharonim, including the *Chazon Ish* (op. cit.), *Teshuvot Beit Ephraim* (O.C. 28), *Teshuvot Maharam Schick* (O.C. 168), *Teshuvot Tzemach Tzedek* (O.C. number 8), and *Teshuvot Avnei Neizer* (op. cit.) subscribe to this more lenient version of the *Tevu'ot Shor's* stringency. Only one side of the *tzurat hapetach* in New Haven was less than ten *amot* away from the wall.

SECOND ARGUMENT IN SUPPORT OF THE NEW YALE ERUV ROUTE

Many Acharonim, including the *Tosefet Shabbat* (363:10), *Chayei Adam* (48:11), and *Aruch Hashulchan* (O.C. 362:36), reject the stringency of the *Tevu'ot Shor*. These Acharonim are supported by various Rishonim, including the *Tosafot Rabbeinu Peretz* (Eruvin 11a s.v. *mavui*), who runs explicitly counter to the *Tevu'ot Shor*. Inferences are made that the Rashba (Eruvin 14b s.v. *shamat*), Ritva (Eruvin 10b s.v. *shamat*), and Rabbeinu Yehonatan (4a in the pages of the Rif) run counter to the *Tevu'ot Shor*. Rav Hershel Schachter (in his lectures to Yeshiva University rabbinical students in 5749 and 5779) believes that the Halachah follows the Acharonim who reject the stringency of the *Tevu'ot Shor*.[12]

---

[12] Rav Schachter (personal communication) rules that in assessing the gap to determine if it is less than ten *amot* long, one must estimate ten *amot* as measured following the direction of the wire to the connecting wall. However, Rav Mordechai Willig (personal communication) rules that one may measure the ten *amah* gap using the most direct route from the pole where the wire ends to the nearby wall. Interestingly, Rav Zvi Lieberman of the Edgeware section of London, England told me that he

THIRD ARGUMENT IN SUPPORT OF THE NEW YALE ERUV ROUTE

Finally, the *Ba'al Hatanya* (*Teshuvot Harav*, number 24) writes that the widespread custom runs counter to the *Tevu'ot Shor*. He records that in practice no one is concerned for the stringent view. The fact that the *Aruch Hashulchan* (who is generally sensitive to prevailing custom) rejects the *Tevu'ot Shor* may also indicate that the widespread custom in pre-war Europe was not to follow the ruling of the *Tevu'ot Shor*.

A BREAK OF FOUR TEFACHIM WHERE "RABIM BOKIM BO"

Even if this location in New Haven does not require a *tzurat hapetach*, it may still require a different halachic adjustment. The location in question is subject to foot traffic, what is known in halachic terminology as *rabim bokim bo*. This poses a problem, as the area in question might be regarded as a *mavui*, an alleyway that leads from a group of *chatzerot* (courtyards) to a street. Even in a *mavui* that has a break of only four *tefachim*, the *Shulchan Aruch* (O.C. 365:2) requires one to correct the break if the area in question is subject to foot traffic. (It goes without saying that such is the case if the breach is greater than ten *amot* wide even if the area in question is not subject to foot traffic. However, the type of correction will differ depending on the size of the gap.) By contrast, the *Shulchan Aruch* (O.C. 365:3) rules that a

---

and Dayan Chanoch Ehrentreu, the Av Beit Din of the London Beth Din, had a similar disagreement regarding the creation of the *eruv* in the Hendon section of London. Rav Lieberman agrees with Rav Schachter, and Dayan Ehrentreu agrees with Rav Willig.

chatzer does not need to be corrected if there is a break of less than ten *amot*, even in a place where *rabim bokim bo*. The break between the light post and the building in New Haven is larger than four *tefachim*, and the area has the potential to qualify as a *mavui* through which many people trod.

The question is whether we regard a contemporary street as a *mavui* or *chatzer*. The Rama (O.C. 363:26) rules that we regard a contemporary street as a *chatzer*. If so, breaks of ten *amot* or less in our communities do not require any halachic intervention. However, the *Magen Avraham* (365:4) understands the Rama as ruling that we regard our streets as *chatzerot* only when such a designation results in stringency. When the *chatzer* designation would otherwise result in leniency, we are concerned that the area in question is a *mavui* and deal with it accordingly.

The *Even Ha'ozer* (O.C. 365) disagrees and understands the Rama as defining our communities as *chatzerot* even when such a designation results in leniency, such as a four *tefachim* break in an area where people trod. Rav Bloi (*Netivot Shabbat* 20:15 footnote 34) cites *Teshuvot Avnei Neizer* and "many Acharonim" who rule in accordance with the *Even Ha'ozer*.

However, even the *Even Ha'ozer* does not permit a break of four *tefachim* or more in an area where people trod if there is more than one such opening on one side of the *eruv* or on the second side of the *eruv*. Nonetheless, Rav Meir Arik (*Minchat Pitim* 363 and 365) is inclined to be lenient even in such a case, and Rav Bloi (*Netivot Shabbat* 20:14 footnote 32) notes that "many Acharonim" agree with Rav Meir Arik's more lenient approach.

Since the *Ba'al Hatanya* (O.C. 365:2), *Mishnah Berurah* (363:11), and *Aruch Hashulchan* (O.C. 363:45 and 365:6) all do not accept the approach which does not require one to correct a more than four *tefachim* wide breach in an area where people trod, we prefer not to rely on this most lenient view. The problem is, as we noted at the beginning of our discussion, that the New Haven community does not have permission to add this type of infrastructure.

A viable option is to follow the compromise view of Rav Hershel Schachter (personal communication). In a case where there is an opening that is more than four *tefachim* but less than ten *amot* wide in an area where people trod, Rav Schachter suggests that a solitary *lechi* should be installed. It should be noted that this *lechi* does not serve to fill in the breach. Rather, the *lechi* serves to notify people of the breach.

Rav Schachter's suggestion is in accordance with the ruling of Rav Shlomo Kluger (*Teshuvot Ha'elef Lecha Shlomo* O.C. 159). Rav Kluger reasons as follows: If the area is regarded as a *chatzer*, then a break of ten *amot* or less does not pose a problem. If the area is defined as a *mavui*, then it may be corrected with a single *lechi*. This approach is followed in practice in the Teaneck community *eruv*. This is a very practical option, as there are often existing *lechis* on the pole, and we rule that *lechi ha'omeid mei'eilav*, a *lechi* not erected to serve a halachic purpose nevertheless constitutes a valid *lechi* (*Shulchan Aruch* O.C. 363:11).

In the case in New Haven, a single *lechi* was added to a light post (on its side that faces the building) that was already designated to serve as the side post for the *tzurat hapetach*. Logistically speaking, this did not pose a problem as the light post was public property, regarding which permission was granted to adapt for use in the *eruv*. Following Rav Shlomo Kluger's ruling, no additions had to be affixed to the building itself, private property regarding which the community did not have permission to modify in its construction of its *eruv*.

CONCLUSION

There is considerable and formidable support in favor of the new configuration of the Yale *eruv* route. In fact, Rav Hershel Schachter and Rav Mordechai Willig both told me that they rule in accordance with the *Aruch Hashulchan's* rejection of the *Tevu'ot Shor*. The *eruv* that encompasses the Yeshiva University campus is made in accordance with the lenient opinion. Thus, I encourage and support the new route for the New Haven *eruv* by simply adding a solitary *lechi*, in conformity with the ruling of Rav Shlomo Kluger.

Nonetheless, I told Rav Ozar and Rav Roth to maintain the old *eruv* route along with the new *eruv* route. This is because the *Mishnah Berurah* (363:23) rules that one should ideally conform to the opinion of the *Tevu'ot Shor*. *Teshuvot Beit Shlomo* (O.C. 41) and *Teshuvot Aryeh D'vei Ilai* (O.C. 4) agree.

Rav Yaakov Bloi (*Netivot Shabbat* 19:16, note 37) prefers the strict version of the *Tevu'ot Shor*.[13] This means that ideally we should avoid relying on even just one side of a *tzurat hapetach* located within ten *amot* of a wall. Thus, those who wish to follow the strict view may continue to do so and use the old narrow portal that satisfies the stringency of the *Tevu'ot Shor*. However, one has a halachic right to rely on the more lenient view, if he chooses. In any event, it is a good idea to create a backup for

---

[13] This seems to be the opinion of the *Mishnah Berurah* as well. In his *Sha'ar Hatziyun* (363:16), he cites the compromise position of the *Netivot* in brackets but does not seem to rule in accordance with this view.

those who would mistakenly stray out of the old *eruv* path to the hospital.

In conclusion, both those who wish to follow the lenient and strict views can happily coexist regarding their use of the new and old *eruv* routes to the hospital. This is most appropriate regarding the hospital, where there is considerable need for the *eruv* for the entire Jewish community.[14]

POSTSCRIPT - USING A TZURAT HAPETACH TO FILL IN A THREE TO FOUR TEFACH-WIDE GAP

Rav Moshe Heinemann (as recorded in the Star-K *eruv* webinar) rules in accordance with those Acharonim (such as the *Tosefet Shabbat* 362:25 and *Kaf Hachaim* O.C. 362:94) who forbid having a three to four *tefach* break in a *mechitzah*.[15] A break that is three *tefachim* or less is acceptable through the principle of *lavud*. However, some Acharonim argue that a break that is between three and four *tefachim* wide is not acceptable, since we find in *Hilchot Mezuzah* that a gap less than four *tefachim* is not defined as a *petach* (opening). Thus, since such a gap is not defined as a halachic opening, it is unable to be corrected with a *tzurat hapetach*, which can only serve to fill in a halachic gap in a *mechitzah*.

However, we should note that the *Aruch Hashulchan* explicitly permits the use of a *tzurat hapetach* to correct a break

---

[14] I presented this approach to Rav Mendel Senderovic who found it reasonable and fair.

[15] Rav Herschel Schachter (as stated in the lectures on *Hilchot Eruvin* he delivered to Yeshiva University rabbinical students in 5779) subscribes to this view as well.

that is between three and four *tefachim* wide. Interestingly, the *Mishnah Berurah* does not address this issue in *Hilchot Eruvin*. In *Hilchot Sukkah* (630:9), he writes that *"yeish omerim,"* "there are those who say," that a minimum of four *tefachim* is needed to create a *tzurat hapetach*. His omission of this opinion in *Hilchot Eruvin* and characterization in *Hilchot Sukkah* of this view as only a *"yeish omerim"* indicates that in the context of *Hilchot Eruvin*[16] there is room to be lenient with regard to this issue.

---

[16] We might reconcile the discrepancy between *Hilchot Eruvin* and *Hilchot Sukkah* by suggesting that that the *Mishna Berurah* felt the need to be more strict in regard to *Hilchot Sukkah*, which is a Torah-level obligation, as opposed to the laws of *tzurat hapetach* in *Hilchot Eruvin*, which only apply in areas where it is forbidden to carry only on a rabbinic level.

THE 'ALL-AMERICAN' ERUV IN CHAMPAIGN-URBANA

The Champaign-Urbana *eruv* is one of my favorite *eruvin* that I help maintain nationwide. Rav Shlomo and Rabbanit Ahava Schachter serve as the Orthodox Union's JLIC couple on campus at the University of Illinois Champaign Urbana (UICU) and work tirelessly to enhance Orthodox Jewish life on campus. Their efforts to successfully create and maintain a high-quality *eruv* serve as a model for other communities worldwide.

THE CREATION PROCESS
Rabbanit Ahava contacted me in November 2016 about constructing an *eruv* on the UICU campus. As a first step, I informed the Schachters of the various practicalities that must be taken into consideration when considering the construction of an *eruv*. I then shared a list of Torah material from which Rav Shlomo could hone his practical *eruvin* knowledge before we met in person.

The Schachters then visited my Teaneck home in December 2016, where I provided a tutorial based on dozens of *eruv* pictures. I then showed them interesting and enlightening portions of the Teaneck, Englewood, and Tenafly *eruvin* so they could see how the relevant *halachot* are applied in the field.

Rav Shlomo then worked tirelessly to create a route and detailed construction plan for the *eruv*. He consistently contacted me with on target questions on how to apply our learning to the Champaign-Urbana scene. One issue that arose was the presence of many cornfields scattered throughout the town's landscape, especially on its outer portions. We decided, upon direction from Rav Mordechai Willig, to draw the Southern *eruv* border at Curtis Road (see Figure 3). The small cornfields north of this street may be considered part of the town and therefore may be included in the *eruv* (based on the ruling of the *Teshuvot Dvar Shmuel* mentioned in an earlier chapter). However, the cornfields south of this street are not part of the *dirah* (inhabited area) and must be excluded from the *eruv*.

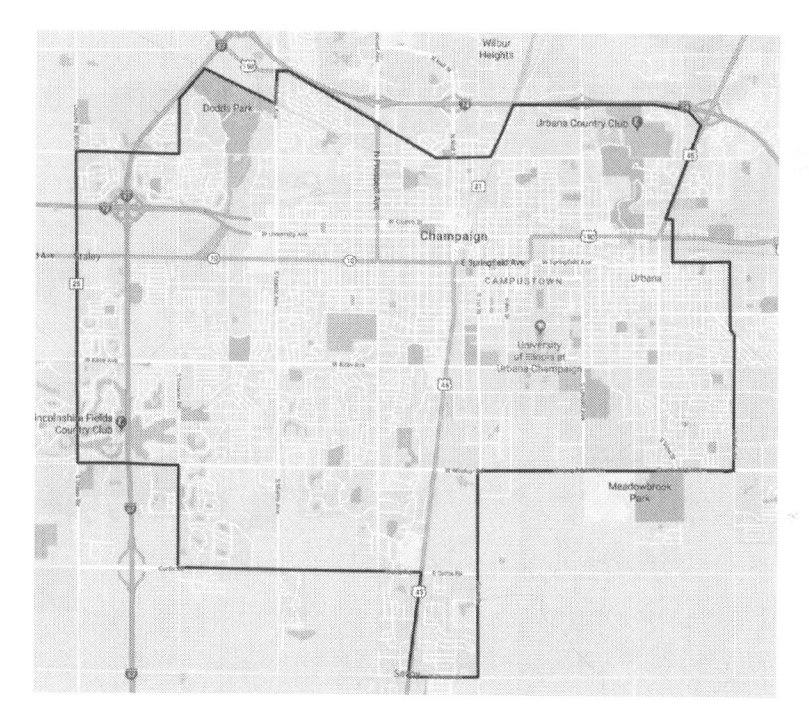

Figure 3: The Champaign-Urbana *eruv*

I visited for two days in June 2017 to review the plan. I was satisfied with almost the entire plan; only a few tweaks were needed. I then returned in August 2017 for a gala ceremo-

Walking the Line

ny, during which we conducted a *sechirat reshut* with a high ranking official of Champaign County, publicly made an *eruv chatzeirot* for the observant Jews in the community, and reviewed the tweaks to the *eruv*.

The *eruv* is inspected each week, and I make a thorough in-person annual review of the entire *eruv*. Rav Shlomo poses questions to me on a regular basis throughout the year regarding the *eruv*.

ACHDUT

Three Orthodox outreach organizations operate on the UICU campus: OU JLIC, Chabad, and JET-Aish HaTorah. The Schachters succeeded in making everyone feel comfortable with the *eruv* and its halachic standards. Each group participated in the aforementioned gala ceremony.

Rav Shlomo created a very large *eruv* to serve as much of the Jewish community in Champaign-Urbana as possible. In fact, the rabbis of the non-Orthodox congregations also joined us at the August 2017 ceremony as well, expressing their buy-in to the *eruv* forged in a great moment of Jewish unity.

THE BROADER COMMUNITY

The mayor of Champaign Urbana, Deborah Frank Feinen, has been very supportive of the *eruv* as a means of broader inclusion and diversity.

Communities in North America rely upon the utility poles to create the *eruvin*, with minor modifications made as necessary. The local utility company, Ameren, graciously helped in the construction of the Champaign-Urbana *eruv*.

When a small portion of the encompassed area was missing utility poles upon which to base the *eruv*, Ameren installed the poles. This proved to be beneficial for both parties when, a few months later, there was a power outage. The added poles which bridge the gap in the *eruv* prevented power from being lost in parts of the enclosed area.

Even the local mass transit company, the Champaign Urbana Mass Transit District, helped with the *eruv*. Signage for a bus stop was installed in a location that was a win-win for both riders and the *eruv*, since the signpost also serves as a *lechi*.

STUDENT INVOLVEMENT

Rav Shlomo uses the *eruv* as a means of student involvement and engagement. He enlists the students to inspect and maintain the *eruv*. For example, each *lechi* and wire must be plumblined each year to ensure proper alignment. A dedicated cadre of students has joined Rav Shlomo in this project which involves considerable effort.

Not all students find it easy to sit for hours poring over a Gemara or Tanach. For many, involvement in a Torah field project such as an *eruv* is an enjoyable way to actively connect to Torah learning. Ideas such as *tzurat hapetach* and *mechitzot* come alive while enjoying the many hours spent outside working on the *eruv*. I know of at least one young man who was somewhat distanced from Jewish practice who returned to full observance due to his positive active involvement with the *eruv*.

CONCLUSION – AN 'ALL-AMERICAN' ERUV

I refer to the Champaign-Urbana *eruv* as an 'all-American' *eruv*. It serves more than merely rendering the enclosed area into a *reshut hayachid*. It serves as a beacon and model for an essential component for a fully dedicated and enjoyable Torah life. It creates an authentic community bond which serves to spiritually elevate the Jewish community both within and outside its boundaries.

Rabbi Chaim Jachter

THE LECHI UNDER THE CABIN EAVES AT CAMP RAMAH DAROM

The challenge was considerable. On the one hand, Rav Shmuel Khoshkermann of the Atlantic Kashrut Commission wanted the updated *eruv* for Camp Ramah Darom (CRD) in northern Georgia to be constructed to high standards to satisfy all potential guests. On the other hand, Camp Ramah Darom is a world class facility blessed with extraordinarily beautiful scenery, from which we could not detract when creating the new *eruv*.

The question became whether we could attach *lechis* to CRD's many cabins. The *lechis* would then be situated beneath eaves (see Figure 4), an unacceptable arrangement according to some opinions. If we would have adopted the stringent view, much more construction would have become necessary, making a very challenging project even more difficult. Upon investigation, it emerged that there was much room to be lenient regarding this issue, even not in a case of great need, all the while maintaining high *eruv* standards. In this chapter, we will examine the justification for using such *lechis* as a part of the Camp Ramah Darom *eruv*.

LECHI IN A RESHUT HAYACHID

The concern is that the eaves create halachic walls through the concept of *pi tikra yoreid v'soteim*, that the lip of the roof (in our case, the eaves) extends to the ground and creates a halachic wall. If so, the *lechi* would then have to penetrate a halachic wall, a situation that is subject to considerable debate.

Figure 4: Lechi under a cabin eave

The *Mishnah Berurah* (363:113) cites the *Netivot* (*Tikkun Eruvin*), who invalidates a *tzurat hapetach* which is partially encompassed by a *reshut hayachid*. The *Mishnah Berurah* accepts his ruling as normative Halachah.

The *Netivot* sets forth two possible reasons for this strict ruling. One might argue that the *tzurat hapetach* is not noticeable (*nikar*) if it is situated within a *reshut hayachid* (such as a private yard). Alternatively, one might claim that the walls or fences that encompass a *reshut hayachid* are halachically viewed as extending "all the way to the heavens" (*k'man d'malya*; see Shabbat 7a), so the airspace above a *reshut hayachid* is halachically impenetrable. For example, a horizontal wire that passes through a backyard enclosed by a fence would be invalid according to this reason, as it is halachically blocked by the "upward extension" of the fence.

Other Acharonim disagree with the *Netivot's* stringency. The *Aruch Hashulchan* does not mention this stringency, and the *Teshuvot Chatam Sofer* (O.C. 91 and 96) and *Teshuvot Maharsham* (1:207) rule leniently regarding this issue when the *lechi* is noticeable (*nikar*). *Teshuvot Chavatzelet Hasharon* (1:20) writes that the custom is to be lenient in regard to this issue. He adds that his father, who was exceedingly strict concerning most halachic matters, likewise ruled leniently in this instance.

Rav Hershel Schachter (lecture at Yeshiva University) relates that Rav Mendel Zaks told him that the custom in Europe was indeed to be lenient. *The Laws of an Eruv* (p. 108) notes that it is apparent from many responsa that the custom in pre-war Europe was to be lenient. However, Rav Schachter strongly urges communities to be strict in this matter. This issue has not yet been resolved, and practices vary from community to community.

Accordingly, the stringency introduced by the *Netivot* raises concern regarding the installation of a *lechi* beneath an eave. It should be noted that there are two primary interpretations of the *Netivot's* stringency. The issue of placing a *lechi* that is noticeable underneath an eave only arises according to the stricter interpretation, which regards halachic walls (such as those "created" via the principle of *pi tikra*) the same as physical walls. However, Rav Yaakov Bloi (*Netivot Shabbat* 19:19, footnote 44) argues that the *Netivot's* stringency only applies to actual walls and not to halachic walls.[17] Nevertheless, *Teshuvot Beit Shlomo* (O.C. 55:4) adopts the strict view regarding this matter.

---

[17] In addition, one could argue (as noted by Rav Hershel Schachter in his lectures on *Hilchot Eruvin* delivered to Yeshiva University rabbinical stu-

Rav Aharon Kotler (cited by Rav Moshe Heinemann in a speech to a convention of Young Israel rabbis in the 1990s and in *The Laws of an Eruv* ad. loc.) adopts the same lenient view as Rav Bloi. Nonetheless, Rav Moshe Feinstein is cited (ibid.) as adopting the strict view in accordance with the *Beit Shlomo*.

We decided to permit the installation of *lechis* on the cabins only in situations where the *lechi* is positioned under one eave. We did not install *lechis* on cabin corners, where two perpendicular eaves meet. This approach, as we will explain, satisfies the position of the *Beit Shlomo* and Rav Moshe Feinstein.

PI TIKRA YOREID V'SOTEIM

The reason for this distinction lies in the scope of the principle of *pi tikra yoreid v'soteim*. While Rashi (Shabbat 94b) believes that we apply *pi tikra* even if there is only one *mechitzah* (as depicted in Figure 4), *Tosafot* (Shabbat 94b s.v. *bishtei ruchot*) and Rambam (*Hilchot Eruvin* 17:35) argue that *pi tikra* applies only if there are at least two adjacent walls. The Rama (O.C. 361:2) rules in accordance with *Tosafot*. The *Kaf Hachaim* (O.C. 361:31) rules that Sephardic Jews may follow this opinion as well.

Accordingly, since the Halachah follows *Tosafot*, there is concern for *pi tikra* only when a *lechi* is placed beneath two adjoining eaves above two adjacent walls. Since the Halachah does not follow Rashi, *pi tikra* does not result in the creation of a halachic wall when a *lechi* is placed under a single eave. We there-

---

dents in both 5749 and 5779) that halachic walls are intended to be applied only in a lenient direction. For example, the *Mishnah Berurah* (632:20) rules (based on Rashi to Sukkah 9b s.v. *mai l'meimra*) that the halachic principle of *lavud* is not to be applied in a strict direction.

fore could affix *lechis* along the sides of the cabins in such locations.

RAV YAAKOV KAMINETSKY'S STRINGENCY

Rav Yaakov Kaminetsky (*Emet L'yaakov*, O.C. 361:2) rules strictly even in a case where a *lechi* is located beneath only one eave. However, with the great respect owed to Rav Yaakov, this seems to constitute an excessive stringency.

Rav Yaakov's position assumes a quadruple stringency. It assumes that the Halachah is concerned for the stringency of the *Netivot*, the stricter version of the *Netivot's* stringency, the *Beit Shlomo's* strict application of the strict version of the *Netivot*, and the lone view of Rashi regarding *pi tikra* (which is not cited in the *Shulchan Aruch* as normative Halachah). Such stacking of stringencies in a case of a rabbinic law (as previously noted, *eruvin* consisting of *tzurot hapetach* may be constructed only in an area in which it is forbidden only on a rabbinic level) seems unreasonable.

CONCLUSION

Even though we made a great effort to create a very strict *eruv* at Camp Ramah Darom, we permitted *lechis* to be attached to cabins where the *lechi* rests beneath only one eave. The Satmar *posek*, Rav Shulem Weiss (*Tikkun Eruvin* 4:4) permits such an arrangement even not in a case of great need, despite the strong inclination of the Satmar community (as communicated to me by Satmar Dayan Rav Mendel Silber in 1992) to follow the strict rulings of the *Beit Shlomo*.

Rav Moshe Heinemann (as reported by Rav Micha Shotkin) and Rav Hershel Schachter (personal communication in

1989) agree with this ruling as well. Rav David Feinstein (cited in *The Laws of an Eruv* ad. loc.) permits the placement of a *lechi* only under one eave in a case of need. Our situation at CRD qualified as a situation of need, and we therefore followed the view that permits the installation of *lechis* under single eaves.

Rabbi Chaim Jachter

THE DELATOT OF CANARSIE, LONDON, MATTERSDORF, & OAKLAND

In 1989, I was shown the *eruv* in the Canarsie section of Brooklyn designed by Rav Moshe Faskowitz, who was then the rabbi of the Young Israel of Redwood.[18] My fellow Yeshiva University Kollel member, Rav Yitzchak Eisenmann, had told me that Rav Faskowitz had created a high quality *eruv* in Canarsie and I was very eager to see it. I was especially interested since Rav Faskowitz was guided in the creation of this *eruv* by the renowned *posek* Rav Gedalia Zinner. I very much wanted to see approaches that differed from the ones I was taught at Yeshiva University by my Rebbeim, Rav Hershel Schachter and Rav Mordechai Willig.

The visit did not disappoint. Indeed, the Canarsie *eruv* was a very high quality *eruv*. It was, on the one hand, stricter than the standards that I was taught, as no breaches wider than three *tefachim* were tolerated. On the other hand, it was more lenient in that it relied on what is referred to in the Halachic literature as *delatot*.

The *eruv* was attached to the South Shore High School building and followed the walls of the building until the nearby fences. Some of these fences had openings wider than ten *amot* and were open during the day. Rav Zinner, it turns out, permitted relying on the fact that these fences were closed at night as a sufficient means to create a halachic boundary. Rav Schacher and Rav Willig, by contrast, do not permit relying on *delatot* in

---

[18] This *eruv*, to the best of my knowledge, is defunct as of this writing.

Walking the Line

this manner. In this chapter, we will explore the varying approaches to the use of *delatot* in community *eruvin*.

YERUSHALAYIM'S GATES

The Gemara (Eruvin 6b, 22a, and 101a) presents Rabbi Yochanan's oft-cited teaching that "had Yerushalayim's gates (*delatot*) not been locked at night, [the city] would have been considered a *reshut harabim*."[19] This Gemara teaches that an area's designation as a *reshut harabim* may be removed through the use of *delatot*.[20] In such cases, the *delatot* serve to fill in breaches that are wider than ten *amot*. The *Shulchan Aruch* (O.C. 364:2) codifies this rule as normative Halachah.

---

[19] A most interesting implication of Rabbi Yochanan's teaching is that it was forbidden on a rabbinic level to carry in Yerushalayim. In other words, the sages of the time did not take the necessary steps to permit carrying in Yerushalayim, such as establishing an *eruv chatzeirot*. This is shocking, considering the fact that the Gemara (Eruvin 68a) teaches that we must create an *eruv* wherever possible. Rav Moshe Feinstein (*Teshuvot Igrot Moshe* O.C. 1:139) offers a most interesting explanation which he uses as part of his refusal to permit the creation of an *eruv* in Manhattan. However one explains the absence of an *eruv* in Yerushalayim of ancient times, Yerushalayim today boasts of both a city wide and neighborhood *eruvin* endorsed both by Israel's Chief Rabbinate and the Edah Chareidit of Jerusalem. In fact, in many sections of contemporary Yerushalayim, *tzurot hapetach* are simply ubiquitous. Indeed, the famed Rav of mid-twentieth Jerusalem, Rav Zvi Pesach Frank (*Teshuvot Har Zvi* 2:24) does not subscribe to Rav Moshe's approach to the Yerushalayim *eruv* of old and its application to twentieth century Manhattan.

[20] See the discussion below in regard to the *Chazon Ish's* interpretation of this Gemara.

The standard explanation, as presented by the *Mishnah Berurah* (364:6), is that since the *delatot* inhibit the traffic flow at times, the area they enclose cannot be described as a *reshut harabim*.

DALETOT RE'UYOT LINOL

The Rishonim, though, engage in a major debate regarding how to understand and apply this idea. The Rif (Eruvin 2a in the pages of the Rif) and the Rosh (Eruvin 1:8) seem to imply that the doors have to be closed every evening. The Rambam (*Hilchot Shabbat* 17:10), however, writes that it is sufficient for there to be potential for the doors to be locked at night (*delatot re'uyot linol*) to transform the enclosed area into a *reshut hayachid*.[21]

The *Shulchan Aruch* (op. cit.) presents the opinion of the Rif and Rosh as the primary opinion and the Rambam as the secondary opinion. Rav Yosef Karo here follows his celebrated formula that he sets forth in his introduction to the *Shulchan Aruch*, to use the Rif, Rambam and the Rosh as his *"beit din"* and to follow the majority when they disagree.

The *Mishnah Berurah* adds (*Sha'ar Hatziyun* 364:9) that the fact that the Rama does not express an objection indicates that he, too, subscribes in practice to the stricter rulings of the Rif and the Rosh. The *Mishnah Berurah* assumes that the Rama's silence in regard to this ruling of the *Shulchan Aruch* represents a retraction of his ruling in accordance with the Rambam that he

---

[21] For further discussion of the Rambam's approach to this issue see the *Magid Mishnah* to Rambam's *Hilchot Eruvin* 1:1 and Rav Baruch Simon's *Imrei Baruch, Eruvin UReshuyot*, pp. 83-84.

included in his *Darkei Moshe* commentary to the *Tur Shulchan Aruch* (364).

THE PRACTICE IN PRE-WAR EUROPE

Many communities in pre-war Europe (as reported by *Teshuvot Avnei Neizer*, O.C. 273-278 and *Chazon Ish* O.C. 78:1) relied upon *delatot re'uyot linol*.[22] This seems to run counter to the rulings of the *Shulchan Aruch* and Rama.

However, the *Aruch Hashulchan* (O.C. 364:1) rules in accordance with the more lenient view of the Rambam. He supports this ruling from the fact that the *Tur* endorses the approach of the Rambam. The *Shulchan Aruch Harav* (364:4) also essentially rules in accordance with the Rambam, though he strongly prefers accommodating the stricter view. His ruling that baseline Halachah is in accordance with the Rambam is based on the Rama's approach that appears in the *Darkei Moshe* (O.C. 364).

Moreover, Rav Yaakov Bloi (*Netivot Shabbat* 23:1, note 10) argues that even the stricter views of the Rif and Rosh require the gates to be locked at night only when *delatot* are used to remove the area's designation as a *reshut harabim*. However, when *delatot* are used (as was done in Europe) as *mechitzot* in a *karmelit*, all would agree that *delatot re'uyot linol* suffice.[23]

---

[22] These communities relied on *delatot* because the authorities did not permit them to install *tzurot hapetach*.

[23] According to Rav Bloi's approach, Sephardic Jews would also be able to rely upon *delatot re'uyot linol* to enclose a *karmelit*, even though the *Shulchan Aruch* favors the stricter opinion of the Rif and the Rosh.

In addition to surrounding the community with *tzurot hapetach*, Jerusalem's neighborhood of Mattersdorf maintains a door (the *Mishnah Berurah* 364:7 cites opinions that one door suffices) on Panim Me'irot street to bolster the status of its *eruv*. The community's spiritual leadership cites a ruling it received from none other than Rav Moshe Feinstein who regards this door as satisfying the stricter opinions of the Rif and Rosh, who require the doors to be actually locked, even though this door is locked only for Shabbat and not every evening.

Rav Moshe is cited as arguing that the point of the requirement of the doors being locked at night is that the doors should serve a highly significant function. In the times of the Talmud, having the doors locked at night protected ancient Jerusalem from the invasion of bandits at night. The door of Mattersdorf, argues Rav Moshe, also serves a significant function since it prevents cars from entering the community and thereby desecrating the holy Shabbat.

Interestingly, Rav Moshe's argument serves to reject a suggestion made at the lecture on *eruvin* in Israel delivered by Ashkenazic Chief Rabbi Rav David Lau at Yeshivat Otniel. Rav Re'eim HaCohen, the Rosh Yeshivah of Otniel, suggested to Rav Lau that *delatot* should be installed around Israeli cities and be momentarily closed at three in the morning on a daily basis.

Rav HaCohen argued that this would satisfy even the strict opinion of the Rif and Rosh, since they do not state that the *delatot* must be closed throughout the entire evening. Rather, they merely require that the *delatot* be closed every evening, without specifying a minimum period of time during which the *delatot* must be closed.

According to Rav Moshe, a momentary closing of the doors does not serve any significant non-*eruv* function. Thus, the "doors" such as the ones described by Rav HaCohen would not at all satisfy the opinion of the Rif and the Rosh, even if these doors would be closed for a minute each early morning.

DELATOT WITHOUT TZUROT HAPETACH

The *Chazon Ish* vociferously objected to the pre-war European practice of relying upon *delatot re'uyot linol*. The *Chazon Ish* argues that the Gemara teaches only that *delatot* relieve an area of its *reshut harabim* status. However, *delatot* alone do not render an area as a *reshut hayachid* and therefore permitted to carry within. The Chazon Ish supports his contention that the Gemara never presents *delatot* as a means to render an area as a *reshut hayachid*. However, it should be noted that the straightforward readings of the aforementioned Rambam and *Shulchan Aruch* directly run counter to the opinion of the *Chazon Ish*.

Additionally, the *Chazon Ish* notes that the *Chatam Sofer* (O.C. 88) disagrees and rules that the use of *delatot* even without *tzurot hapetach* suffice to permit one to carry within the enclosed area. This view is supported by the fact that the Gemara never mentions a requirement to supplement *delatot* with *tzurot hapetach*.

Teshuvot Teshuvah Mei'ahavah (2:245) and *Teshuvot Brit Avraham* (number 18) agree with the *Chatam Sofer*. The famous Radzhiner Rebbe, Rav Gershon Henoch Leiner, published an essay entitled *Delatot Sha'ar Ha'ir* (printed at the end of his celebrated work, *Ein Ha'techeilet*) supporting the ruling of the *Chatam Sofer*.

Netivot Shabbat (23:3, note 16) notes that the many Acharonim who support the pre-war European practice regarding *delatot* also disagree with the ruling of the *Chazon Ish*. Moreover, Dayan Yitzchak Weisz (*Teshuvot Minchat Yitzchak* 4:41) argues that the *Chazon Ish* was strict only in regard to *delatot* that serve to enclose a *reshut harabim*. However, in regard to serving as *mechitzot* within a *karmelit*, *delatot* suffice without *tzurot hapetach*.[24]

We should note, though, that the *Chazon Ish* is hardly a lone voice. *Teshuvot Chessed Le'avraham* (O.C. 2:35) and *Teshuvot Divrei Malkiel* (3:15) explicitly agree with the *Chazon Ish*, and Rav Yaakov Bloi (*Netivot Shabbat* 23:3, note 15) believes that the *Sefat Emet* (Eruvin 6b) does, as well. Rav Moshe Feinstein is also cited in agreement (*The Laws of an Eruv*, p. 118), but Rav Yaakov Kaminetzky (*Emet Le'yaakov*, O.C. 364) is unsure as to whether the *Chatam Sofer* or *Chazon Ish* is correct.

THE GATES IN CANARSIE

Returning to the gates in Canarsie, it emerges then that Rav Zinner ruled in accordance with the many Acharonim who adopt the lenient view of the *Chatam Sofer* permitting a *delatot* without accompanying *tzurot hapetach*. The fact that these gates were actually closed each evening further supports the ruling of Rav Zinner.

Rav Baruch Simon (*Imrei Baruch, Eruvin UReshuyot*, pp. 88-89) bolsters the ruling of the *Chatam Sofer* by noting that the great Rabbi Akiva Eiger (*Teshuvot Chadashot Le'rabbeinu Akiva*

---

[24] Rav Baruch Simon (*Imrei Baruch, Eruvin UReshuyot*, p. 88) notes that a straightforward reading of the *Chazon Ish* does not support the contention of the *Minchat Yitzchak*. Rav Schachter and Rav Willig agree with Rav Simon's reading of the *Chazon Ish*.

Eiger, number six) supports the view of his son-in-law, the *Chatam Sofer*. Moreover, Rav Simon notes that there are even two Rishonim, the Meiri (Eruvin 59a s.v. *kevar bi'arnu*) and Ritva (Eruvin 22a s.v. *d'rabbanan ad'rabbanan*) who subscribe to the view of the *Chatam Sofer*.

Rav Yosef Gavriel Bechhofer (*The Contemporary Eruv*, third edition p. 100) writes that "the preponderance of *posekim* rule that *delatot* are valid enclosures without *tzurot hapetach* overhead." In addition, the *Aruch Hashulchan* (O.C. 364:1) clearly indicates that he also subscribes to the lenient view.

Nonetheless, Rav Schachter and Rav Willig firmly rule in accordance with the *Chazon Ish*. Rav Zvi Sobolosky ruled this way for an NCSY Shabbaton held on a camping ground. He rules that the fact that the gates of the camping ground were closed at night does not render the area a *reshut hayachid* when the gates are open on Shabbat day.

Moreover, Rav Mordechai Willig (personal communication) rejects a suggested compromise that permits the reliance upon parking lot gates that are closed every evening, as long as the gates are closed when Shabbat begins. This compromise is based on the many Halachot which are determined by the beginning of Shabbat, such as the laws of *muktzeh*.

Rav Willig summarily rejected the idea, noting that *Tosafot* (Eruvin 17a s.v. *ireiv*) do not accept the application of the principle of *shabbat keivan shehutrah hutrah*, that an *eruv* that was intact at the start of Shabbat remains valid for the entire Shabbat, to the context of *mechitzot*. Rav Willig rules that if the parking lot gates are wider than ten *amot* and are open during the middle of Shabbat, the *eruv* is invalidated, despite the fact that these doors were closed at the beginning of Shabbat.

RESOLUTIONS IN ROSLYN HEIGHTS, WEST ORANGE, AND CHARLESTON

The dispute that rages between the *Chatam Sofer* and *Chazon Ish* is difficult to resolve. The absence of discussion in the Gemara makes it difficult to arrive at a definitive ruling. Hence, in practice, I make every effort not to rely on *delatot*, even if they are locked at night, except in case when there is no alternative. In the case of no alternative, we rely upon the many *posekim* who adopt the lenient view and the precedent of the pre-war European communities.

For example, the *eruv* in Roslyn Heights, Long Island, runs along the fences of Christopher Morley Park. However, we redirect the *eruv* to utility wires instead of relying on the portion of the park's parking lot fence which is open during the day, even on Shabbatot when the park fences close before the beginning of Shabbat.

Similarly, in West Orange, New Jersey, the community relies upon a golf course fence for a portion of its *eruv*. However, it redirects the *eruv* to utility poles instead of relying on the portion of the gate where a break of greater than ten *amot* opens during the day to permit cars to enter the parking lot. In Charleston, South Carolina, the community's *eruv* also avoids the *daltot de'uyot linol* at the entrance of the famous Citadel Military Academy.

On the other hand, an *eruv* in Long Island relies on a series of fences that include a parking lot fence which opens during the day and is closed each evening. The community has neither been able to secure permission to install *tzurot hapetach* in the area, nor is there a viable alternative if this community is to be surrounded by an *eruv*. As such, we rely on the many

Acharonim who rule leniently, especially since Rav Bloi leans in favor of the lenient view.

GOVERNMENT LIMITS ON DELATOT

There was considerable debate in pre-war Europe about the validity of the installed *delatot*. As we have noted, many pre-war communities considered these *delatot* to constitute viable *delatot re'uyot linol* in cases where it was impossible to obtain permission to build *tzurot hapetach*.

Teshuvot Yeshu'ot Malko, however, argues that these *delatot* did not meet even the standard of *re'uyot linol*, since the government would not permit the doors to be locked except for extremely brief periods at very limited times. However, *Teshuvot Avnei Neizer* (ad. loc.) defends the validity of these *delatot* despite the limitations imposed by the government.

Rav Baruch Simon (op cit. p. 86) writes that he is inclined to the stricter opinion that such doors are not considered to be *re'uyot linol*. He cites the *Maharsham's Hagahot* to the *Orechot Chaim* (363:11), who writes that "where it is impossible due to government restrictions to close the doors there is no room to be lenient. Despite the fact that I have heard of great Rabbanim who are lenient about this matter, in my humble opinion they do not have upon which to rely."

However, Rav Simon does not cite the *Aruch Hashulchan* (op. cit.) who writes in endorsement of the lenient view that

> even if the city government does not permit the *delatot* to be closed, it does not matter since the *delatot* render the breaks in the *mechitzot* as permitted openings (and not a breach). After *delatot* are installed, the area is considered one enclosed courtyard without the need of adding any *lechis* or *korot*.

It is hardly surprising to discover the *Aruch Hashulchan* endorses the lenient view, as he is very inclined to defend the extant practices of the observant Jewish community.

Moreover, the work *U'l'arev Eiruvo* cites a most interesting practice of Jerusalem's Edah HaCharedit to maintain police barricades at the side of the main vehicular entrance to Jerusalem. None other than Rav Chaim Kanievsky is reported to have endorsed the efficacy of these doors as *delatot re'uyot linol*, as a stringency to help ameliorate the status of Jerusalem as a *reshut harabim*. Rav Kanievsky makes this endorsement despite the government's severe limitations and restrictions on using these barriers to close this major thoroughfare.

STRING DELATOT – LONDON AND OAKLAND

Various communities today have a form of *delatot* installed as a stringency to help remove an area's status as a *reshut harabim*. For example, in June 2011, Rav Zvi Lieberman of the London neighborhood of Edgeware showed me the *dealtot* he installed to help overcome concern for his community being considered a *reshut harabim*.

These contemporary *delatot* consist of rolls of thin durable material stored within plastic or metal canisters which are installed to the utility poles that form the *eruv* boundaries. The *delatot* are forty inches high and consist of strings that are not less than three *tefachim* apart. As they can be connected to the adjacent utility pole, they can serve as *delatot re'uyot linol*.

Rav Yaakov Bloi calls into serious question the validity of such *delatot*. He cites *Teshuvot Avnei Neizer* (O.C. number 282) and *Teshuvot Imrei Yosher* (1:110) who require that it be recognizable that the *delatot* serve to enclose the public area. Such de-

latot in canisters hardly seem to satisfy the *Avnei Neizer* and *Imrei Yosher's* requirement.

On the other hand, Rav Eliezer Waldenburg (*Teshuvot Tzitz Eliezer* 14:90) and Rav Shmuel Wosner (*Teshuvot Sheivet Halevi* 4:41) endorse the proposal of the creation of an *eruv* in Amsterdam based solely on such "canister *delatot*." They reason that as long as the doors have the potential to impede traffic in the areas into which they were installed, they enjoy the status of *delatot*. Rav Waldenburg and Rav Wosner approved these installations in situations in which there were no available alternatives.

Much effort has been made to create an *eruv* for the Jewish community of Oakland, California. Due to safety concerns for earthquakes, the local government authorities do not permit the installation of *tzurot hapetach*. As such, *delatot* remain the only viable option. Rav Judah Dardik asked Rav Zinner if he may rely on such *delatot* in Oakland, where there is no other way to create the *eruv*. Rav Zinner extended his approval in such circumstances, and Rav Willig ruled that we may rely on Rav Zinner's ruling.

Unfortunately, the Oakland community, as of this writing, is still awaiting the long sought permission from the local authorities to install even these *delatot*. The community has invested considerable sums to create halachically viable *delatot*, and we remain hopeful the approval will soon be forthcoming.

CONCLUSION

Rav Waldenburg writes in the context of the proposed *eruv* for Amsterdam that we are mandated and directed by the great *posekim* of earlier and later generations to expeditiously create community *eruvin* which have some basis in Halachah, even when it is debatable, since, thereby, one prevents hundreds and thousands of Jews from wittingly or unwittingly violating Shabbat in an area without an *eruv*.

Although every effort should be made to create the highest quality *eruv* that a community can implement and sustain, in some cases there is no choice but to rely upon lenient approaches. In regard to *delatot*, every effort should be made to accommodate the stricter approach of the *Chazon Ish*; however, when there is absolutely no other choice, we have a tradition from pre-war Europe and the support of first rate *posekim* to rely on *delatot*. This applies to even the more debatable *delatot* such as when the government severely limits the times the *delatot* may be closed, and even regarding string *delatot* rolled up into a canister attached to utility poles.

Section 4

Diversity in *Eruvin*

SEPHARDIC STANDARDS FOR DEFINING A RESHUT HARABIM

As discussed in our first section, Rashi holds that only an area with more than 600,000 residents has the potential to be designated as a *reshut harabim*. In this chapter, we will discuss whether Rashi's standard for a *reshut harabim* was accepted by the Sephardic halachic tradition.

THE OPINION OF RAV YOSEF KARO

Although Rav Yosef Karo presents Rashi's leniency merely as a second opinion in *Shulchan Aruch* O.C. 345:7, his view is somewhat unclear, as he appears to contradict himself in O.C. 303:18, where he writes that no location today qualifies as a *reshut harabim*. Presumably, the reason is that he requires the presence of 600,000 people to create a *reshut harabim*.

Sephardic authorities throughout the generations have debated which view should be regarded as the opinion endorsed by Rav Karo. The *Chida* (*Birkei Yosef*, O.C. 345:2) regards the stricter opinion as the one accepted by Rav Karo, and thus the Halachah for Sephardic Jews. However, Rav Yitzhak Taieb in his *Erech Hashulchan* (O.C. 345:2) disagrees and argues that Rav Karo accepts Rashi's lenient opinion requiring the presence of 600,000 people in order to render an area a *reshut harabim*.

This argument persists until this very day. Rav Shalom Messas (*Teshuvot Tevu'ot Shemesh* 1:65) rules that Rav Karo accepts the stricter opinion, while Rav Ovadia Yosef (*Teshuvot Yabia Omer* 9 O.C. 33) rules that Rav Karo accepts the more lenient view.

RAV OVADIA AND RAV MESSAS'S ENDORSEMENT OF AMERICAN COMMUNITY ERUVIN

Both Rav Ovadia (ibid.) and Rav Messas (*Teshuvot Shemesh U'magen* O.C. 3:84) urged the local rabbis to establish a community *eruv* in Deal, New Jersey.[1] They both stated that their motivation derived from the fact that many Jews carried on Shabbat even though an *eruv* did not yet exist in the area, in a blatant breach of the laws of Shabbat.

Despite the fact that both Rav Ovadia and Rav Messas strongly encouraged the creation of this *eruv*, however, their respective approaches were significantly different. Rav Messas regarded the *eruv* as intended only for those who already carry without the *eruv*. He strongly encouraged others to refrain from relying on the *eruv*, since he fundamentally rules that the presence of 600,000 people is not required to create a *reshut harabim*. Rav Ovadia adopted a more lenient view. While he writes that it is preferable to adopt the strict view and refrain from using a standard community *eruv*, he concludes that according to the baseline Halachah, *tzurot hapetach* suffice to render an area a *reshut hayachid*.

Rav Ovadia further notes that the *Kaf Hachayim* (O.C. 345:37), who maintains that Sephardic Jews essentially do not rely on the lenient view requiring the presence of 600,000 people to constitute a *reshut harabim*, writes that one may rely upon this lenient view if a supplementary lenient consideration exists. Rav Ovadia bolsters the lenient view requiring 600,000 people with the lenient consideration set forth by the *Chazon Ish*

---

[1] Rav Ovadia's endorsement appears in a letter archived at www.erub.org/c_services.

(O.C. 107:5-7) that the arrangement of buildings in modern cities creates a situation in which our cities constitute a *reshut hayachid* on a Torah level, rendering it permissible to create an *eruv* consisting only of *tzurot hapetach* in the area. Rav Ovadia writes that with the *Chazon Ish*'s approach as an adjunct to the lenient view, "there certainly exists a great basis upon which to create an *eruv* consisting only of *tzurot hapetach*."[2]

LARGE CITY ERUVIN

Interestingly, Rav Ovadia records that he encouraged the creation of an *eruv* in Los Angeles, despite the fact that far more than 600,000 people reside there. Rav Ovadia is lenient even in this case, since he rules that people riding in cars do not count towards the number 600,000. Rav Ovadia even endorsed the idea of an *eruv* in Flatbush, New York. This approach would also justify the city-wide *eruv* of Jerusalem, despite the fact that its residents now exceed 600,000 people.

THE VIEW OF THE RAMBAM

An additional potentially challenging factor for Sephardic acceptance of community *eruvin* is the view of the Rambam (*Hilchot Shabbat* 16:16), who maintains that a *tzurat hapetach* spanning more than ten *amot* is valid only if the majority of the *eruv* consists of wall.[3] It is quite difficult to satisfy the Rambam's

---

[2] We should note that in suburban towns such as Deal, there might not be a majority of wall on three sides. Thus, the area is not a *reshut hayachid* on a Torah level.

[3] See, though, *Teshuvot Minchat Yehuda* (number 26), which states that in a community where the buildings form a majority of wall on at least three sides, the *eruv* is acceptable even according to the Rambam. This respon-

Walking the Line

opinion in a typical community *eruv*. However, the *Shulchan Aruch* (O.C. 362:10) presents the Rambam only as a secondary opinion, and the *Kaf Hachayim* (362:91) rules that while it is preferable to abide by the Rambam's strict ruling, one may rely on the majority of Rishonim who disagree.

A SPECIAL SEPHARDIC ERUV
In a letter explaining his endorsement of the Sephardic Flatbush *eruv*, the renown Syrian Jewish community leader Rav Shaul Kassin notes that the Sephardic *eruv* consists of a majority of actual wall. To accommodate the opinion of the Rambam, the *tzurot hapetach* represent only a minority of the *eruv* boundary.

Moreover, Rav Kassin notes that *delatot* were posted throughout the area enclosed by the *eruv* (*delatot re'uyot linol*). Rav Kassin assured that the doors of the *eruv* would indeed be locked periodically. See our earlier chapter on *The Delatot of Canarsie, London, Mattersdorf, and Oakland* for further discussion of this principle.

CONCLUSION
It is significant that Rav Ovadia Yosef does not say that a Sephardic Jew may rely only on a community *eruv* that consists mostly of walls and is surrounded by doors with the potential to be closed. Indeed, as we noted above, the *Kaf Hachayim* writes

---

sum is cited as authoritative by the *Kaf Hachaim* (Orach Chaim 362:92). *Netivot Shabbat* (19:2 footnote 10) infers that *Teshuvot Maharsham* (1:206) agrees with this approach.

that one may rely on the majority of *Rishonim* who disagree with the Rambam.

Thus, it is clear from Rav Ovadia's writings that although it is preferable for a Sephardic Jew to refrain from using a communal *eruv* on Shabbat, he has significant basis upon which to rely on even in the case of a standard community *eruv*, without the enhancements made in the Flatbush *eruv*.[4]

---

[4] In varying degrees, Rav Ovadia (ibid.), Rav Shalom Messas (*Teshuvot Shemesh U'Magen O.C.* 3:84), Rav Mordechai Eliyahu (comments to Rav Zechariah Ben-Shlomo's *Orot Hahalachah*, p. 1236), and Rav Ben Tzion Abba Shaul (*Teshuvot Ohr L'tzion* 1: O.C. 30 and 2:23:12) permit relying on a community *eruv*. Rav Ben-Shlomo told me that it is generally accepted among Sephardic *posekim* that Sephardim are permitted to use a community *eruv*, but they all agree that it is preferable to avoid relying on a community *eruv* when possible.

ERUV STANDARDS ACCORDING TO SEPHARDIC MEASUREMENTS

As discussed in the previous chapter, it is much more difficult to create a community *eruv* based on Sephardic halachic standards, which may accept a stricter view of what constitutes a *reshut harabim*. An additional issue relates to the size of an *amah* and *tefach*. The size of an *amah* is vigorously debated among the *posekim*, and a significant difference exists between Sephardic and some Ashkenazic traditions. Those building and maintaining *eruvin* should keep this in mind so that their *eruvin* satisfy both Sephardic and Ashkenazic traditions.

GAPS OF TEN AMOT AND WALLS OF TEN TEFACHIM

The building of an *eruv* in the Jewish State, where we are at home and government authorities are supportive, is generally not very complicated.[5] Outside of Eretz Yisrael, however, especially in smaller Jewish communities, *eruvin* must be built in the least intrusive manner possible. Every effort is made to use existing structures, such as utility poles (especially those with a wire running on top), very steep slopes, and fences. In such situations, gaps will often exist when seeking to continue the *eruv* from a fence to poles to steep slopes, etc. The Halchah tolerates a gap of up to ten *amot* in such circumstances (*Eruvin* 1:1; Shul-

---

[5] See the chapter in which I describe my visit to the Modiin *eruv*.

chan Aruch, Orach Chaim 362:9; Aruch HaShulchan, Orach Chaim 362:30, 36 and 363:45).[6]

The length of an *amah* and *tefach* has ramifications for another aspect of *eruvin* as well. To be part of an *eruv*, a wall must be ten *tefachim* high (Eruvin 1:9; Shulchan Aruch, O.C. 345:2), and there are six *tefachim* in an *amah*. But how long is an *amah* in terms of feet and inches?

CHAZON ISH, RAV MOSHE FEINSTEIN, AND RAV AVRAHAM CHAIM NA'EH

Twentieth-century *posekim* intensely debate the equivalent of an *amah* and *tefach* in contemporary terms.[7] The three primary opinions are those of the *Chazon Ish*, Rav Moshe Feinstein, and Rav Avraham Chaim Na'eh. The *Chazon Ish* and Rav Na'eh were contemporaries who lived in Eretz Yisrael and engaged in vigorous debate about this topic from 5703 (1943) until 5713 (1953), the year in which both of these sages passed to the next world. Rav Moshe Feinstein issued his ruling on this issue in 1956 when he lived in the United States, independent of and without relating to the debate between the *Chazon Ish* and Rav Na'eh.

---

[6] There is considerable debate as to whether we may tolerate a gap of ten *amot* between a *tzurat hapetach* and a wall; see *Biur Halachah* 363:6, s.v. *tzarich*.

[7] The very wide range of opinions on this matter is summarized in the *Encyclopedia Talmudit*, s.v. *amah*.

	Amah (length of forearm)	***Tefach*** (handbreadth)
Chazon Ish (O.C. 39)	24 inches (60.96 cm)	4 inches (10.16 cm)
Rav Moshe Feinstein[8] (*Teshuvot Igrot Moshe*, O.C. 1:136)	21.25 inches (53.98 cm)	3.54 inches (9 cm)
Rav Chaim Na'eh (*Shiurei Torah* 3:25)	18.9 inches (48 cm)	3.15 inches (8 cm)

SEPHARDIC AND ASHKENAZIC APPROACHES

In Eretz Yisrael, the custom among Ashkenazic authorities is to apply the stringencies resulting from the views of both the *Chazon Ish* and Rav Avraham Chaim Na'eh.[9] Thus, they will require a fence that is part of an *eruv* to be 40 inches high (following the *Chazon Ish*'s measurement of a *tefach*), but they will not permit a gap greater than 15 feet and 9 inches (following Rav Na'eh's measurement of an *amah*).

In the United States, Rav Hershel Schachter and Rav Mordechai Willig essentially follow Rav Moshe's ruling (*Teshuvot Igrot Moshe*, O.C. 1:136). Accordingly, they require a fence to be 36 inches high and permit a gap of up to 18 feet. *The Laws of an Eruv*

---

[8] The *Aruch HaShulchan*'s measurement of an *amah* (*Yoreh De'ah* 201:3 and 286:21) is almost identical to that of Rav Moshe, and the *Mishnah Berurah* (358:7) agrees (as explained at www.asif.co.il/download/kitvey-et/kol/kol-30/1-29.pdf).

[9] As reported in *The Laws of an Eruv*, p. 264, and *Techumin* 32:413.

(p. 264) reports that "many *posekim*" in the United States adopt a similar approach.

Sepharadim, however, follow the opinion of Rav Avraham Chaim Na'eh.[10] Rav Shalom Messas (*Yalkut Shemesh* 137-138) writes that the smaller *shiurim* of Rav Na'eh should be adopted.[11]

CREATING AN ERUV ACCEPTABLE FOR SEPHARDIC JEWS

There is no problem for Sepharadim to rely on *eruvin* created by Ashkenazic *Rabbanim* in Eretz Yisrael, since they accommodate the opinion of Rav Na'eh when it results in stringency. Thus, it is not surprising that in many contexts, the *Yalkut Yosef* permits reliance on the community *eruv* without any provisos that the *eruv* conform to Sephardic standards (see, for example, *Yalkut Yosef*, O.C. 584; *Hanhagot Rosh Hashanah* 2). Rav Ovadia Yosef considers it acceptable for Sepharadim to rely on *eruvin* built according to Ashkenazic specifications without adjustments to accommodate Sepharadim.

However, this might not be true of *eruvin* created in the United States under the auspices of Ashkenazic *Rabbanim*, since many

---

[10] A letter from Rav Ovadia Hadaya is cited by Rav Na'eh in the introduction to his *Shiur Mikveh* vigorously confirms that the Sephardic tradition is in full accordance with the views set forth by Rav Na'eh. Not surprisingly, the *Yalkut Yosef* rules that it is sufficient for *hadassim* and *aravot* to be three *tefachim* long according to the measurements of Rav Na'eh (*Yalkut Yosef*, O.C. 650).

[11] The Yemenite *posek* Rav Eli Kady reports that the Yemenite practice also conforms to the opinion of Rav Na'eh.

of the *eruvin* in the United States do not accommodate the stringent result of Rav Na'eh's measurements. It might therefore be improper for a Sephardic Jew to rely upon a community *eruv*, unless the *eruv* conforms to Rav Na'eh's measurements (i.e., gaps do not exceed 15 feet and 9 inches).

Any community that is blessed with a Sephardic congregation should endeavor to comply with Rav Na'eh's measurements and ensure that gaps do not exceed 15 feet and 9 inches. As the *Rav Hamachshir* (supervising rabbi) of the Englewood *eruv* (which includes a significant Sephardic community), I ensure that the *eruv* conforms not only to Rav Moshe's measurements, but also those of Rav Avraham Chaim Na'eh. In my service on the Rabbinic board of the Teaneck *eruv*, I similarly ensure that there are no gaps wider than 15 feet and 9 inches in the *eruv*.[12] When we had the honor of hosting Chief Rabbi Rav Shlomo Amar at Congregation Shaarei Orah in August 2017, he told me that he agrees that an *eruv* that services Sephardic Jews should ensure that gaps not be wider than 15 feet and 9 inches.[13]

---

[12] Whenever possible, in the more than sixty community *eruvin* that I help supervise, every effort is made to conform to Rav Na'eh's *shiur* when it results in stringency.

[13] Rav Ike Sultan, however, reports that Rav Zecharia Ben-Shlomo told him that in a case of great need, a Sephardic Jew may carry in an *eruv* that conforms to Rav Moshe Feinstein's *shiurim* (see *Orot Hahalachah*, p. 581). The basis of this ruling may be the convergence of two rabbinic decrees (*trei d'rabbanan*), as Rav Mordechai Willig argues (see below in the text). We may also suggest (based on the *Chazon Ish*, *Kuntres Hashiurim*, O.C. 39) that the measurements of *amah* and *tefach* are by definition flexible and vary from country to country. Thus, since America's greatest *posek*, Rav Moshe Feinstein, determined that in the United States an

It is important to note that Chabad-affiliated Jews also follow the opinion of Rav Na'eh. Thus, if an *eruv* includes a Chabad community, it behooves the broader community leaders to ensure that there should be no gaps in the *eruv* wider than 15 feet and 9 inches.

It is also important to note that most Ashkenazim rely on Rav Na'eh's opinion in a lenient direction in the context of the size of *hadassim* used on Sukkot. Most of the *hadassim* sold in the United States conform to Rav Na'eh's opinion—they are *meshulash*, with all three leaves on the same level, on a majority of the rows for at least 9.45 inches (3 *tefachim*). Those that conform to the *shiur* of the *Chazon Ish* are *meshulash* on at least 12 inches. Thus, many, if not most, of the members of many Orthodox synagogues nationwide rely on Rav Na'eh's view in a lenient direction regarding fulfillment of the Torah obligation to take *hadassim* on the first day of Sukkot. It seems logical that Rav Na'eh's opinion should thus be accommodated in a strict direction regarding community *eruvin*, even in a completely Ashkenazic community.[14]

Rav Mordechai Willig told me that he makes every effort to ensure that the Riverdale *eruv* (which he supervises) satisfies

---

amah is 1.8 feet, that measurement might also be relevant for Sephardic Jews.

[14] Rav Zvi Sobolofsky told me that the community relies not upon Rav Na'eh's smaller *shiur*, but rather on the smaller *shiur* for a *tefach* in the context of *hadassim* and *aravot* (as presented in Sukkah 32b and *Shulchan Aruch*, O.C. 650:5). The three *tefachim* required for *hadassim* and *aravot* according to Rav Moshe Feinstein are a bit smaller than what Rav Na'eh regards as the conventional three *tefachim*.

Rav Na'eh's opinion when it results in a stringency.[15] However, Rav Willig defends those communities whose *eruvin* do not satisfy Rav Na'eh's opinion, but rather only that of Rav Moshe. He argues that since the situation involves two converging rabbinic laws (*trei d'rabbanan*), there is room to adopt the lenient approach.[16] The prohibition to carry in an area that is suitable for an *eruv* consisting significantly of *tzurot hapetach* (such as almost all city *eruvin* today) constitutes a rabbinic prohibition (according to baseline Halachah), and the invalidity of a gap of more than ten *amot* when a majority of the side of the *eruv* is enclosed (*omed merubah haparutz*) also constitutes only a rabbinic prohibition according to baseline Halachah (Rav Chaim Ozer

---

[15] Rav Shaul Shalom Deutsch, the head of Brooklyn's Living Torah Museum, told me that he has found no less than twenty seven pieces of archaeological evidence that Rav Avarahm Chaim Na'eh's *shiurim* are the historically accurate *shiurim*. Rav Deutsch told me that when he shared his discoveries with Rav Yosef Shalom Eliashiv, he reacted "now we know that Rav Avraham Chaim Naeh's *shiurim* are the accurate ones." This is consistent with what Rav Eliashiv writes about Rav Naeh's *shiurim* constituting the primary Halachah in *Kovetz Teshuvot* (2:30). However, I recall from my years of learning at Yeshivat Har Etzion hearing the claim that investigators discovered that the measurements discovered on *Har Habayit* perfectly matched the *shiurim* of the *Chazon Ish*. For further discussion of the role of archaeology in Halachic decision making, see my *Gray Matter* 3:249-267.

[16] Many Ashkenazic Jews in North America rely on Rav Naeh's *shiur* in a lenient direction (for example, to rely on a fence as a valid *mechitzah* if it is ten *tefachim* high according to Rav Naeh's *shiur* but not according to Rav Moshe's standard. Rav Mordechai Willig and Rav Baruch Simon told me that it is permissible to do so in case there is no viable alternative; on the other hand, Rav Hershel Schachter felt it is not proper to do so.

Grodzinsky, *Teshuvot Achi'ezer* 4:8; the *Chazon Ish*, op. cit. and O.C. 107:5-7; and Rav Moshe Feinstein, *Teshuvot Igrot Moshe*, O.C. 2:90).

Walking the Line

CHABAD AND COMMUNITY ERUVIN

There is a misconception that the custom of Chabad is not to accept community *eruvin*. This misconception emerges from a misunderstanding of Rav Shenuer Zalman of Liadi's opinion regarding the use of community *eruvin*. Rav Shenuer Zalman of Liadi was the founding Rebbe of Chabad and his work, the *Shulchan Aruch Harav*, serves as a baseline for much of Chabad Halachah.

However, upon further investigation, it turns out that the *Shulchan Aruch Harav* adopts the same approach as the *Mishnah Berurah* to community *eruvin*. Both of these great authorities prefer that we avoid using communal *eruvin* (see *Shulchan Aruch Harav* 345:11 and 362:19 and *Mishnah Berurah* 345:23 and 362:59); however, they do not reject the use of community *eruvin* by the broader Jewish community. In this chapter, we will briefly examine the Chabad approach to community *eruvin*.

TWO REASONS TO AVOID USING A COMMUNAL ERUV WHEN POSSIBLE

Both the *Shulchan Aruch Harav* and *Mishnah Berurah* agree that there are two considerable problems with the use of communal *eruvin*. The first problem is that communal *eruvin* almost always are composed of *tzurot hapetach*, which can only enclose *karmeliyot*. As many Rishonim, such as the Rif and Rambam, do not adopt Rashi's lenient position that an area can be defined as a *reshut harabim* only if more than 600,000 people reside there, both the *Shulchan Aruch Harav* and *Mishnah Berurah* urge halachically scrupulous individuals to avoid carrying even within communities enclosed by *eruvin*. That being said, both the *Shul-*

chan Aruch Harav and *Mishnah Berurah* fundamentally recognize that the accepted custom is to rely on the lenient opinion.

In addition, the Rambam (*Hilchot Shabbat* 16:16) severely limits the efficacy of *tzurot hapetach*. He rules that they be relied upon only if the majority of the side in question is enclosed by valid *mechitzot* (such as actual walls, very steep hills, or fences). Only then may the *tzurot hapetach* fill in the missing pieces.

The *Shulchan Aruch Harav* and the *Mishnah Berurah* prefer that we satisfy the opinion of the Rambam. At the same time, they recognize that the fundamental Halachah conforms to the *Shulchan Aruch* (O.C. 362:10), who rules in accordance with *Tosafot* (Eruvin 11a s.v. *ileima*) and the Rosh (Eruvin 1:13), who disagree with the Rambam. The *Aruch Hashulchan* (O.C. 362:30) notes that most *posekim* subscribe to the view espoused by *Tosafot* and the Rosh.

Not surprisingly, Chabad adherents who create *eruvin* in their summer camps, bungalow colonies, and backyards make the *tzurot hapetach* no wider than ten *amot*. We should note, though, that this measure satisfies only the *Chatam Sofer's* (*Teshuvot Orach Chaim* 88) understanding of the Rambam. However, Rav Chaim Soloveitchik (to the Rambam *Hilchot Shabbat* 16:16) and the *Chazon Ish* (O.C. 79:6) argue that according to the Rambam, even a succession of *tzurot hapetach*, in which each individual *tzurat hapetach* does not exceed a width of ten *amot*, does not enclose the area unless a majority of valid *mechitzah* encloses that side of the area.[17] According to this understand-

---

[17] Rav Baruch Simon (*Imrei Baruch, Eruvin UReshuyot*, pp. 95-97) demonstrates that the disagreement between these Acharonim finds its roots in a dispute between the Rishonim. We should also note that the *Kaf Hacha-*

ing, the Rambam does not treat *tzurot hapetach* as valid *mechitzot* in and of themselves. Rather, the *tzurot hapetach* can only serve to fill in gaps in pre-existing *mechitzot*.

THE POLICY CONCERNS OF THE SEVENTH LUBAVITCHER REBBE

Accordingly, we have seen that there is no long-standing Chabad tradition to eschew communal *eruvin* for the broader Jewish community. The current widespread reluctance among Chabad adherents to rely on community *eruvin* stems from policy concerns of the seventh and most recent Lubavitcher Rebbe, Rav Menachem Mendel Schneerson.

As is apparent from the collection of the Rebbe's halachic writings known as *Shulchan Menachem* (O.C. 196), the Lubavitcher Rebbe felt that the precedent to establish *eruvin* in European communities should not be followed in America. The Lubavitcher Rebbe was fundamentally concerned that the American Jewish community in his time was dramatically weaker, spiritually speaking, than their European antecedents. Thus, he was very concerned that the creation of community *eruvin* would lead to Jews forgetting about the prohibition of carrying on Shabbat (see Shabbat 139b and Eruvin 59a with Rashi ad. loc. s.v. *v'shel rabim* as a precedent for such concern). The Rebbe was afraid that people would be so accustomed to

---

im (O.C. 362:92) cites the *Orchot Chaim* who argues that even the Rambam would accept an *eruv* when the broader area is surrounded by walls on a majority of three sides. Such situations exist in many communities, especially in more urban areas where there is little or no space between buildings.

relying on their community *eruv* that they would rely on it even on Shabbatot when the *eruv* was down and even if they moved to another neighborhood or city that did not have an *eruv*. As we have mentioned in a previous chapter, the Rebbe was not alone among the great twentieth century American Rabbanim in this regard.

On the other hand, the Rebbe did leave the decision to create an *eruv* to the rabbis of each community. They should weigh, he wrote, whether it will be to the benefit or detriment of the community. In practice, of course, the pro-community *eruvin* view of Rav Zvi Pesach Frank (*Teshuvot Har Zvi*, O.C. 2:24) Rav Moshe Feinstein, and Rav Yosef Eliyahu Henkin (*Kitvei Harav Henkin* 2:32-33) prevailed in North America.

Nonetheless, many of the lessons may and should be derived from the Rebbe's writings. First, he notes that a community *eruv* requires the active involvement of a Rav who has specialized knowledge in the area of *eruvin*. How correct this assertion is! Just as the areas of divorce, circumcision, *kashrut*, conversion, *mikva'ot*, and *dinei Torah* require specialized knowledge training and experience, so, too, creating and maintaining a high quality community *eruv* demands a Rav who has invested his proverbial "10,000 hours" in halachic communal *eruv* activities.

He also writes that if a community *eruv* already exists, the Rabbanim must ensure that it remains on a high halachic standard. How correct is this advice as well! In my more than three decades of experience with community *eruvin*, I am witness to the fact that high *eruvin* standards are maintained only if Rabbanim maintain an ongoing effort to uphold the *eruv's* standards.

In addition, to a certain extent, *eruv* awareness is often lacking in our communities. While the practice of calling the *eruv* down once a year may not be feasible for many or even most communities, *eruv* education is paramount. Events such as biking around the *eruv* and other activities to learn about the *eruv* will help address this concern and keep the prohibition to carry on Shabbat on people's minds even if their neighborhood is blessed with an *eruv*.

CONCLUSION
Rav Avrohom Bergstein, one of the Chabad *shalichim* in Fair Lawn, NJ, informs me that Chabad families typically follow the approach of the respected Rav Yaakov Landa of Bnei Brak to community *eruvin*. Rav Landa advised for Chabad that women and children may rely on a community *eruv* but that the men should follow the stricter opinion.[18]

This approach seems to both fit with the *Shulchan Aruch Harav's* preference to avoid relying on community *eruvin* and the policy concerns of the Lubavitcher Rebbe. If the men do not rely on the *eruv*, the community will not lose consciousness of the prohibition of carrying and all of its attendant problems. On

---

[18] Interestingly, I was told that when Rav Mordechai Willig created the *eruv* in the Riverdale section of Bronx, New York, he told his wife that he did not want to be one of those husbands whose wives relied on the *eruv* while they themselves did not. Rav Willig asked Rebbetzin Willig if she wished to rely on the *eruv* and that if she would, he in turn would rely on the *eruv*. Rebbetzin Willig responded that she would not rely on the *eruv*, and, thus, both Rav and Rebbetzin Willig do not rely on community *eruvin* in order to satisfy the stricter opinions regarding the community *eruvin*.

the other hand, women with small children will not be confined to their homes for Shabbat and children will have the flexibility of relying on the community *eruvin*.[19]

---

[19] Rav Bergstein also sent me a recording of a ruling issued by Rav Gedalia Oberlander, a leading Lubavitcher halachic authority who resides in Cleveland. Rav Oberlander agrees that Lubavitch women may rely on a properly constructed *eruv*. He explains that it is essential for contemporary women to be able to get out of the house with their small children on Shabbat, and thus they may rely on a proper *eruv*.

THE MODI'IN ERUV & ERUVIN STANDARDS IN THE JEWISH STATE

In January of 2019, I was given a tour of the Modi'in *eruv* by Rav Eli Haddad. As I have been involved with *eruvin* in North America since 1989, I was eager to see how my Israeli counterparts manage their *eruvin*. In this chapter, we will note some of the differences between *eruvin* construction in North America and Israel, with a particular focus on the Modi'in *eruv*.

CREATIVE CONTROL YIELDS HIGHER HALACHIC STANDARDS

I was pleasantly surprised and even shocked to discover the very high quality of Modi'in Eruv. In North America, we are grateful when utility companies and municipalities grant us permission to make minor infrastructure changes when creating our own *eruvin*. For the most part, we utilize the existing utility wires and, when necessary, make certain modifications to conform to the demands of *Hilchot Eruvin*. In Israel, by contrast, the municipalities (for the most part) grant free reign for *eruv* designers and builders to create the highest quality *eruvin* possible. In Israel, utility poles and wires are not used in *eruvin*. Instead, specially constructed *tzurot hapetach* are constructed, thus enabling the creation of *eruvin* that conform to the highest possible halachic standards.

PERFECTLY STRAIGHT WIRES AND BOXING OUT KARPEFIYOT IN MODI'IN

In Modi'in, Rav Haddad devotes loving care to maintaining the highest quality *eruv* possible. I saw no sags in the Modi'in *eruv*, thereby satisfying the stringency of the *Teshuvot Mishkenot Yaakov*[20] that is almost impossible to meet when using the preexisting utility poles and wires.[21] Additionally, the *eruv* poles and wires are perfectly straight, thus satisfying another stringency that is nearly impossible to fulfill in North American *eruvin*.

Likewise, a field just outside of Modi'in is readily excluded from the *eruv* due to concern for *karpeif*, an issue that is significantly more difficult to manage in North America. In addition, any gaps larger than three *tefachim* between sections of the *tzurat hapetach* are halachically "sealed" to satisfy the stringency of the *Tevu'ot Shor*.[22]

HIGH ERUVIN STANDARDS THROUGHOUT THE ENTIRE COUNTRY

Modi'in is not home to many Charedi Jews. Nonetheless, the *eruvin* standards maintained by the community are significantly higher than those of many Charedi communities in the United States. For Rav Hadad, *eruv* work is a passion, and the Modi'in *eruv* is clearly his pet project, which he lovingly maintains at a very high level.[23]

---

[20] See our earlier chapter, *Constructing the Tzurat Hapetach*, for a further discussion of the *Mishkenot Yaakov's* stringency regarding sagging wires.

[21] Rav David Lau reports (in the aforementioned lecture at Yeshivat Otniel) on the efforts he and Rav Haddad make to keep the wires straight in the Modi'in *eruv*.

[22] See our earlier chapter, *The Stringency of the Tevu'ot Shor and the Yale New Haven Eruv*, for further discussion.

[23] There is a significant downside to Israeli *eruvin*. Rav Haddad describes Fridays as a day of a *milchamah* (war; i.e. extraordinary effort) he must

Although I was not privileged to be given a tour of the Ramat Beit Shemesh *eruv*, a community with a very high concentration of Chareidi Jews, I did notice on a visit that every few blocks seemed to be enclosed by separate *eruvin*. I assume this is done to satisfy the stringency of the Ramban, who writes that one should have a sense of being enclosed inside the *eruv* (i.e. the *eruv* does not encompass an unusually large area; see our earlier chapter on *The Maximum Size of an Eruv*). Even in the middle predominantly secular Tel Aviv, I saw a *tzurat hapetach* installed outside the *Hashalom* train center.

Of course, one would not list high *eruv* standards as one of the most important accomplishments of the Jewish State. However, it does reflect a very important reality. Israel, simply put, is our home. Since we are in our home in Israel, within reason, we can do as we please. Rav Haddad told me that he works hard to maintain the *eruv* on a high level of aesthetics as well as Halachah so it should not upset those concerned with maintaining the high aesthetic quality of Modi'in. Nonetheless, the freedom and flexibility accorded by the authorities to Rav Haddad cannot be matched in North America, which is not, let us be honest, our true home. Moreover, it is none other than the Israeli government that pays for the *eruv* construction maintenance, as it is an expected amenity of the Jewish State.

---

wage to ensure that the *eruv* is in tip top shape. In North America, where the *eruvin* consist mainly of relatively minor adjustments made to existing utility wires, such a major struggle is not standard fare.

CONCLUSION

A number of years ago, a friend explained his decision to make *aliyah*. He told me that one need not be a major Torah scholar to recognize that Hashem wants us to move to Israel. The Siddur and Chumash are both most definitely Israel-centric and we should follow suit. A review of Israeli *eruvin* leads one to the same conclusion.

Walking the Line

THE MACHMIR & THE MEIKEL MAKING ALLOWANCES FOR EACH OTHER

It is a deceptively simple story. After the Mishnah (Sukkah 25a) teaches that one is permitted to eat a snack (*achilat arai*) outside the Sukkah, the subsequent Mishnah (Sukkah 26b) relates that Rabban Yochanan ben Zakai was given a small quantity of food to taste and that he asked that the food be brought to the Sukkah for him to eat.

Similarly, Rabban Gamliel was offered two dates to eat and some water to drink, and he requested that these items be brought to the Sukkah for him to eat. On the other hand, when Rabbi Tzadok was offered a snack to eat on Sukkot, he chose to eat it outside the Sukkah, in accordance with the rule articulated in the previous Mishnah.

The Gemara (Sukkah 26b-27a) explains that the stories in the Mishnah teach that one has options regarding snacking outside the Sukkah. One option is to follow the baseline Halachah and eat snacks outside the Sukkah. Another legitimate and halachically meaningful action is to be strict and refrain from consuming even small amounts of food outside the Sukkah. The Rambam (*Hilchot Sukkah* 6:6) and the *Shulchan Aruch* (O.C. 639:2) codify both of these approaches as entirely legitimate Halachic options.

THE DESTRUCTION OF THE SECOND BEIT HAMIKDASH
The Mishnah seems to simply be communicating the options men have in regard to eating snacks outside a Sukkah during Sukkot. However, upon further reflection, we may notice that

206 | *Diversity in Eruvin*

the characters in this Mishnah are central rabbinic characters involved in the stories surrounding the destruction of the second *Beit Hamikdash* (see Gittin 55b-56b).

Is it possible that this Mishnah implicitly presents a remedy to the spiritual malaise that was in part responsible for the destruction of the second *Beit Hamikdash*? As is well known, Chazal (Yoma 9b) state that the sin of *sinat chinam*, baseless hatred, caused the destruction of the Second Temple.

The Netziv, in his introduction to Sefer Bereishit, elaborates that the Jews of the time were very pious and assiduously studied Torah. However, they regarded anyone who differed from them in their style of *yirat shamayim* as heretical. In other words, the *machmir* (strict individual) and the *meikel* (lenient individual) made no allowances for each other.

Our Mishnah presents a remedy to this spiritual malady, as it presents two equally legitimate and viable options in the manner in which one may observe the *mitzvah* of Sukkah. We do not regard either option as "too frum" (*mechzei k'yuhara*), or "too liberal and modern." The *machmir* and the *meikel* make allowances for each other in this Mishnah.

KEEPING "THE PUCK WITHIN THE BLUE LINES"

This is not saying that the Halachah is a "free for all," where anything goes. There are limitations. Chazal (*Bemidbar Rabbah* 13:16) teach that there are seventy faces to the Torah. It is significant to note that they do not say that there are infinite faces to the Torah. While there is a wide range of interpretation, there are boundaries. The seventieth approach is valid. The seventy-first is not.

Walking the Line

A Sukkah, at minimum, must be at least ten *tefachim* high and, at maximum, twenty *amot* high. While there are boundaries, there is an ample range between them. Nevertheless, that which falls beyond the boundaries lies beyond the pale. Rav Mordechai Willig is fond of illustrating this principle with a hockey metaphor: We must keep the puck within the blue lines, otherwise one is called for offsides.

RAMIFICATIONS FOR COMMUNITY ERUVIN

Machmirim and *meikilim* need to make allowances for each other in regard to all areas of Torah life, but especially in the context of community *eruvin*. I have heard of unfortunate incidents on both sides of the aisle (or, in this case, the wire).

Sadly, I know of one community leader who makes every effort to hinder the efforts of the rabbi of a neighboring synagogue in the latter's effort to adjust the *eruv* to satisfy stricter standards, especially in regard to *tachuv*. At the other extreme, I know of a son who refuses to bring his family to visit his widowed mother for Shabbat because the *eruv* in her community relies on *tachuv*.

An *eruv* should satisfy all of the area's communal rabbis' standards. Otherwise, the *eruv* will serve as a source of controversy and friction— both elements that are to be avoided. Indeed, Rav Moshe writes (*Teshuvot Igrot Moshe*, O.C. 4:86) that one of the reasons he endorses the *eruv* in the Kew Garden Hills section of Queens, New York is that all the neighborhood rabbis support it. However, provided that the community Rabbanim are operating within the proverbial "blue lines," those who wish for the *eruv* to meet stricter standards and those who suffice with more lenient standards must make allowances for each other.

SATISFYING EVERY OPINION?

Unlike *mikva'ot* (ritual baths), where the common practice is to satisfy all opinions (see *Gray Matter* 2:258-261), it is impossible to create a communal *eruv* that satisfies all opinions. For example, Rav Moshe Heinemann is renowned for setting high standards for the *eruvin* he creates in North America. However, even the standards that Rav Heinemann sets forth are not accepted by all opinions. For example, he follows (as he stated in an address to a conference of Young Israel rabbis in the 1990's, and as evident from his creation and maintenance of an *eruv* in Baltimore) Rav Moshe's opinion that an *eruv* may be created in a community where the population is less than 2.4 million. However, Rav Yosef Shalom Eliashiv (cited in *The Laws of an Eruv*, p. 156) believes that an *eruv* made of *tzurot hapetach* should not be made in cities whose population is larger than 600,000 people. Moreover, *The Laws of an Eruv* (p. 150) notes that Rav Aharon Kotler believed that *eruvin* should not be created altogether in the United States, as many Rishonim reject the 600,000 person leniency.

In addition, he relies on Rav Aharon Kotler's opinion that permits a slanted *eruv* wire that is less than 45 degrees steep; Rav Yaakov Bloi (*Netivot Shabbat* 19:27 note 60), however, does not accept a slant greater than 22 degrees. Rav Heinemann permits a top-side wire, something that *The Laws of an Eruv* (p. 102) cites Rav Moshe as not permitting. Rav Heinemann permits a minor sag in an *eruv* wire, in contrast to the aforementioned *Mishkenot Yaakov's* adamant rejection of the practice. Rav Micha Shotkin reports that Rav Heinemann permits (following the ruling of Rav Aharon Kotler cited in *The Laws of an Eruv*, p. 108) the use of a *lechi* placed under an eave, a practice rejected by Rav Yaakov Kaminetzky (ibid. pp. 108-109). Finally, Rav Shmuel Khoshkerman reports that Rav Heinemann permits the Atlanta *eruv* to rely on a very thin grounding wire as a *lechi*, a practice strongly objected to by Rav Hershel Schachter.

We are not criticizing Rav Heinemann for following any of these leniencies. We merely are clarifying that even the *eruvin* that follow Rav Heinemann's fine standards do not satisfy all opinions.[24] All would agree, though, that an *eruv* should be made

---

[24] Even the *mehudar eruvin* in Israel do not satisfy all opinions. Although *Teshuvot Avnei Yashfeh* 2 O.C. 43 states that he created a *mehudar eruv* in Netivot that satisfies every opinion, the reality is that it does not satisfy every view. Even *mehudar eruvin* in communities which make sure that there is a majority of wall on three sides in order to define the area as a *reshut hayachid* on a Torah level assume that breaks on the *eruv* wall greater than ten *amot* (when there is a majority of wall on each side) constitute only a rabbinic level prohibition. However, while many leading *posekim* adopt this approach, it is, in fact, a hotly debated topic.

Teshuvot Mishkenot Yaakov (O.C. 121) famously and vigorously argues that ten *amot* or more breaks constitute a problem on a Torah level. This opinion was strongly contested by *Teshuvot Beit Ephraim* (O.C 27) in a famous correspondence with the *Mishkenot Yaakov*. There are major Rishonim that support the view of the *Mishkenot Yaakov*. The *Gaon Yaakov* (Eruvin 11a s.v. *v'ha* and s.v. *shaminan*) infers this is the opinion of Rashi (Eruvin 94a s.v. *chatzeir*) and the Rashba in his *Avodat Hakodesh*. The *Mishkenot Yaakov* infers this opinion from the Rambam (*Hilchot Shabbat* 16:16 and 18) as well. This is also inferred from *Rabbeinu Chananel* (Eruvin 101b) and *Tosafot* (Bava Metzia 53b s.v. *d'naful*). Although the *Tosafot Harosh* (Eruvin 17b s.v. *araba'ah*) explicitly states that a breach of more than ten *amot* constitutes a problem only on a rabbinic level, nonetheless it seems that

to the highest standards feasible and must satisfy all of the area's communal rabbis. Otherwise, the *eruv* will serve as a source of friction and controversy.

---

many Rishonim support the *Mishkenot Yaakov's* opinion (for further discussion of the position of the Rishonim on this matter, see Rav Baruch Simon's *Imrei Baruch, Eruvin UReshuyot*, pp. 22-25).

One may further support the view of the *Mishkenot Yaakov* with the following argument: The *Biur Halachah* (345:7 s.v. *v'yesh omerim*) notes that communities in the time of Chazal were not encompassed by *eruvin*. He argues that had the communities been encompassed by *eruvin*, there would have been no need for Chazal to forbid blowing Shofar and taking Lulav on Shabbat lest we come to carry either object. Accordingly, we may ask why did Chazal not make *mehudar eruvin*? One could argue that the reason is that Chazal believed that a *pirtzah* wider than ten *amot* constitutes a problem on a Torah level, and, therefore, even *mehudar eruvin* are ineffective.

Indeed, *The Laws of an Eruv* (p. 55) does not note that even a *mehudar eruv* does not satisfy all opinions. Interestingly, the authors do write that although the *Mishnah Berurah* says that a *ba'al nefesh* (a halachically scrupulous individual) should not rely on a community *eruv* consisting of *tzurot hapetach*, he raises the possibility that a *ba'al nefesh* might be able to rely on a *mehudar eruv*. In summation, it is impossible for a community *eruv* that incorporates public roads wider than sixteen *amot* to satisfy all opinions.

This is not to say that *mehudar eruvin* are not to be commended. Those involved in the creation of such *eruvin* should be highly commended for making the extraordinary effort to create such an *eruv* of high standards. However, at the same time, not every community is able to meet these standards.

Walking the Line

CONCLUSION

Each community should ensure that its *eruv* is up to the best standard possible (as determined by an expert in *Hilchot Eruvin* in conjunction with the local *Rabbanim*) for that community. **The goal should be framed as the creation of the best community *eruv* possible, not the creation of a community *eruv* that satisfies each and every opinion. Regarding the latter, such an *eruv* cannot and does not exist.** Chazal's teaching that *"echad hamarbeh v'echad hama'amit uvilvad sheyechavein libo lashamayim,"* whether one does little or a lot what matters is whether one devotes his heart to Hashem (Berachot 17a), is particularly salient in this context. In any event, as long as a competent rabbinic authority is followed, the *machmir* and the *meikel* should make allowances for each other.

As a concluding note, it is rare to find something in Tanach or Chazal described as being hated by Hashem. One of the few incidences is *machloket* (strife). Hashem is described by Rashi (*Bereishit* 11:9 s.v. *umisham hefitzam*) as hating *machloket*. As such, the *machmir* and the *meikel* must follow the example set by Rabban Yochanan Ben Zakai, Rabban Gamliel, and Rabbi Tzadok by making allowances for each other. This is the remedy to the destruction of the Second Temple and the path to the ultimate redemption.

Rabbi Chaim Jachter

FIGHTING PRICE GOUGING BY ADOPTING A LENIENT OPINION

It is possible that if community Rabbanim feel that local merchants are taking advantage of the Jewish community by overcharging for various religious-based needs, they may instruct the community to instead rely on lenient halachic opinions that do not require the merchants' services. Precedent for adopting a lenient approach to fight price gouging may be found in Pesachim 30a, Sukkah 34b, Keritut 8a, *Teshuvot Tzemach Tzedek* 28, *Kaf Hachaim* 242:12 and Rav Meir Mazuz (*Techumin* 35:91-102).

PRECEDENTS FOR THE PRACTICE

The Gemara presents cases where Rabbanim advised following more lenient opinions regarding *chametz* after Pesach, *hadassim*, and the number of *korbanot* required of a woman who gave birth to multiple children. In the contemporary context, Rav Meir Mazuz (a major halachic authority in the Sephardic community) argues for relying on the *heter mechirah* (the sale of Israeli land by the Israeli Chief Rabbinate to avoid *shemitah* prohibitions) rather than being forced to purchase poor quality products at unreasonable prices that satisfy the stricter approach to *shemitah*.

FISH ON SHABBAT AND SEPHARDIC STANDARDS OF SHECHITAH

Rav Yaakov Chaim Sofer, in his work *Kaf Hachaim*, addresses a situation in which a particular community was being overcharged for fish for Shabbat. As is well known, the Gemara (in the famous story of Yosef Mokir on Shabbat 119a; the Kabbalah enthusiastically encourages this practice) indicates a preference for us to eat fish on Shabbat. The *Kaf Hachaim* writes that the community leadership can decide to forego fish on Shabbat if they believe the community is being taken advantage of. The *Kaf Hachaim* mentions an opinion that limits the permission to where there is at least a one third price gouge; however, he himself does not subscribe to this limitation. Instead, he leaves it to the judgment of the leadership of the impacted community.

It would seem also that if community leaders deem butchers to be charging Sephardic Jews unreasonable prices for Beit Yosef *chalak* meat, they may advise congregants to purchase meat that satisfies the not as strict Ashkenazic standard of *glatt kosher*. Although Rav Ovadia Yosef strongly encourages Sephardic Jews to consume only *chalak* meat, he permits relying on the more lenient Ashkenazic version of *glatt* in case of great need (*Teshuvot Yabia Omer* 5, Y.D. 3).

RELEVANCE TO ERUVIN

I applied this idea when reviewing an *eruv* in the Midwestern United States. The community is forced to use a specific company to install *lechis* when needed on utility poles, as the company is the only one approved by the local utility provider to perform this work on its poles. Taking advantage of the situation, the company charges exorbitant prices for its services ($200 per *lechi*; the usual charge ranges from $50 to $75 per *lechi*).

I told the community that in such a case, they may rely on the lenient approach of Rav Moshe Feinstein who believes that a *lechi* is not necessary unless there is a significant change in direction in the wire used for the *eruv*. Rav Zvi Pesach Frank and Rav Mordechai Willig agree with Rav Moshe.[25] While in ordinary circumstances we make considerable effort to accommodate Rav Hershel Schachter's opinion that *lechis* should not be more than .05 to 0.1 miles (roughly one to two blocks) apart, in case of great need we may rely on the more lenient view of Rav Moshe, Rav Zvi Pesach, and Rav Willig.

Those who provide halachic based services to the Jewish community deserve to make a proper living like anyone else. However, it is intolerable for them to take advantage of the community by price gouging. There is ample basis in the Gemara and contemporary *posekim* for the community to fight back by relying on lenient views. May we never have the need to wage this battle and hope that pricing conflicts, along with all conflicts, be resolved peacefully without resorting to drastic measures.

---

[25] See the earlier chapter, *A Lechi on Every Pole*, for a full discussion of this issue.

Section 5

Eruv Maintenance

∝

Rabbi Chaim Jachter

A COMMUNITY MODEL FOR ERUVIN MAINTENANCE IN SHARON, MA

I am often asked which community's *eruv* is my favorite. I currently serve as an *eruv* consultant for more than sixty communities throughout North America, and I have seen more than a hundred *eruvin* on three continents. Which do I like best? Hands down, without a doubt, it is the *eruv* created and maintained by the Young Israel of Sharon, Massachusetts.

Why is it my favorite? The answer is simple. The community aspires to attain the high *eruvin* standards set by Rav Moshe Heinemann of Baltimore, meticulously maintains those standards to the best of its abilities, and in addition to regular rabbinic involvement, more than 35 lay members of the community regularly are involved in the ongoing weekly inspection and upkeep of the *eruv*. In this chapter, we will take a look at how this stellar community maintains its *eruv*.

HIGH STANDARDS

The Sharon, MA *eruv* maintains very high halachic standards. A *lechi* is attached to every pole, unless a utility wire runs atop a pole. Also, breaks in a *lechi* of less than three *tefachim* are not tolerated. There are no barriers (*chatzitzot*) between the *lechis* and wires, *tachuv* is not relied upon, and there are no openings more than three *tefachim* wide between *tzurot hapetach* and *mechitzot*.

For many communities, the adoption of such strict standards is not feasible. It would simply result in much too many installations to properly monitor and maintain. How is the Sharon community able to sustain such high standards?

THE FOUNDING RAV – RAV MEIR SENDOR

Rav Meir Sendor, the founding Rav of the Sharon *eruv*, from the very beginning successfully fostered a culture of high level community involvement in the *eruv*. In most other communities, one person is hired to inspect the *eruv* each week. Most often, it is nearly impossible to find even a second individual to help with the *eruv's* weekly inspection. It is very difficult for a lone *eruv* inspector to maintain hundreds of installations. By contrast, in Sharon, MA, where more than twenty people inspect the *eruv* weekly, each inspector is assigned only a few dozen *eruv* components to monitor. Each inspector requires approximately a half an hour to complete his section, which again is a reasonable undertaking.

Rav Sendor insisted from the beginning that responsibility for the *eruv's* upkeep be shared by the community members. To everyone's credit, the Sharon community bought into the idea. In general, it is challenging for a community rabbi to institute such a policy for an already existing *eruv*. The Sharon *eruv* policy continues to succeed since it was instituted at the very inception of the community *eruv*.

THE COMMUNITY MEMBERS

The Sharon *eruv* is divided into more than twenty sections. Community members rotate each week in their inspection of their small portion of the *eruv*. Each portion is inspected on foot to insure proper upkeep. Rotating inspectors keep everyone honest and alert. In most other communities, the weekly inspection is conducted by car. Although this is an acceptable practice (as long as one person drives and the other inspects), it is not the best practice. There is no substitute for a walking inspection, during which one is far more likely to notice nuanced and subtle issues with the *eruv* than he would if he were whizzing by at thirty miles per hour.

THE CURRENT COMMUNITY RAV – RAV NOAH CHESES

In many communities, the community Rabbanim are not involved with the *eruv* on a regular basis. The inspection process is farmed out to an individual and the Rav is consulted if there are any problems. Hopefully, the community Rav will at minimum conduct a yearly walking inspection of the entire *eruv* together with a Rav with considerable experience with *eruvin*.

Rav Noah Cheses of the Young Israel of Sharon, by contrast, is a hands-on community rabbi who often is involved with *eruv* maintenance and repair. He occasionally reviews portions of the *eruv* to keep inspectors "on their toes" and helps with emergency repairs on Fridays.

THE OUTDOOR SHARON CULTURE

An advantage of the Sharon community is that the prevailing culture is one of love of hiking and outdoor activities even in cold weather. Many people choose to live in this community due to its rich open spaces. Thus, *eruv* inspections fit with the prevailing Sharon culture. Active involvement with the *eruv* enhances the sense of community and commitment to careful observance of Halachah. Devotion and attention to the details of the *eruv* spills over to other areas of Halachic observance. In a day and age when people crave active religious activities, *eruv* inspection perfectly fits the bill.

CONCLUSION

The Sharon *eruv* continues to maintain a high standard regarding many areas of halachic dispute regarding *eruvin*. Indeed, the Sharon, Massachusetts community serves as a model for communities worldwide of how the synergy between the local Rav, experienced outside Rabbanim, and the involvement of a large percentage of lay community members helps create and maintain a top-notch community *eruv*.

All communities should consider implementing at least some of these standards. While it is difficult to change practices midstream, people are often receptive to slow change. In the meantime, all communities should ponder the benefits reaped by the Sharon community from its *eruv* policies and at least consider how to introduce at least some of these practices to their communities.

Rabbi Chaim Jachter

MANAGING AN ERUV EMERGENCY IN CAMBRIDGE, MA

Whenever I receive a phone call late Friday afternoon from an out of town caller, it is typically about an *eruv* emergency in one of the many communities whose *eruvin* I advise. One Friday, the rabbi from Cambridge, Massachusetts called with the following conundrum: The Boston area had suffered from a major storm and about a dozen points in the *eruv* needed to be repaired.

Since the *eruv* repair company also services the much larger greater Boston *eruv*, the company attended to the many repairs needed by the greater Boston *eruv* first, and, only on Friday afternoon, did the work begin on the Cambridge *eruv*. The non-Jewish technician reported to the community about an hour and half before sunset that he was unsure if he would complete the repairs before Shabbat.

ASKING A NON-JEW TO REPAIR THE ERUV

The first question is whether it is permitted for the community to ask the *eruv* repair person to complete the work even after Shabbat has already started. The answer is a resounding yes, as stated explicitly by the *Mishnah Berurah* (276:25). It is clear from the Gemara that one may ask a non-Jew to do work on Shabbat if the work is necessary to benefit the community.

The classic case is recorded on Gittin 8b, where the Gemara permits one to ask a non-Jew to write a deed to acquire property in Eretz Yisrael. We see that we may ask a non-Jew even to perform Biblically forbidden activities on Shabbat for community needs.

THE HALACHIC NE'EMANUT OF THE NON-JEWISH REPAIRMAN

The Halachah accords *ne'emanut*, credibility, only to those Jews who observe Halachah; a non-Jew, therefore, does not enjoy halachic *ne'emanut*. Could the community rely on the presumption that the non-Jewish professional completed the work? We should note that the *eruv* committee and the *eruv* repairman have enjoyed a very satisfactory relationship for many years. The repairman has always followed through in a superlative manner when asked to perform repairs on the *eruv*. We should also clarify that the location where the repairs were needed is quite distant from where people live and is not readily accessible for inspection on Shabbat.

Since the prohibition to carry without an *eruv* in the area is only rabbinic in nature, I felt that the community could assume that the repairman had completed his work.[1] In such a situation, one may rely on a non-Jewish worker due to a convergence of three halachic principles:

1. *Mirtat* (Avodah Zara 61b): The fear of being discovered. The repairman knows that if he does not complete his work, his dereliction will be discovered the next time the *eruv* is inspected, which will in turn lead to his termination.

2. *Uman lo mara anafshei*: A professional does not risk his reputation (see Chullin 97a, *Tosafot* s.v. *samchinan*).

---

[1] The enclosed area is a *karmelit*, as discussed in our first chapter.

3. *Milta d'avidi le'igaluyei* (Bechorot 36a): People do not lie when the lie may be easily discovered.

Regarding rabbinic prohibitions, we may assume that a *shaliach* (representative) has fulfilled his mission (Eruvin 31b and *Shulchan Aruch* Y.D. 331:34). Even though a non-Jew is not regarded as a *shaliach* (Kiddushin 41b), as we are speaking of a *po'eil*, a trusted hired worker, we may assume that he has done the work (at least according to the *Machane Ephraim, Hilchot Sheluchim* number 11 and *Minchat Chinuch* 216:6 based on Bava Metzia 10a). Rav Baruch Simon (personal communication) believes that one may rely on this in a rare case of special need (as was this situation).

MAY WE ASSUME THE ERUV IS UP ONCE SHABBAT HAS BEGUN?

The question then emerged if we may assume that the *eruv* was completed before Shabbat. Perhaps we may argue that since we are dealing with a doubt (*safek*) regarding a rabbinic prohibition, we may be lenient. This, however, is subject to great dispute as to whether we may rely on the principle of *safeik d'rabanan l'kula* when there is a *chezkat issur* (a status quo of being prohibited). The *Aruch Hashulchan* (Y.D. 110:106) rules that if there is a *safek* as to whether an act occurred that would render the situation permissible (such as ours), one must rule strictly.

CONCLUSION

I advised the Cambridge community to announce that one should refrain from relying on the *eruv* on that particular Friday evening, as there was a doubt as to whether the *eruv* repairs were completed. However, on Shabbat day, I felt they may rely on the *eruv*, since at that point they could safely assume the *eruv* repairs were completed. In ordinary circumstances, though, an observant Jew must verify a repair to the *eruv* if it was performed by either a non-Jew or non-observant Jew.

Rabbi Chaim Jachter

THE FRIDAY AFTERNOON THE RABBI DISCOVERED THE ERUV WAS BROKEN

Upon driving myself and children home from an idyllic Friday bowling expedition, I noticed something very disturbing about our community *eruv*: One of the poles along the *eruv* route was severely damaged. I safely parked near the site of the broken pole and began to investigate. Lo and behold, there was a serious problem with our *eruv*: approximately six feet of the bottom of the *lechi* was missing! With only two and a half hours until Shabbat, my mind began to race with calculations as to how to handle the situation. As a first step, I called the administrator of our *eruv* in Teaneck, New Jersey, Rav Micha Shotkin. Fortunately, Rav Shotkin "happened" (I view this as *siyata d'shmaya*) to be located only fifteen minutes away, and he quickly changed course and made his way to Teaneck. Rav Shotkin made the repair quickly and efficiently, and the *eruv* was up and ready for Shabbat. Had I not noticed the damaged pole and gone to investigate, thousands of Jews would have unwittingly relied on a subpar *eruv* throughout that Shabbat. In this chapter, we will analyze this incident to glean some vital lessons for *eruv* maintenance.

RABBINIC INVOLVEMENT WITH ERUV MAINTENANCE

I currently advise more than sixty communities in regard to their *eruvin* and have thirty years of experience dealing with community *eruvin*. One lesson I have seen repeatedly in community after community, is that the quality of a community's *eruv* depends a great deal on the involvement of the local Rabbanim. Communities where the local rabbi pays little or no attention to the *eruv* often are of poor quality, sometimes being completely disqualified or marginally acceptable at best. On the other hand, communities where the rabbis are actively involved on a regular basis are maintained at a high level.

Community rabbis are most often extremely busy tending to an extraordinarily diverse set of communal and individual needs; nevertheless, it is vital for the local Rav to oversee the religious needs of the community. For example, the Gemara (Beitzah 16b) relates that Avuha D'Shmuel made an *eruv tavshilin* for his entire town of Nahardei'a, and Rabi Ami and Rabi Asi made an *eruv tavshilin* for their entire town of Teveriah. In more recent times, it is related that both the *Chafetz Chaim* (*Dugmah Midarkei Avi zt"l* 63:14) and the *Chazon Ish* (*Pe'eir Hador* 2:136 and 285) every week inspected their respective community's *eruv*.

In Teaneck, our inspector does an excellent job of meticulously inspecting the *eruv* each week. It is clear that the problem arose after he completed the inspection on Thursday. In the wake of this incident, I sent a note to all of the Teaneck community Rabbanim to remind them to be alert to any unusual phenomenon in regard to the *eruv*. Those Rabbanim who participate in our twice a year walking inspection of the *eruv* are best equipped to notice such suspicious alterations. Regular walking tours provide Rabbanim with a perspective on what the *eruv* is supposed to look like, which sensitizes them to be alert to any abnormalities.

THURSDAY ERUV INSPECTION

Ideally, a community *eruv* should be inspected on Friday (*Teshuvot Doveiv Meisharim* 2:28). However, in practice, many *eruvin* are inspected on Thursday to allow time for any necessary *eruv* repairs. The Teaneck *eruv* and most community *eruvin* with which I am familiar are sufficiently stable such that we may rely upon Thursday inspections. However, Rabbanim[2] should remain alert to problems, even after the inspection has been completed.

After I completed creating an *eruv* in the community in which I resided in 1989, I asked Rav Schachter if I was required to look at the *lechis* on the streets that I happened to pass on Friday, after the *eruv* was inspected for the Shabbat. Rav Schachter replied that it is not necessary to obsessively repeat the inspection of the *eruv*. However, this does not mean we can blithely ignore an obvious problem.

WHAT IF THE PROFESSIONAL IS NOT AVAILABLE?

What are the Rav's options if the professional repairman is not available to fix the *eruv*? In such situations, advance preparation is in order. Rabbanim should maintain a stockpile of forty inch (the equivalent of ten *tefachim*) *lechis* that are ready to be installed on the poles by laymen in situations similar to our case. There may not be sufficient time to make such repairs by "laymen" if the *lechis* are not prepared in advance.

In such situations, the Rav might not have the equipment or ability to safely install the *lechis* the entire way to the wire. He also may not be able to insure that the ten *tefachim* high

---

[2] Rav Hershel Schachter advises educating community members about the *eruv* route and to encourage them to notify their rabbis if they see utility workers working on the utility wires along the *eruv* route. In this manner, the entire community is enlisted in the effort to maintain the *eruv*.

lechis are plumblined beneath the wire. In such a situation, one could temporarily rely on an eyeball estimation that the *lechi* is placed precisely beneath the wire. (I heard this ruling directly from none other than Rav Shlomo Zalman Auerbach; see our chapter on *Constructing the Tzurot Hapetach*.)

RELYING ON B'DI'EVED STANDARDS

What if we were even unable to make the "layman" repair? The Rabbanim should be aware of standards upon which they can rely in a pinch, or at the very least have a Rav whom they can consult. In our case, the top portion of the *lechi* remained intact and extended approximately twenty-five feet down from the wire, while the bottom six feet were missing. In such a situation, the community may be able to rely upon the opinion of *Chatam Sofer*, who permits relying on the principle of *gud achit mechitzta*.[3]

Rav Hershel Schachter told me that he is not comfortable relying upon the *Chatam Sofer* in this instance; however, Rav Mordechai Willig believes that in a case of great need (*besha'at hadechak*) this ruling may be followed. Indeed, the *Chatam Sofer's* ruling seems compelling: Just as *tzurat haptach* may be created via the mechanism of *gud asik* (the halachic extension of a *lechi* upwards towards the wire; at least according to the *Mishnah Berurah* 362:62), so too it may be created relying upon *gud achit*.

Had the *lechi* in question not been able to be repaired before Shabbat, the Teaneck Rabbanim would have faced a di-

---

[3] See our earlier chapter, *Gud Achit Mechitzta and Lavud*, for a more complete treatment of the *Chatam Sofer's* opinion, in addition to our presentation of the *Chazon Ish's* dissenting view.

lemma as to whose ruling, that of Rav Schachter or Rav Willig, should be followed. Fortunately, we have a formal *eruv* council consisting of the local Rabbanim with considerable experience managing community *eruvin*. The question would have been submitted to the *eruv* council for a decision whether to announce the *eruv* as functional for that Shabbat.

OCCASIONALLY ANNOUNCING THE ERUV IS DOWN
Some Rabbanim might have been inclined to use the opportunity to announce that the *eruv* is down. There is an acute need to educate the community about the prohibition to carry on Shabbat and *eruvin*. For example, in my teaching experience, I have encountered many youngsters who are not aware of the distinction between Shabbat and Yom Tov in regard to the *issur hotza'ah*.

However, Rav Mordechai Willig does not subscribe to this approach. Sadly, in our communities, not everyone can be expected to observe the *issur hotza'ah* in case the *eruv* is not functional. Public *chillul Shabbat* (desecration of Shabbat), heaven forbid, would be most detrimental to the community. In fact, I once heard from Rav Willig that the camp Rav at Camp Morasha suggested the *eruv* be called down upon encountering a very serious problem with the camp *eruv* late Friday afternoon. Rav Willig insisted, though, that every effort be made to repair the *eruv* in time for Shabbat so as not to need to call the *eruv* down.

CONCLUSION
Due to *siyata dishmaya* along with proper advance planning and organization, a problem with the Teaneck *eruv* was noticed and

repaired expeditiously, Baruch Hashem, thus avoiding a situation in which thousands of observant Jews would rely on a less than excellent *eruv* for a Shabbat.

Moshe Rabbeinu, upon seeing the unusual sight of a bush on fire that was not consumed, made it his business to investigate. As a result, the process of our redemption from Egypt was initiated. When you think you see something awry with the *eruv*, say something and do something. Follow Moshe Rabbeinu's example and investigate.

POSTSCRIPT - A RELATED INCIDENT WITH THE ENGLEWOOD, NEW JERSEY ERUV

Daniel Lubat, while inspecting the Englewood *eruv* on a Thursday evening, noticed utility workers working on poles along Route 9W near Sage Street in Englewood Cliffs. He alerted me that the area required reinspection on Friday, since although intact on Thursday, the workers constituted a *rei'uta* (halachic detriment) to the presumed-valid status of the *eruv*. I subsequently inspected the area on Friday and found an *eruv* wire that was down, which was dealt with accordingly. Daniel's wise decision to inform me when he noticed a situation that had the potential to adversely affect the integrity of the *eruv* paid off. He even followed up with me to ensure that nothing fell between the cracks.

"Alertness avoids catastrophe" is an apt slogan promoted by security experts. The same is true regarding community *eruvin*. One may not assume that once the *eruv* is constructed that it will remain intact indefinitely. Constant vigilance is a *sine qua non* for maintaining a quality community *eruv*.

Rabbi Chaim Jachter

ERUV THROUGH THE STORM

On Friday, Shushan Purim 5778, calls were pouring in. The calls were coming from Rebbeim from communities throughout the Northeastern United States when a fierce nor'easter hit their respective communities with winds that exceeded forty miles an hour. The burning question on everyone's mind was whether we must announce that the *eruv* is down due to concern that the *eruv* might not be able to withstand the storm.

The issue in halachic parlance is whether to view the storm as a *rei'uta*, a legal detriment, to the *chezkat kashrut*, the presumptive valid status, of a community *eruv*. The answer, as Rav Mordechai Willig noted in a personal conversation, depends to a great extent on the community. Some community *eruvin* rely on dozens of their own wires (fishing line is typically used due to its resilience) strung from pole to pole, while other communities' *eruvin* rely almost exclusively on utility wires. The latter group is far less vulnerable than the former. In this chapter, we present how I instructed some of the various communities hit by the storm.

SHARON, MA

This *eruv* relies, in part, on utility wires, but also consists of many *tzurot hapetach* constructed through heavily wooded areas. Trees sway more in the wind than utility poles. Therefore, strings that are attached to trees are more likely to break than strings that are attached to utility poles. Rav Cheses of the Young Israel of Sharon informed me that Rav Moshe Heinemann ruled that if the winds exceed forty miles per hour, the *chezkat kashrut* of the *eruv* is removed. While this is not necessarily true for every community *eruv*, it is a reasonable standard regarding the Sharon *eruv*. Not only might the wind knock down an *eruv* wire, it is also not unlikely that a tree branch would fall on one of the *eruv* lines and render it invalid. Therefore, I advised Rav Cheses to declare the *eruv* down for that Shabbat. I would advise the same for an *eruv* whose many wires run along an oceanfront, making the *eruv* especially susceptible to breakage by severe winds that come from the ocean during a storm. I also would advise a community that has wires running through wooded areas to consider finding an alternative less vulnerable route to bolster the stability of their *eruv*.

SOUTHERN WASHINGTON, D.C. AND FORT LEE, N.J.
The *eruv* in southern Washington, D.C. mostly consists of utility wires, with less than a dozen of its own added wires spread throughout the city. These wires are located in non-wooded areas where falling branches are not a risk. The *eruv* wires have historically withstood even the fiercest of winds, making us confident that the *eruv* would remain intact through the Shabbat despite the nor'easter. Thus, I felt that there was not a compelling reason for Rav Hyim Shafner to declare the *eruv* inoperable for the Shabbat. I advised Rav Zev Goldberg to adopt the same approach in Fort Lee, New Jersey for similar reasons. Only three added wires in Fort Lee are essential to the *eruv*. Historically, these wires have not broken during storms, and could thus be relied upon to weather a severe storm.

I would like to share one note about a fishing line strung between two light posts. One summer, while conducting a walking review of the Cambridge, MA *eruv*, we watched in horror as a very large dump truck had its crane up heading towards an *eruv* line. The crane ran forcefully into the line and we expected the worst. However, to our surprise, the wire bounced back into a straight trajectory after being stretched quite far. I was surprised to learn the extent of the resilience of a fishing line stretched in such a manner.

TEANECK, NJ

I conferred with fellow Teaneck eruv council member Rav Michael Taubes, who felt that if the utility wires remain up and the power remains on, then we may assume the Eruv remains intact. The power remaining on is a reasonable indicator that the wires upon which the eruv relies are still intact. Since the Teaneck eruv consists almost entirely of utility wires and virtually every wire we install has some halachic backup (Rav Willig is particularly enthusiastic about creating backups for the various components of the Eruv he administers in Riverdale), we decided that we need not declare the eruv down unless there was a power outage or trees were down.

STAMFORD, CT

This *eruv* also consists predominantly of utility wires. However, there was a power outage in Stamford, leading me to suspect that the *eruv* might not have remained intact. Rav Willig, though, cautions that ideally one need not assume that the utility wires used in the *eruv* are down just because one power line is down. He reasons that one may follow the majority, and since the majority of wires remain intact, one may assume that the utility wires upon which the *eruv* relies upon are not broken. I suggested to Rav Daniel Cohen that in such a situation one could write to the community that it is preferable not to rely on the *eruv*, but those who wish to may rely on the Eruv despite the storm.

ALLENTOWN, PA

Rav David Willensky told me that an alert congregant noticed that a large tree branch had fallen on a utility wire that constitutes a component of the community *eruv*. The police had closed the street off to traffic as the branch perched precariously on the wire. In my judgment, this represented a significant *rei'uta* to the status of the *eruv* and I felt it best to announce that the *eruv* was down.

SHABBAT KEIVAN SHEHUTRAH HUTRAH

What if one were confident that the *eruv* remained intact at the beginning of Shabbat but feared that the intensifying storm broke the *eruv* in the midst of Shabbat? Rav Shlomo Kluger (*Teshuvot Ha'elef Lecha Shlomo* numbers 153, 162, and 172) rules that if the *eruv* was up at the beginning of Shabbat, one may rely on the *eruv* even if it came down during Shabbat, via the principle of *shabbat keivan shehutrah hutrah*, which states that an entity permitted at the beginning of Shabbat is permitted throughout the entire Shabbat (Eruvin 70b).

Perhaps we can rely on Rav Shlomo Kluger as a component of a *sefek sefeika*, a double doubt. There is a doubt if the *eruv* is intact, and there is an additional doubt if Rav Shlomo Kluger is correct in applying the principle of *shabbat keivan shehutrah hutrah* to *tzurot hapetach*. Unlike Rav Shlomo Kluger, the *Tosafot* (Eruvin 15a s.v. *lo savar* and 17a *ireiv*) rule that *shabbat keivan shehutrah hutrah* applies only to the *eruv chatzeirot*, but not to *tzurot hapetach* and *mechitzot*.

The story is told of Rav Aharon Lichtenstein, the late co-Rosh Yeshiva of Yeshivat Har Etzion, visiting his students during their time of their active military service and being informed that his co-Rosh Yeshiva Rav Yehuda Amital had told the students they may rely on Rav Shlomo Kluger's ruling. Rav Lichtenstein is said to have reacted in shock in light of the aforementioned *Tosafot*. When he next saw Rav Amital, he inquired as to the basis of his ruling. Rav Amital replied that in Europe the custom was to rely on this leniency of Rav Shlomo Kluger.[4]

While I have very deep respect and love for Rav Amital, I find this ruling untenable. It is clear from the Rambam (*Hilchot Eruvin* 3:25) that he agrees with *Tosafot*. Moreover, the Gemara (Eruvin 17a) explicitly states that the *mechitzot* must remain intact in order to apply the principle of *shabbat keivan shehutrah hutrah*.

The sole apparent basis for Rav Shlomo Kluger's approach is a responsum of the *Mahari Weil* (*Dinim Vehalachot*, number 12) who limits the requirement that the *mechitzah* remain intact to a *mechitzah* excludes a *reshut harabim* from the enclosed area. However, if only a *karmelit* is excluded, then one may apply the rule of *shabbat keivan shehutrah hutrah* even if the *mechitzot* do not remain intact.

The problem is that the *Shulchan Aruch* (O.C. 374:2) explicitly states that the *mechitzot* must remain intact even if only a *karmelit* is excluded. None of the major commentaries to the

---

[4] Rav Yoel Amital, son of Rav Yehuda Amital, confirmed that this is his father zt"l's ruling (personal conversation at Yeshivat Shaalvim in January 2019).

Shulchan Aruch dissent. Thus, it seems that one may not rely upon Rav Kluger's leniency since it runs counter to a ruling of the *Shulchan Aruch* and all its commentaries. Even Rav Kluger himself expresses uncertainty about his ruling and uses his approach in two of his responsa only as a prong of a *sefeik sefeika*. Indeed, Rav Hershel Schachter told me that one may not rely on this leniency of Rav Shlomo Kluger even in case of great need. Rav Schachter believes that it cannot even be relied upon as a *senif l'hakeil*.

TWO PRACTICAL POINTS

We conclude with two practical recommendations. Rav Willig advises that whenever an *eruv* wire needs to be installed, one should install an extra one or two wires as a backup. As Shlomo HaMelech teaches, "*Tovim hashanayim min ha'echad v'chut hameshulash lo bim'heirah yenateik*," "Two are better off than one, in that they have greater benefit from their earnings, and a threefold cord is not readily broken" (Kohelet 4:9 and 12).

Our second piece of advice relates to Kohelet 2:14 – "*Hachacham einav b'rosho*," "A wise man has his eyes in his head." If one sees a serious storm developing, it is best to alert the community early on Friday that the *eruv* might be called down for Shabbat. Our communities today are so accustomed to relying upon an *eruv* that it becomes very challenging to function on Shabbat without one. Thus, everyone should be alerted early when there is concern that the *eruv* will need to be declared down to give time for community members to adjust their plans to meet the challenge.

Rabbi Chaim Jachter

THE PROPER WAY TO CHALLENGE AUTHORITY DURING ERUV INSPECTION

In Parashat Shofetim, we are commanded to listen to whatever the Beit Din instructs and "not deviate either to the right or left" (Devarim 17:11). We must listen, Rashi explains, even when the Beit Din tells us that right is left and left is right. Nonetheless, there are times when we may, nay must, challenge rabbinic authority. There are times when failing to challenge rabbinic authority is itself sinful (see Horiyot 2a).

SEE SOMETHING, SAY SOMETHING

A positive example occurred at a summer camp where one of my students worked a few years ago. In the kitchen where the student worked, he felt that despite having a stellar certification of *kashrut*, the protocols for separating milk and meat were a bit behind the curve. He contacted me, and I in turn raised the issue with the certifying *kashrut* agency. The *kashrut* supervisor investigated the issue, and, lo and behold, an upgrade in the standards was in order and immediately implemented. Had the student merely assumed that the *mashgiach* (*kashrut* supervisor) had everything under control, the *kashrut* at the program would not have been at its best standard. The policy of "see something, say something" certainly worked out very well in this situation.

A similar situation occurred when reviewing an *eruv* in the Southern United States a few summer ago. While inspecting a shrub-covered *lechi*, I declared that the *lechi* was properly positioned beneath the wire. One of the much younger rabbis present said he thought the *lechi* was not under the wire but he submits to my authority. I responded that my authority should not be invoked in such circumstances. I advised that we devote more time to examining the locale. Lo and behold, after a careful inspection, it turned out that the younger rabbi was correct and that the situation needed correction.

INAPPROPRIATE DEFERENCE TO AUTHORITY YIELDS MISTAKES

Proper management permits and encourages creating an environment where younger and less-experienced staff members feel comfortable to challenge senior staff. Dan Senor and Saul Singer's *Start Up Nation* reports that part of the Challenger space shuttle disaster was due to the failure to create such an environment. The book reports how members of the Challenger junior management were aware of the problems that caused the terrible tragedy, but were nevertheless intimidated to raise the issue with their superiors. They assumed that their superiors were aware of the issue and that it did not pose a threat to the mission. Malcolm Gladwell's *Outliers* similarly describes how airplane crashes frequently occurred in a particular country due to a culture of excess deference towards authority.

By contrast, *Start Up Nation* notes how Israeli firms create a culture where everyone is encouraged to say something if they see something that they perceive to be wrong. Similarly, Rav Aryeh Lebowitz of Yeshiva University reports that OU Kosher is an environment where *mashgichim* are encouraged to speak up if they believe a policy seems not to be working in practice. Rav Lebowitz explains that the strength of OU Kosher lies not only in its senior *posekim*, but in its dozens of middle management rabbinic coordinators and hundreds of rabbinic field representatives. All work together as a team to ensure that the best *kashrut* practices are in place.

I noticed an example in the opposite direction when visiting a Conservative Jewish administered camp *eruv* in Europe in the summer of 2014. A young Conservative rabbi wrote an extensive description of the camp *eruv*. However, he noted one section of the area relied upon a *tel hamitlaket*. He wrote that while it seemed to him that the area was insufficiently steep to constitute a valid *tel hamitlaket*, he submitted to the authority of a revered leading Conservative rabbi who had in years past surveyed the area and deemed it a proper *tel hamitlaket*. During my visit (there was a request to bring the *eruv* under Orthodox auspices), I asked to first view this section. I measured the area in question and not surprisingly I found it to be an inadequate *tel hamitlaket*.

A BALANCING ACT

Of course, proper respect must be shown when calling rabbinic authority into question. In addition, if a panel of competent Rabbanim overrules a challenge, the decision must be respected even if it appears to us that the panel is telling us that right is left and left is right, as per the dictum set forth in Parshat Shofetim. As with anything in life, proper balance is in order. Rav Nahman of Breslov famously teaches, "*kol ha'olam kulo gesher tzar me'od*," the entire world is a very narrow bridge. In other words, life is a big and delicate balancing act. In our case, the trick is to respect authority while knowing when and how to properly challenge authority.

ERUV INSPECTIONS FOR YOM TOV

Despite the fact that the full prohibition of carrying applies only on Shabbat, some communities still inspect their *eruvin* before Yom Tov as well. Rav Hershel Schachter (personal communication) holds that one should inspect the community *eruv* each Erev Yom Tov, while Rav Mordechai Willig and Rav Elazar Meyer Teitz (personal communication) do not feel that it is not necessary. In this chapter, we will attempt to explain the basis for both opinions.

THE CONCEPT OF MITOCH – RASHI VS. TOSAFOT
The Mishnah (Beitzah 1:5) teaches:

> Beit Shammai say that one may not carry a child, a *lulav*, or a *Sefer Torah* into the street on Yom Tov. Beit Hillel say that this is permitted.

Beit Shammai and Beit Hillel disagree as to whether one may carry non-food items on Yom Tov. The Gemara (Beitza 12a) explains that according to Beit Hillel, "since (*mitoch*) you can carry for eating, you can also carry for non-food-related purposes." In other words, once carrying is permitted for purposes relating to food preparation (*ochel nefesh*), it is also permitted for all other purposes. This principle is known as *mitoch*. The Rishonim debate the scope of this expansion of the permission to carry.

For what purposes may one carry on Yom Tov? Rashi (Beitzah 12a, s.v. *ela*) explains that the principle of *mitoch* teaches us that on a Torah level, carrying on Yom Tov is completely permitted, even for no specific reason.

Tosafot (Ketubot 7a s.v. *mitoch* and Beitzah 12a, s.v. *hachi garas*) disagree. They explain:

> Since it was permitted for food-related purposes, it was also permitted for non-food-related purposes" – provided that it fulfills a need for the enjoyment of the day or a need to fulfill a *mitzvah* on Yom Tov, such as in the case of carrying a child to circumcise him, a Torah scroll to read from it, and a *lulav* to fulfill the *mitzvah* with it. However, [the act of carrying] not for any need of the day at all, is not permitted. For example, one who carries out stones would be liable... It appears to Ri that carrying a baby out to walk casually is considered a need of the day.

According to *Tosafot*, the Torah permitted carrying on Yom Tov only when fulfilling a Yom Tov purpose. Thus, an empty container of food or medicine would have to be removed from one's pocket before Yom Tov since it is not meeting any Yom Tov need.

The Rama (O.C 518:1) rules in accordance with *Tosafot* that one may carry on Yom Tov only for some Yom Tov need. However, he notes that one may carry anything (provided that it is not *muktzeh*) if one established an *eruv* in the area. Hacham Yitzhak Yosef (*Yalkut Yosef*, O.C. 518:1-4) states that the same rules apply for Sephardic Jews. Accordingly, Rav Schachter rules that one should inspect the *eruv* before Yom Tov to permit all carrying. Moreover, since many are not aware of this limitation, it is important to ensure that the *eruv* is functional to permit to carry all non-*muktzeh* items on Yom Tov.

Rav Teitz, though, responded that one may rely on a combination of the *chezkat kashrut* (presumption that the status quo has not be disturbed) and the opinion of Rashi that *mitoch* permits all carrying on Yom Tov on a Torah level. Of course, even those who adopt the lenient approach would conduct an *eruv* inspection if an event such as a major storm occurred between Shabbat and Yom Tov, which would disrupt the *eruv's* presumed-valid status.

PRE-YOM KIPPUR INSPECTION

All would agree that under normal conditions, the *eruv* should be inspected before Yom Kippur. The seriousness of Yom Kippur demands we make the extra effort to be sure the *eruv* remains intact.

When inspecting my community's *eruv* on Erev Yom Kippur in 1993, I discovered a crew of utility employees working on lines upon which the *eruv* relied. I felt this sufficiently disturbed the presumed status of the *eruv* to warrant further inspection. Lo and behold, upon further examination, I discovered that the *eruv* was broken and in need of repair. I worked on the *eruv* until quite late, and was able to return home with only just enough time to quickly wolf down some food as my *seudah hamafseket* (the meal before the fast). I even arrived at the synagogue after Kol Nidrei had already begun (imagine the sight of a young assistant rabbi entering the synagogue late for Kol Nidrei – it caused quite a stir). This experience conveys a poignant message: There is ample reason to inspect an *eruv* on Erev Yom Kippur.

PRACTICAL CONSIDERATIONS

Each community should consult its Rav regarding the necessity of inspecting its *eruv* before Yom Tov. The decision might depend on the stability of the particular *eruv*. The level of an *eruv's* stability might vary depending on the extent of utility pole construction occurring in the area at a particular time.

In general, an *eruv* which relies almost entirely on pre-existing utility wires is more stable than an *eruv* for which special wires were installed. An *eruv* with its own special wires is far more vulnerable. In addition, *eruvin* in communities that have made arrangements with local utility companies to inform them when they are working on the utility wires and have placed notices on the *lechis* to not remove without informing the community (and these notices are respected by the utility workers) are much more reliable, regarding which all might agree that they do not require inspection before Yom Tov.

CONCLUSION AND A COMPROMISE

Each community Rav, accordingly, should assess the situation regarding his community to determine whether the *eruv* should be inspected before Yom Tov. In many situations, all may agree that it may not be necessary to inspect an *eruv* when Yom Tov begins on a Sunday night, as utility employees most likely did not work on the poles since Shabbat.

GUIDELINES FOR ERUVIN MAINTENANCE

In this chapter, we present an outline of experience-based protocols for community *eruvin* maintenance. Proper halachic standards can be met by strictly adhering to the outlined protocols. We shall focus our discussion on four components that are crucial to the success of a community *eruv*: the *posek*, the community Rav, the weekly inspectors, and the community. The standards for *eruvin* inspectors are discussed in the next chapter.

THE POSEK

Creating and maintaining proper *eruvin* involves complex halachic issues. A *posek* of eminent stature must be consulted to issue halachic rulings regarding a community *eruv*. The qualifications of someone to serve as a *posek* for a community *eruv* are as follows:

1. He must be expert in Gemara and Rishonim as well as the many Acharonim (especially the *Chazon Ish*, who is widely regarded as having great authority perhaps even more than the *Mishnah Berurah* in this area of Halachah) who discuss the practical details of *eruv* design and construction.

2. He must have extensive practical experience in dealing with North American community *eruvin*, such as working in the field with utility poles.

3. He must be widely recognized in the Orthodox community as an authority in the field of *eruvin*.

4. He or his delegate must be available to occasionally visit the *eruv* and field questions as they arise.

The *posek* must set standards and protocols for the community. He must set optimal standards as well as emergency (*sha'at hadechak*) standards such as when a problem arises shortly before the onset of Shabbat. He must establish protocols in determining the standards for both the creation and continuous maintenance of the *eruv*. For example, he must establish how often utility wires be inspected and, if river banks are used, how often they must be checked to ensure that they remain at a proper angle and height to serve as part of the *eruv* (*tel hamitlaket*). No change in the *eruv* should be made without consulting the *posek*.

THE LOCAL RAV

The continuous integrity of the *eruv* largely depends on the involvement of a competent local community rabbi. The following section lists some of the baseline requirements for a rabbi to serve as a part of the *eruv* team:

1. He must have extensive theoretical and practical training and knowledge of *Hilchot Eruvin*. We cannot rely solely upon the fact that a Rav of eminent stature designed and once inspected the *eruv*. *Eruvin* are quite vulnerable to weather, vandalism, and the reconfiguration of utility poles and wires. *Eruvin* become disqualified quickly and often, especially if the *eruv* in question is very large. The community depends on the local Rav to facilitate and supervise repair of the *eruv* in a proper manner. **The local Rav must educate him-**

self in the area of *eruvin* and seek out an appropriate mentor who can share practical insight to enable him to reach the level of expertise necessary to maintain a proper *eruv*.

2. He must ensure that there is an extensive and clear precise written record that details how the *eruv* is constructed. Every change in the *eruv's* construction must be duly noted in writing.

3. He must be intimately familiar with every detail of the *eruv*.

4. He must be involved in the inspection of the *eruv* on a regular basis. Ideally (although it is most often impractical), the Rav should be the one who inspects the *eruv* each week as the *Chazon Ish* in Bnei Brak reportedly did every Friday morning even in the most inclement weather (*Pe'eir Hador* 2:136 and 285). Similarly, the *Chafetz Chaim's* son (*Dugma Midarkei Avi zt"l* 63:14) writes that his father "scrupulously supervised the *eruvin* in his city." Experience teaches that when community rabbis do not attend to the community *eruv*, the validity of the *eruv* deteriorates. The community Rav and *posek* should conduct a full walking inspection of the *eruv* at least once a year (Rav Yona Reiss is correct in his assessment that it should be done twice a year). **The proper way to conduct a yearly inspection of an *eruv* is to inspect it on foot.** One who is driving does not notice peculiarities with the *eruv* as easily as one who is walking. This inspection must take place together with the *eruv* inspector to ensure that he remains thoroughly acquainted with all of the details of the *eruv*. "Fresh eyes" (people who have never viewed the

eruv before) should be included in this review so that nuances will be noticed that might be overlooked due to familiarity with the *eruv*.

5. He must understand when it is appropriate to consult the *posek* that supervises the *eruv*.

6. He must ensure that the *eruv* adheres to the highest standards of ethics and safety. Rav Yosef Dov Soloveitchik insists (heard directly from the Rav speaking to community rabbis visiting him in 1985) that any portion of the *eruv* should not be constructed without obtaining the necessary permission. *Eruvin* must be a source of *Kiddush Hashem* in the community. Rav Hershel Schachter believes (personal conversation, 1989) that claiming "*zeh neheneh v'zeh lo chaser*," "that this one gains and this one does not lose," (Bava Kama 20) is an inadequate excuse to defend placing a *lechi* on another individual's property without permission. He explains that in a case of "*zeh neheneh v'zeh lo chaser*," Beit Din does not compel payment, but that it does not imply that one is permitted *ab initio* to benefit from another's property without permission (see *Pitchei Teshuvah* C.M. 363:6 and *Aruch Hashulchan* C.M. 363:16).

7. Alternative routes to the *eruv* must be explored in case of recurrent problems in specific portions of the *eruv*.

8. He must ensure that *sha'at hadechak* standards do not evolve into becoming the conventional standards for the *eruv*. For example, a *lechi* that was attached to a utility pole shortly be-

fore Shabbat in a less than optimal fashion should not remain as a permanent component of the *eruv*.

9. He must ensure that the *eruv chatzeirot* and *sechirat reshut* remain up-to-date and cover the entire area encompassed by the *eruv*.

10. There is great pressure on a Rav to ensure that the *eruv* encompasses all members of the community. He must ensure that any expansion of the *eruv* does not compromise its halachic standards and integrity and/or become too large and unwieldy to properly supervise.

11. Experience teaches that a community that does not yet employ a Rav should exercise great caution before it establishes an *eruv*. Although there is great motivation to establish an *eruv* in order to attract people to the community, without on-site rabbinic supervision, *eruvin* easily and quickly fall into disrepair. The involvement of a rabbi from a neighboring community might provide a solution to this problem.

12. When a community is "in between rabbis," the *eruv* should not be relied upon unless other rabbinic supervision of the *eruv* can be provided. Changes to the *eruv* should certainly not be made during this time. I have witnessed the disastrous results when this policy is not adhered to.

13. He must network and familiarize himself with the challenges and strategies of rabbis of other communities in regard to their *eruvin*.

14. Be sure that the rabbis in the community agree to the *eruv* in general and all of its halachic details (see *Teshuvot Igrot Moshe* O.C. 4:86).

15. He must deal sensitively and effectively with those who wish to be strict and not rely on a community *eruv*. (See *Biur Halachah* 345:7 s.v. *v'yeish omerim* and *Mishnah Berurah* 362:59.)

16. He must educate the community about what an *eruv* permits and what it does not permit, such as carrying umbrellas and ball-playing.

17. He must ensure that the community is well-informed about the boundaries of the *eruv* and that members know to avoid those streets where one can easily stray out of the *eruv*.

18. He must make a great effort to ensure that the *eruv* is designed in a manner that community members will not be confused and mistakenly carry outside the *eruv*. When feasible, communities should try to follow Rav Mordechai Willig's practice to include "back-ups" for the *eruv* (especially for somewhat "unstable" or "fickle" portions of the *eruv*) in case of failure.

19. Any suspicion or concern the Rav has regarding the *eruv* should be raised with the *posek*. If something seems to be wrong, it very likely is wrong. One should not assume that the *posek* reviewed the *eruv* and thus there is no need for concern – the matter may simply have escaped the notice of the *posek*.

20. Rabbanim should ensure that the halachic level of the *eruv* does not deteriorate over time. Rav Schachter has commented that, as time goes along, efforts should be made to ensure that, if possible, halachic improvements should be introduced to the *eruv*.

THE COMMUNITY OF USERS

In addition to the guidance of a *posek* and a local Rav, the community that uses the *eruv* also plays an important role in its continuous maintenance. The community of users should be aware of the following considerations:

1. The community should realize that the maintenance of a community *eruv* requires a very significant amount of time, resources, and effort devoted to the *eruv* on an ongoing basis. The price of a kosher *eruv* is eternal vigilance. All too often, communal enthusiasm regarding an *eruv* wanes after it is constructed. Ongoing attention ensures that the *eruv* does not fall into disrepair.

2. The community should, as suggested by Rav Hershel Schachter, be aware of the route of the *eruv*, so that they can alert potential problems such as utility pole construction to their Rav and *eruv* committee. By way of example, I once heard on a traffic report on a Thursday night that there was a downed utility pole in a community that is located twenty-five miles from where I reside. I happened to know that the *eruv* in that community ran along the street mentioned on the radio report and informed the Rav of that community. It turned out that the *eruv* was disturbed by this incident and

my call enabled the community to repair the *eruv* in time for Shabbat.

3. The community might consider adopting the recommendation of Rav Pinchas Teitz, to declare the *eruv* not to be in operation once a year to educate the community that carrying is forbidden on Shabbat. Otherwise, a generation is raised not knowing about the prohibition to carry on Shabbat (see Eruvin 59a). For example, a woman who grew up in a community surrounded by an *eruv* told me that she never knew that there is a difference between Shabbat and Yom Tov with regard to the prohibition of *hotza'ah*. An off-Shabbat for the *eruv* would be a fine opportunity for Rabbanim in a community to discuss the basic rules of the *eruv* and its precise borders. Not all Rabbanim, though, favor this practice.

4. The community should network and familiarize themselves with other communities' challenges and strategies with *eruvin*.

5. The community should deal with the broader community (both Jewish and non-Jewish) with intelligence and sensitivity.

6. A good notification system needs to be put in place to inform the community of any problems with the *eruv*, especially at the last minute. Many communities email out the status of the *eruv* before Shabbat.

7. An *eruv* map should be posted on the web as well as in a prominent place in the shuls of the community.

8. The community must be prepared to assist the Rav in various tasks such as charting the details of the Eruv route.

9. It is the community's responsibility to ensure that the *eruv* is properly funded and insured.

10. The community should properly manage, in cooperation with the community Rav, issues concerning potential expansion of the *eruv* and those who are not included in the *eruv*. It should be noted that some people purchase a house just outside the *eruv* since the price will be significantly lower and then hope to successfully pressure the local *eruv* committee to expand and include them in the *eruv*.

PARTIAL LIST OF ISSUES TO BE DISCUSSED WITH THE POSEK

The local Rav should discuss the issues listed below with a *posek* before attempting to construct an *eruv* in his community, to determine what standards are feasible for the community to adopt. Where possible, we have included references to the relevant chapters in this work.

1. Is the area that is to be encompassed by the *eruv* as a *karmelit* or *reshut harabim*? See our chapter, Defining the Four Domains.

2. Are *delatot* required and how should they be constructed? Are *delatot re'uyot linol* sufficient or are *tzurot hapetach* required to supplement them? See our chapter, The Delatot of Canarsie, London, Mattersdorf, and Oakland.

3. Are any of the highways encompassed by the *eruv* classified as a *reshut harabim*? Additionally, the exclusion of bridges from the *eruv* should be discussed with the *posek*. See our chapter, Highways, Railroads, and Ground Levels.

4. The issue of ground levels and the exclusion of bridges from the *eruv*. See the previously cited chapter.

5. Are any areas included in the *eruv* defined as a *karpeif*? See our chapters, Karpeif, Eruv Chatzeirot, and Sechirat Reshut and Karpeif and Bodies of Water.

6. Should the *eruv* rely on *tachuv*? See our chapter, The Use of Tachuv in Contemporary Community Eruvin.

7. What standard should be adopted for wires that sag and/or sway in the wind? See our chapters, Constructing the Tzurot Hapetach and Sagging Wire in the Yeshiva University Eruv.

8. What standard should be adopted for the maximum distance between *lechis*? See our chapter, A Lechi on Every Utility Pole?

9. What standard should be adopted for the maximum size of a *lechi* (Netivot Shabbat 19:17)?

10. How large and strong should the *lechis* be? See our chapter, Lechi Strength.

11. What position should be adopted in regard to *lechis* that are *mei'achorei hakotel*? See our chapter, Mei'achorei Hakotel in Long Island.

12. What types of materials are acceptable for use as a *lechi*? See our chapter, *Lechi Strength*, as well as *Sha'ar Hatziyun* 363:22 and *The Contemporary Eruv* p. 70 note 141. The *posek* should be consulted about the use of thick paint as a *lechi* in case of very great need.

13. Which approach should be adopted in regard to the use of signs and other "non-rabbinic" structures as *lechis*? See our chapters, *The All-American Eruv in Champaign-Urbana*, *A Tree as a Lechi*, and *A Defense of the Top-Side Wire*.

14. *Lechis* that serve *l'achzukei tikrah*, to support the ceiling, be used as a part of the *eruv*? (*Beit Yitzchak* 25:94-96).

15. What precisely is defined as a legitimate extension of both a horizontal pole and the vertical pole? See our chapter, *A Defense of the Top-side Wire*.

16. Can one rely on *lavud* and *gud achit mechitza* in regard to the vertical pole? See our chapters *Gud Achit Mechitzta and Lavud* and *The Friday Afternoon the Rabbi Discovered the Eruv Was Broken*.

17. Must the *lechi* extend all the way to the wire? See our chapter, *Constructing the Tzurot Hapetach*.

18. How often must utility wires and other "non-rabbinic" or "pre-existing" components of the *eruv*, such as buildings, fences, or river banks, be inspected? See our chapter, *Eruv Through the Storm*, for an overview of potential issues that may detract from the presumed-valid status of the *eruv*.

19. What standard should be adopted for measuring the precise location of a *lechi*? Is eye-sight sufficient, or is a plumb line required? See our chapter, *Constructing the Tzurot Hapetach*.

20. Must the surface area beneath a *tzurat hapetach* be flat (*Beit Yitzchak* 25:98-99)?

21. Are obstructions between the *lechi* and the *eruv* wire acceptable? See our chapter, *A Defense of the Top-Side Wire*.

22. How much change in direction of the *eruv* wire is acceptable? See our chapter, *Constructing the Tzurot Hapetach*.

23. How slanted may the vertical or horizontal wires be? See the previously cited chapter.

24. Can a *tzurat hapetach* be placed in a *reshut hayachid*? See our chapter, *The Lechi Under the Cabin Eaves at Camp Ramah Darom*.

25. The issue of a *tzurat hapetach* through which one cannot easily walk. See our chapter, *Defending the Use of the Boardwalk Railing in Long Branch, NJ*, for a brief discussion of this issue.

26. Can one rely upon the bottom of a tapered pole as a *lechi* in case of extraordinary need? See our chapter, *Constructing the Tzurot Hapetach*.

27. Where should the *eruv chatzerot* be stored? See our chapter, *Karpeif, Eruv Chatzeirot, and Sechirat Reshut*.

28. Where should a *lechi* be precisely placed at a point where the overhead wire changes direction? When and how should two *lechis* be placed on a single pole to "catch" the change in wire direction?

29. How and with whom should the *sechirat reshut* be conducted? How long should a *sechirat reshut* last? See our chapter, *Karpeif, Eruv Chatzeirot, and Sechirat Reshut*.

30. The issue of *siluk mechitzot* should be discussed with the *posek* (*B'ikvei Hatzon* 13:8).

31. Can highway overpasses be used to form halachic walls via the principle of *pi tikrah yoreid v'soteim*? (*Teshuvot Igrot Moshe* O.C. 1:140 and *Imrei Baruch, Eruvin Ureshuyot*, pp. 28-31).

32. How to identify situations that are defined as *nifratz b'milu'oh* and *nifratz l'makom ha'assur lo* (*Netivot Shabbat* 14:6 and *Journal of Contemporary Society* 5:21).

33. How to identify and manage a *pitcha b'keren zavit*. See our chapter, *Pitcha B'keren Zavit*.

34. How wide can a gap be in an area subject to frequent foot traffic? How should such a gap be corrected? See our chapter, *The Stringency of the Tevu'ot Shor and the Yale New Haven Eruv*.

35. How wide can a gap in an *eruv* composed of *tzurot hapetach* be? See the previously cited chapter.

36. What is the minimum area that a *tzurat hapetach* or *mechitzah* must cover? (Rav Schachter, personal conversation in 1989, is concerned where there is a wall within four *tefachim* of a *tzurat hapetach* in the direction that is encompassed by the *eruv*. Such a wall bounds the area so that it is less than the minimum space that can be designated as a *reshut hayachid*.)

37. What is the precise definition of a *tel hamitlakeit* (*Beit Yitzchak* 25:83-84)? Also see the discussion in our chapter, *Islands and Waterfronts*.

38. How large is an *amah* and *tefach* (*Encyclopedia Talmudit* 20:659)? Also see our chapter, *Eruv Standards According to Sephardic Measurements*.

39. May the *eruv* be inspected earlier than Friday (*Teshuvot Doveiv Meisharim* 2:28 and *The Contemporary Eruv* p. 89 note 181)? Also see our chapter, *The Friday Afternoon the Rabbi Discovered the Eruv Was Broken*.

40. Should the *eruv* be inspected before Yom Tov? See our chapter, *Eruv Inspections for Yom Tov*.

41. Can one ask a non-Jew to fix the *eruv* on Shabbat (*Mishnah Berurah* 276:25)? Also see our chapter, *Managing an Eruv Emergency in Cambridge, MA*.

42. How one should inform the community on Shabbat if it is discovered that the *eruv* is down (see Rav Ezra Schwartz's

essay in the Spring 2004 issue of the *Journal of Halacha and Contemporary Society*).

43. Should one rely upon disputed leniencies accepted by the previous Rav of the community (*B'ikvei Hatzon* number 12)?

44. What is the maximum area that may be enclosed by the *eruv*? See our chapter, *The Maximum Size of an Eruv*.

45. Can a waterfront be used as one of the sides of the *eruv*? See our chapter, *Islands and Waterfronts*. Also see *Ba'eir Heiteiv* 363:9.

46. How to manage a sea-wall and beaches as a part of the *eruv* (*Shulchan Aruch* O.C. 363:29 with commentaries). Also see our chapter, *Islands and Waterfronts*.

47. May one rely upon utility workers to report the repair of a wire? See our chapter, *Managing an Eruv Emergency in Cambridge, MA*.

48. Be certain that *gud asik mechitzta* is measured straight up and not according to the angle of the *lechi* (*Chazon Ish* 71:6). **This is a very common problem!**

49. Be aware of the applications of the principle of *ati avira d'hai gisa v'hai gisa u'mevatel lei L'Mechitzah* (*Netivot Shabbat* 14:7).

50. Be aware of the application of the concept of a *tzurat hapetach ba'avir* (*Imrei Baruch, Eruvin UReshuyot*, pp. 131-132.

HIGHLY RECOMMENDED READING

1. *Netivot Shabbat* by Rav Yaakov Bloi.

2. *Hilchot Eruvin* by Rav Elimelech Lange.

3. *Halachos of the Eruv* by Rav Shimon Eider.

4. *The Contemporary Eruv* by Rav Gavriel Bechhoffer.

5. Rav Hershel Schachter's essay in the Spring 1983 edition of the *Journal of Halacha and Contemporary Society*; and *Teshuvot* 12 and 13 in his *B'ikvei Hatzon*.

6. Rav Mordechai Willig's essay in volume 25 of *Beit Yitzchak*.

7. Dr. Bert Miller's (of Baltimore) *Eruv Manual*.

8. Rav Baruch Simon's *Imrei Baruch, Eruvin UReshuyot*.

9. *The Laws of an Eruv* by Rav Shlomo Francis and Rav Yonason Glenner.

10. The sources cited in each of these works, especially from the *Mishnah Berurah* and *Chazon Ish*.

A BALANCE BETWEEN THE COMMUNITY & THE RABBI

In contemporary Orthodox communities in North America, an *eruv* is an expected amenity. The responsibility falls on the community Rav to properly maintain the *eruv*. Indeed, the Halachah expects that an *eruv* should be established wherever it is possible to do so (see Eruvin 67b-68a, *Mordechai* Eruvin number 515, *Teshuvot Harosh* 21:8, *Teshuvot Chatam Sofer* O.C. 89 and

Teshuvot Har Zvi O.C. 2:24). However, not all community members are sufficiently sensitized to the time and effort that is necessary to achieve the goal of maintaining a proper community *eruv*. Many (if not most) Rabbanim are severely overburdened and cannot in most cases be expected to maintain the *eruv* without abundant and generous communal support. This support should be two-fold: financial and the dedication of time to ensure the success of the *eruv*. On the other hand, community members cannot be expected to successfully maintain an *eruv* at an appropriate halachic level unless the local Rav is involved with the *eruv* on an ongoing basis. The synergy of Rav and community will ensure that the *eruv* remains at the same high standards it was at the time of its creation.

Rabbi Chaim Jachter

STANDARDS FOR COMPETENT INSPECTION OF COMMUNITY ERUVIN

The *eruv* requires weekly inspection by a competent individual. He must meet all of the following requirements to serve as an *eruv* inspector:

1. Optimally, the *eruv* inspectors should be Talmidei Chachamim who are well-versed in the theory and practice of *Hilchot Eruvin*. At minimum, they should be God-fearing Jews who are highly scrupulous in their observance of Halachah who will inspect the *eruv* meticulously (see Rav Asher Bush's *Teshuvot Sho'el Beshlomo* 1:12, based on Rama Y.D. 127:3). This includes knowledge of the maximum allowance for deflection in the wire, the *lechi*, and *tachuv* (if it is permitted by the overseeing rabbi). To facilitate this, an area should be identified where the maximum allowance occurs to establish a benchmark.

2. They should never make any changes or repairs to the *eruv* without consulting the local Rav. Any change to the *eruv* must be done with the consultation of the rabbinic supervisor of the *eruv* and noted in the written plan of the *eruv*.

3. They must have a thorough knowledge and understanding of every detail of the *eruv*, so that they should be able to spot a potential problem in the *eruv*. Their knowledge of *Hilchot Eruvin* should be sufficient for them to know when to alert the local Rav to a problem.

4. Experience teaches that when *eruv* inspectors do not know exactly how the *eruv* works, the *eruv* falls into disrepair. They cannot inspect that which they do not know! This regrettably happens in "complex" portions of *eruvin*. Rabbanim must ensure that *eruv* inspectors know how each portion of the *eruv* works. This includes the location of every *lechi* along with the entire *eruv* plan (i.e. how pole x uses wire y to connect to pole z). If an inspector does not know how a section of the *eruv* works, he must ask the supervising rabbi to review the area with him.

5. They must record where the *eruv* is most vulnerable and must inform the Rav of recurrent problems in specific locations.

6. They must be alert to specific halachic issues that arise from time to time, such as entangling of wires in trees during springtime, cable wires becoming pulled out of alignment by service lines when they are attached to homes, and the appearance of brand new utility poles, all of which adversely affect the presumed-valid status of the *eruv*.

7. They must not (except for special circumstances, see below) drive a car and inspect the *eruv* simultaneously. In general, inspectors who drive while inspecting the *eruv* neither inspect nor drive properly.

8. Candidates for *eruvin* inspectors should be tested to determine competency in this task.

9. The Rav and *posek* should be consulted as to whether the *eruv* can be inspected earlier than Friday in case of great need (see *Teshuvot Doveiv Meisharim* 2:28, who states that *eruvin* should be inspected on Friday).

10. If something seems wrong, the inspector should not assume that the supervising rabbi or *rav hamachshir* set everything properly and that all is well. Rather, he should ask for an explanation. It is insufficient for the *eruv* plan to be documented in the formal *eruv* record. It must also be understood and etched in the minds of all those responsible for the *eruv*. This also requires that the documentation be constantly updated to match the facts on the ground.

11. Inspectors should conduct a yearly walk (preferably twice a year) with the *rav hamachshir* and conduct a thorough walking review of the entire *eruv* to refresh their knowledge of how the *eruv* works. It is a daunting challenge to inspect a large community *eruv*. Slight and nuanced changes can invalidate the *eruv*. The yearly walking inspection allows the inspector to develop a good sense of what the operational *eruv* is supposed to look like (*tevi'at ayin*), so, while conducting the weekly *eruv* inspection, he will be able to readily identify any problems. *Eruv* inspectors need to be experts in the *eruv* they supervise in order to make such quick decisions, which is absolutely necessary during the weekly *eruv* inspection when the hundreds of components of the *eruv* are inspected.

12. Safety is primary in regard to *eruv* inspection and installation. Chazal (Chullin 10a) teach *"chamira sakanta mei'isura"*, we are more careful in regard to safety than Torah prohibitions.[5] The *eruv* inspector (and any accompanying individuals) must wear reflective vests while inspecting the *eruv*.

13. The inspectors should be subject to oversight by a rabbinic authority that is knowledgeable and familiar with the *eruv*. The inspector should be in regular contact with the rabbi and not just once or twice a year during the walkthrough(s) of the *eruv*. The rabbi must engage some *active* oversight so that the inspector will be more motivated to do a good and thorough job.

14. Rav Mordechai Willig encourages the creation of backups for community *eruvin*. However, there is an inherent danger when it comes to backups. One must exercise caution to not be tempted to conduct a less than excellent inspection and haphazardly rely upon the backup. Particular care should be taken when relying upon a backup; the backup portion of the *eruv* must be thoroughly inspected. This is reminiscent of the Gemara (Eruvin 3a) that a *kidra d'vei shutefi*, a pot managed by more than one person, is neither hot nor cold as each manager assumes the other is taking care of the pot. This is Chazal's elegant way of expressing the idea of diffused responsibility. Similarly, when not managed properly,

---

[5] Unfortunately, I have been involved in three driving accidents when riding in a car during *eruvin* inspections. The lesson of *chamira sakanta mei'isura* should not be taken lightly.

backups have the potential to slip into disrepair. This is not to say that backups are not appropriate; however, those who oversee the *eruv* should bear this potential problem in mind and be careful not to slip into this pitfall.

STANDARDS FOR WEEKLY INSPECTION

1. Every week, inspectors should scan the *eruv* to check that no changes have been made (ex. wires pulled out by service wire, pole changed, wiring change, and not just obvious changes such as a downed wire or a missing *lechi*). The Sharon, MA *eruv* maintains a record as to where problems have been discovered and conducts an analysis of how to improve the stability of areas that experience frequent problems. Other communities should maintain a repair log as well.

2. Every week, inspectors should check to see if each *lechi* is intact from bottom to top and confirm that it is still below the appropriate wire. This will often require leaving the car to physically inspect a large number of *lechis*. The attachment of *lechis* to the lowest wire and the attachment of a white cap or tape to the top of the *lechi* makes this process much more efficient. Additionally, the use of PVC conduit as *lechis* makes *eruv* inspection much more efficient.

3. It is absolutely critical to realize that a new utility pole is a screaming red light, or severe *rei'uta* to the *chezkat kashrut* of the *eruv*. Whenever a new pole is discovered, the area must be thoroughly inspected to see if the *eruv* remains intact in that section.

4. Utility wires change, sometimes frequently. Inspectors must remain on alert for these changes. One may never assume that the utility wires remain the same and all that needs to be inspected are the installations made by the Jewish community.

5. In order to check a *lechi* from a car (in extenuating circumstances), the following conditions must be met:

   a. The inspector can see the entire *lechi* from the car.

   b. The inspector can confidently ascertain that the top of the *lechi* is under the appropriate wire.

   c. Nothing is obstructing the view of the *lechi* from the car.

6. The *eruv* inspector should be alert regarding the placement of old and new poles. Old and new poles commonly stand side by side, where some of the wires (often the higher electric wires) have been transferred from the old pole to the new pole and others (often the communication wires which are often used by the *eruv*) remain on the old pole. An *eruv* often will utilize the old pole, onto which a *lechi* may be affixed. It is entirely unpredictable when the old pole will be removed: it could remain a year, or it could last ten years. In one instance, the old pole remained intact for ten years and then was suddenly removed. Unfortunately, the *eruv* inspector did not notice the change, and the disqualification of the *eruv* went unnoticed. These situations demand vigilance and being aware that such an alignment of poles is by definition volatile. This is especially so when a pole upon which the *er-*

uv depends has an X spray-painted on it, which indicates that it is slated for removal.

ESTABLISHING A SYSTEM SET FOR SUCCESS

1. Often, the wires upon which the *eruv* relies are difficult to follow. The *eruv* should be simplified to allow for a straightforward inspection. If and when the utility company changes the wires, thus making the inspection more challenging, the *eruv* should be modified to allow for a relatively easier inspection.

2. Wherever possible, the *lechis* should be placed on the outside of the pole facing the street to make it easier for the inspector to notice (if the inspection is conducted by car).

3. The best system is the one used in the Sharon, MA[6] *eruv*. See our chapter on *A Community Model for Eruvin Inspection* for further discussion of their excellent system.

4. There should be a culture of continuous improvement, of always trying to make the *eruv* better.

5. Before introducing a *chumra* to the *eruv*, one should consider whether this addition makes the *eruv* too difficult to maintain. The financial capabilities and limitations of the community are also important factors to take into consideration.

6. Every component of the *eruv* should be catalogued.

---

[6] The Edison-Highland Park *eruv* employs a similar system.

7. *Eruv* administrators must also be mindful that *eruv* inspectors can succumb to burnout. The administrator should make sure that the inspectors are paid adequately, express appreciation towards the inspectors, and ensure that the inspectors are not overburdened. All of these measures will help stave off burnout.

A THOUGHT FOR THE FUTURE

As technology progresses, we should bear in mind the possibility of conducting *eruv* inspections by drones. Communities would have to ensure that the usage of drones would fully comply with all legal and security regulations, in addition to making sure that only qualified technicians operate such drones to minimize any potential damage or harm.

CONCLUSION:
WHY DOES THIS MATTER TO HASHEM?

In concluding our discussion of *Hilchot Eruvin*, it is important to note one last question that arises from the detail-oriented nature of the design, construction, and maintenance of *eruvin*; namely, does Hashem truly care about all these details? Does it truly matter to Him if a wire runs over the pole or ever so slightly to its side? Why the obsession with the minuscule details?

Truthfully, this question can be asked about any area of Halachah. In general, the halachic system is highly detail-oriented. However, the amount of effort and resources put in by communities and their rabbis to ensure that *eruvin* are completely in line with the precise standards of the Halachah makes this question particularly relevant for us. In this concluding chapter, we will suggest a few answers to this important question.

DETAILS AS A UNIFYING FORCE

Throughout the centuries, adherence to details has kept the Jews as one nation. The acceptability of a Yemenite Sefer for all Jews brings home this idea in a most striking manner. In his endorsement of the use of Yemenite *sifrei Torah* by all Jews, Chacham Ovadia Yosef (*Teshuvot Yehave Da'at* 6:56) notes that there are only two differences between the lettering of the Yemenite Torah scroll and that of Ashkenazic and Sephardic Jews. One difference is the Yemenite addition of the letter *yod* in Bereishit 9:29. Yemenite Torah scrolls state *"vayehiyu bnei Noach,"* while others state *"veyehi bnei Noach."* The other difference is in regard to the word *'daka'* (Devarim 23:2). The Yemenite tradition uses an *alef* as the last letter in the word, while the other traditions end the word with a letter *heh*.

Rav Yosef said that there has been considerable dispute regarding the spelling of these two words and there is ample and copious support to both the Yemenite tradition and the Sephardic-Ashkenazic tradition. Thus, he concludes that it is acceptable for all Jews to use the Yemenite Sefer Torah.

Let us consider, though, the bigger picture. It is stunning that despite the many thousands of years and miles apart, the only differences in spelling in the *sefer Torah* is in regard to two letters! We would expect the differences in the lettering to be far more dramatic, given the degree and duration of separation among the Jewish people.

This phenomenon is a dramatic testimony to the dogged determination of all Jewish communities to maintain the integrity of the Torah, despite any and all challenges. In every Jewish community throughout the far-flung Jewish world, scribes, scholars, and ordinary Jews scrupulously paid painstaking attention to the details to preserve the tradition as they passed it down from one generation to another. Rav Saadia Gaon famously asserted that *"ein umoteinu umah ela b'toratah,"* "our nation is a nation only by virtue of its Torah." Torah observance unifies the Jewish people and, more than anything else in Jewish life, the unified Torah text has maintained us as one nation.

The Gemara (Ta'anit 23a) famously relates the cogent and central lesson expressed by an elderly Jew to Honi Hama'ageil: "Just as my ancestors planted for me, so too I plant for my descendants." Jews in every community paid meticulous attention to detail and maintained the Torah text without deviation. In doing so, they bequeathed a precious and unparalleled legacy of Jewish unity. We, the heirs of this divine tradition, are called upon to make every effort to devote deep attention to detail and authentically transmit our holy tradition to future generations, thereby maintaining the unified path of our people through its journey through history towards the ultimate redemption. For this reason, we pay extraordinary attention to detail in regard to all *mitzvot*, including community *eruvin*.

DETAILS MATTER IN LIFE

In every area of serious concern, details matter. To the physician, tiny details often spell the difference between life and death. The same applies to an airplane mechanic. A businessman who does not devote proper attention to the details of his business is doomed to fail. To the scientist, attention to detail can make the difference toward the development of a breakthrough and world-changing product.

Even in the world of sports, details are profoundly important. Imagine the following scenario: A running back in American football carries the ball approximately ten yards, and is very close to achieving what is called a "first down." In such situations, the referees are expected to bring out chains to carefully measure if indeed the first down has been achieved. However, in our imaginary case, the referees decide to make a quick estimate whether the first down was achieved, without bothering to take a careful measurement. They then announce to the fans that it looks as if a first down has been reached, and signal the first down sign.

Even the most moderate sports enthusiast would be outraged at such behavior. If a referee acted in this manner, his

Walking the Line

very life would be placed at risk. A referee who does not devote proper attention to the game's details disrespects the sport. Disregarding the sport's details shows he does not treat it seriously.

OUR LEGACY

As Jews, we are the heirs of the greatest and noblest of legacies. We have the responsibility and privilege of observing and preserving God's law. How can we not take halachic details seriously? Moreover, just as a sports fan revels in the details of the game, we who love Hashem and His Torah revel in the details of Torah observance. Far from being a burden, it is a source of great and genuine happiness and joy.

Just ask the rabbis and community members who devote hours to inspect your community *eruv*. Each rabbi very much enjoys applying the holy words of the Gemara, Rishonim, *Shulchan Aruch*, and *posekim* to the mundane infrastructure of his neighborhood. Transforming the mundane to holy and bringing the Torah to life in its many glorious details is one of the most joyous and satisfying experiences of life. Maintaining the excellent halachic standards of an *eruv* for a community is a labor of profound love.

The same may be said regarding the dozens, if not hundreds, of details we have addressed in this book regarding proper *eruv* design, construction, and maintenance. They all lead to our ultimate goal – respect and love of Hashem and His Holy Torah.

ACKNOWLEDGEMENTS

I love learning about *eruvin*, inspecting *eruvin*, and creating *eruvin*. Anything to do with *eruvin* brings me great joy. My family, friends, congregants, and students all know how much I thoroughly enjoy *eruvin*.

My passion for *eruvin* is related to a fine compliment offered about Rav Shlomo Zalman Auerbach: "He saw Torah in light of reality and he saw reality in light of the Torah." Rav Shlomo Zalman's orientation in his Torah learning was always to have an eye towards how to apply the learning in practice. On the other hand, the reality he encountered was always viewed in the light of the Torah.

The world of *Hilchot Eruvin* is a perfect blend of this idea. The Gemara, Rishonim, *Shulchan Aruch*, and Acharonim are all applied to mundane infrastructure in the field! I vividly remember my reaction when I first saw a utility pole slightly modified to meet *eruv* standards – "there is a *tzurat hapetach* on the telephone pole!" The Gemara comes alive on something so ordinary. The trip must also be made in reverse. We must connect that which appears in the field to that which appears in both the classic and contemporary halachic sources. Every nook and cranny of an *eruv* must be able to fit perfectly into the *Eitz Chaim*, the living tree of the Torah and Mesorah that our great *posekim* have set forth throughout the generations.

In this work, we bring this passion and excitement about *eruvin* to our readers as we take them on an exhilarating ride from the sources to the streets and back.

My guiding principle is *"teshu'ah b'rov yo'etz,"* solutions come from much consultation (Mishlei 11:14). This book collects the views and approaches of a very wide range of contemporary *sefarim*, *posekim*, and *eruv* professionals. *"Mikol melamdai hiskalti"* (Tehillim 119:99), there is so much to learn from so many wise, dedicated, and experienced people. I have culled and distilled best practices from dozens of teachers, all to help communities create proper *eruvin* that can be maintained as such in the long term.

I am especially indebted to my Rebbeim, Rav Hershel Schachter and Rav Mordechai Willig, for answering dozens of questions I posed to them regarding community *eruvin*. I thank them for the great deal of time, patience, and kindness they have shown me during the past forty years in all areas of Torah, but especially in regard to *Hilchot Eruvin*. The turbulent events of the spring and summer of 2020 did not allow time for Rav Schachter and Rav Willig to review our presentation of their views. Any inaccuracies in the citations are my sole responsibility.

Nachum Krasnopolsky has done an extraordinary job in polishing this work. His meticulous and incisive editing and good judgment are a perfect recipe for creating a high-quality product. It is a blessing to have such a dedicated *talmid* who has now helped me introduce two fine *sefarim*.

My son Binyamin deserves a special thank you for taking the time to help me produce the high quality videos for the OU's *All Daf* that help bring *Hilchot Eruvin* to life (and for producing one video himself). A special thank you as well to Rav David Pardo and Rav Moshe Schwed for collaborating to create these wonderful videos.

Additionally, I would like to thank the Rabbanim who have taken the time to review this work. Their many insightful comments and suggestions have added a tremendous amount to *Walking the Line*. Rav Mordechai Djavaheri is owed a special thank you for his outstanding insights. My *talmid*, Dr. Michael Adler, has greatly impacted the book, both through his comments and also by way of the many insights he shared with me from 2010 and 2015, when we collaborated on maintaining the Englewood and Tenafly *eruvin*.

I am grateful to my wonderful wife, Malca. She deserves an extraordinary debt of gratitude for indulging my great passion for *eruvin*. Malca fosters a loving and happy environment in which each one of our family members can thrive. Our children Bracha and Yisrael Perton, Binyamin, Chaya Ziporah, Atara and Hillel eagerly listen to my *eruv* "adventures," encouraging and supporting me all the while in my mission to improve the quality of *eruvin* in the Jewish community (sometimes even joining in on the fun).

I thank my in-laws, Rav Dr. Shmuel z"l and Chana Tokayer, for all of their wholehearted support throughout the last twenty-five years. Their understanding of the time I devote to reviewing community *eruvin* is very much appreciated. My mother in law's inviting smile and warmth uplifts our entire family. It is a privilege to be part of the beautiful family my in-laws created.

Rabbi Chaim Jachter
12 Menachem Av 5780

About the Author

Rabbi Chaim Jachter has earned an international reputation as a consultant for community *eruvin*, a *get* (Jewish divorce) administrator, and a prolific writer. His publications include a series of four well-received books entitled *Gray Matter* on contemporary topics in Jewish Law, in addition to his commentaries on *Sefer Melachim* and *Yonah*. He is a veteran teacher of Judaic Studies at Torah Academy of Bergen County, Rabbi of Congregation Shaarei Orah (the Sephardic Congregation of Teaneck) and *dayan* on the Beit Din of Elizabeth. Rabbi Jachter has lectured on topics of significance at a wide variety of venues worldwide. Rabbi Jachter lives with his wife and five children in Teaneck, NJ.

Other Works by Rabbi Jachter

Gray Matter
Gray Matter II
Gray Matter III
Gray Matter IV

Reason to Believe: Rational Explanations
of Orthodox Jewish Faith

Depths of Yonah: Unleashing
the Power of Your Yom Kippur

From David to Destruction:
Mining Essenial Lessons from Sefer Melachim

Made in the USA
Middletown, DE
25 August 2020